The Official MIVA Web-Scripting Book

By Kent Multer

Shopping Carts
Feedback Forms
Guestbooks
and More

http://TopFloor.com/

The Official Miva Web-Scripting Book

Shopping Carts, Feedback Forms, Guestbooks, and More

SAN#: 299-4550
Top Floor Publishing
8790 W. Colfax, Suite 107
Lakewood, CO 80215 USA

Feedback to the author: feedback@topfloor.com
Sales information: sales@topfloor.com
The Top Floor Publishing Web Site: http://TopFloor.com/
Cover design by Derek Finley, Miva Corp., derek@miva.com

Library of Congress Catalog Card Number: 99-60719

ISBN: 0-9661032-1-1

02 01 00 6 5 4 3 2 1

Acknowledgements

The author wishes to thank Peter Kent of Top Floor Publishing for his patience and support.

About the Author

Kent Multer of Dallas, Texas is a freelance writer, programmer, artist, and musician, not necessarily in that order. His previous works range from *The Official Netscape JavaScript Programmer's Reference* to the science fiction story *Wind Warrior 2000*.

Contents at a Glance

Contents

Foreword

In 1996 when Miva Corporation was founded, talk of doing business on the Internet brought anything from a casual smile to quizzical "what's that" glances. Today the Internet and e-commerce have changed the world—there is no going back. The global rate of Internet growth is so rapid that worldwide connectivity is now an accepted fact.

The Internet is, of course, much more than commerce. The Internet is about communication and easy information exchange between the peoples of the world. In addition to its built-in e-commerce facilities, Miva Script makes the development of Internet database and communication systems easy. The XML-based Miva Script syntax was designed with the look and feel of HTML and the functionality to manage databases, create program logic, read or send e-mail, emulate a browser, and interact with transaction-processing services. This makes Miva Script the full-featured language of the Internet.

Miva Script has been used to create Web sites around the world. Some sell products, while others offer unique communication systems such as lost friend locator services. I invite you to visit Miva Galleria, our showcase of Miva-based sites, to see a sampling of some fantastic Miva applications. You can find the Miva Galleria by visiting our home page and following the Miva Galleria link.

Ken Multer breaks down the elements of Miva Script and describes them in clear, precise language. He uses examples to clearly show how each tag and function can be used in different circumstances. This book not only teaches the novice how to use Miva Script, it can help the expert exploit the power of the language.

Welcome to the world of Miva and Miva Script.

With my best regards,

Joe Austin, Pres/CEO
Miva Corporation

joe@miva.com

Preface

This manual documents Miva Script, a server-side scripting language used for adding active and interactive features to HTML documents. Miva Script provides powerful programming tools, file manipulation, database access, and e-commerce. Its simple syntax of tags and macros is very similar to HTML.

This manual reflects Miva Script version 3.64.

This manual is intended for Web authors and developers who will create and work with scripts. It is assumed that the reader has some familiarity with HTML coding. If you have always done HTML authoring with a WYSIWYG editor, you will need to go "under the hood" and get some familiarity with HTML tags and attributes. Miva Script's grammar is very similar to HTML's.

If you are familiar with any programming languages, such as C, Java, or even BASIC, you will have a head start in understanding the programming concepts. However, even a beginner should be able to pick up the essential concepts from the simple examples in each chapter.

Miva Script Web Sites

Top Floor Publishing provides a companion Web site for this manual at

http://TopFloor.com/miva/

This Web site includes:

- Copies of the script code for all Listings in this manual. If you want to try one of the scripts, you can download it instead of typing it in.
- Hyperlinks to all the online resources listed in the "For More Information" sections of this manual.
- Late updates or corrections to the manual.
- Information about other Web development books from Top Floor Publishing.

For additional information on Miva Script and Miva products, visit the Miva Corporation Web site at

http://www.miva.com/

A number of other useful books and online resources are listed in Appendix D.

Typographical Conventions

Miva Script is a fairly simple language, so this manual only requires a few special typefaces.

- Words that are *italicized* are technical terms that are being introduced and defined, as well as the usual items such as book titles and mathematical expressions. For words whose meaning needs to be emphasized, the manual uses **bold** text.
- Text in `this typeface` represents HTML or Miva Script code that is intended to be written exactly as shown.
- Text in *`this italic typeface`* represents dummy variable names or other prototype code; it is expected that some other value will be written in actual practice.

Additionally, in the Reference section, some use is made of **`this bold typeface`** to represent required items, while optional items are in `nonbold`. These are specifically noted on the pages where they occur.

1

Basic Structure

This chapter describes how the Miva engine processes documents, and the relation between client and server. It also describes the basic organization of documents and scripts.

What is Miva Script?

As the Internet changed from a laboratory curiosity to a daily reality for millions of people, it has begun to provide more advanced services. Often, more advanced means more interactive. The World Wide Web was conceived primarily as a way to store and display documents; but today it is commonly used for interactive communications, such as data management and retail sales or "e-commerce." To support these applications, the HTML document structure needs some additional power. Miva Script provides this power in a form that is very easy to use.

Miva Script uses a grammar of tags, attributes, and macros, very similar to HTML. Miva Script allows a document to perform functions such as reading and writing files, accessing databases, and conducting e-commerce transactions with third-party servers. Miva Script provides standard programming structures such as If-Then-Else and looping. It provides built-in functions for text manipulation, mathematical and logical operations, managing times and dates, and file access.

To run Miva Script, your server must have the Miva engine installed. Two forms of the Miva engine are available:

- Miva Empresa is the primary engine that supports remote access for users of the World Wide Web.
- Miva Mia is an offline version of the Miva engine that users can run on their own computer. Miva Mia is useful for developing and testing scripts. It can also be used to perform operations, such as compressing a database, that are time-consuming and might slow down the server if they were done online.

Client-Side vs. Server-Side

In designing Miva Script applications, it is important to remember the difference between server-side execution and client-side scripts such as Javascript. Figures 1-1 and 1-2 illustrate the difference. For client-side scripting, as shown in Figure 1-1, the user requests a specific URL, and the server responds with an HTML document containing embedded scripts. The user's browser receives the document, displays the HTML, and executes the scripts. The scripts may run while the document is being downloaded. They may also continue to run and interact with the user, long after the download is complete.

Figure 1-1: Document request with client-side scripts

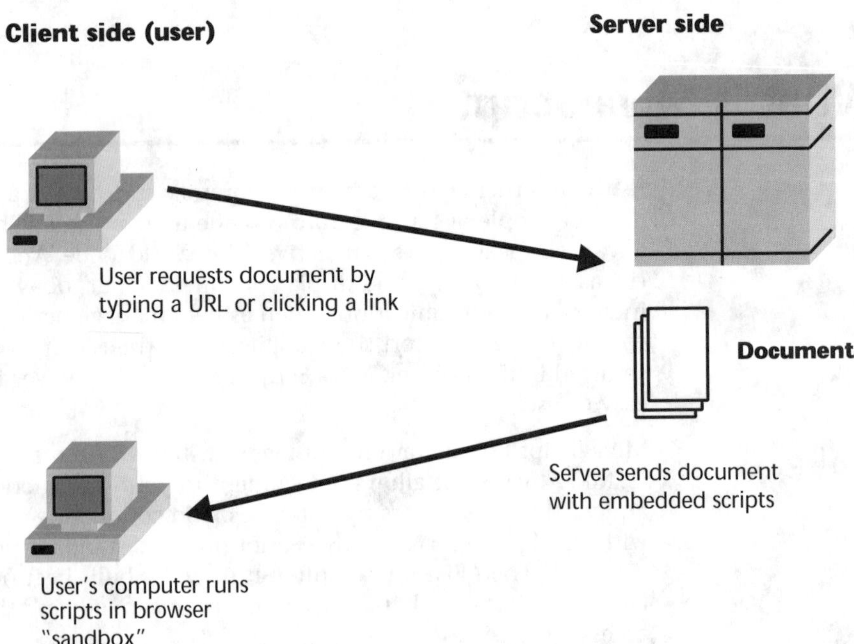
Client side (user)
Server side
User requests document by typing a URL or clicking a link
Document
Server sends document with embedded scripts
User's computer runs scripts in browser "sandbox"

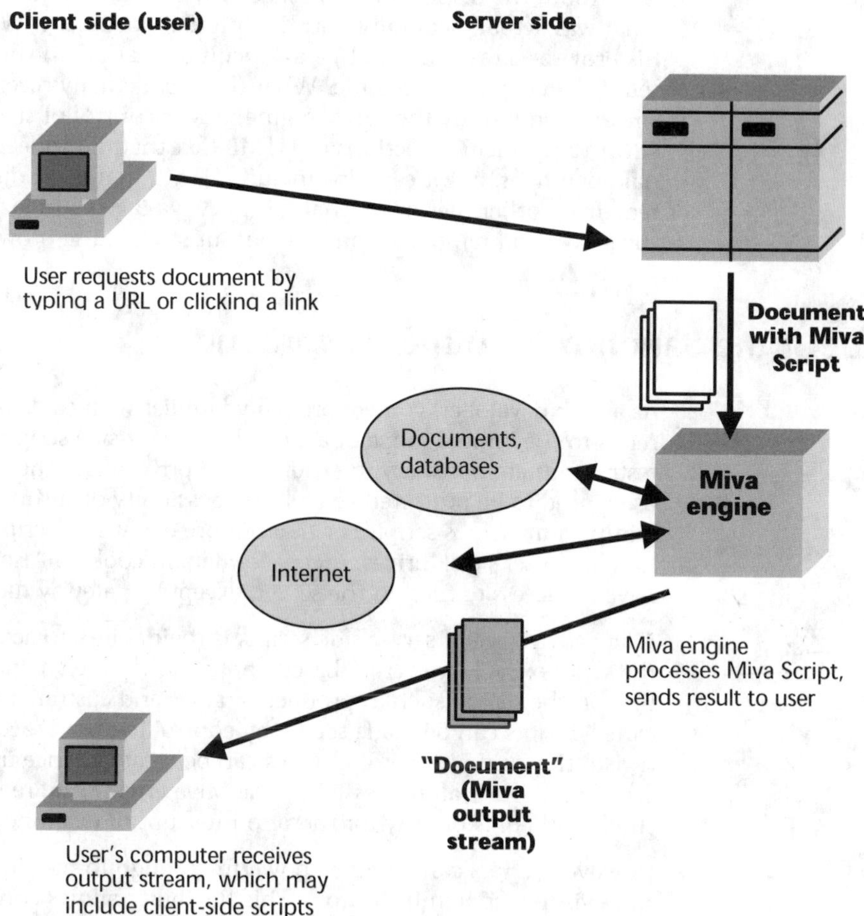

Figure 1-2: Document request with server-side Miva Script

Server-side scripts, on the other hand, operate as shown in Figure 1-2. In this case, after the user requests a document, instead of sending it directly to the browser, the server directs it to the Miva engine. Any embedded Miva Script code (tags or macros) is processed at this time, on the server. Anything other than Miva Script (HTML tags, normal text, etc.) is passed to the browser unchanged. The Miva Script code may perform operations such as:

- Processing data from the query part of the URL, or from files or user data submitted with an HTML form.
- Creating new HTML text and tags, or reading them from other documents, and making them part of the document that is passed to the browser.
- Performing calculations and text manipulation on incoming data.
- Reading and storing information in files and databases.
- Sending and receiving email, and performing e-commerce transactions.

As a result, the display on the user's browser may be quite a bit different from what was actually contained in the original document. What the user sees on his browser screen may not be a "document" at all, in the sense of being a fixed set of data copied from a file. What the user actually receives is the *output stream* produced by the Miva engine, under control of the script. The output stream may include sections of HTML text that did indeed come from the original document, but it can also include HTML that is produced by the script or read from other files. Note that all the Miva tags and macros are processed on the server and removed from the output stream; the browser never sees them.

Out of the Sandbox, into the Playground

As a Web developer, you are probably familiar with the term "sandbox" that refers to the limited range of actions that client-side scripts can take. These restrictions are necessary to ensure users' privacy and the security of their data: users need to be protected against the possibility of surfing to a Web page containing a malicious script. For that reason, client-side scripts can not access any files on a user's disk drives, except for data in cookies. Also, client-side scripts have no access to files on the server, except by gateway mechanisms such as CGI.

A key advantage of server-side scripts is their ability to access resources outside the sandbox. A Miva Script–based application can read and write a variety of files on the server, such as product catalogs and customer orders or "shopping carts." Scripts can be made secure by controlling users' access to these files. User registration and password schemes can be created. Since users never see the Miva Script code—it is all processed by the Miva engine and removed from the output stream—there is no way for them to interrupt or examine the Miva Script.

However, scripts can be made powerful enough to provide full file access for supervisors and administrators. This flexibility allows complete applications to be developed with no program code other than Miva Script embedded in a series of Web pages.

An application can easily use client-side scripts as well as Miva Script; both kinds of code can be written into a single document. Miva Script can even create Javascript or other client-side code "on the fly." However, remember that the behavior of a client-side script may vary quite a bit depending on the brand and version of browser on which it runs. This highlights another advantage of using Miva Script: a single scripting language provides uniform results on all browsers.

Editing and Testing Scripts

Miva Script is easy to edit. Like HTML, it is basically just text; you can edit scripts with a simple text editor such as Unix "vi" or Windows Notepad. You can also use a more sophisticated or WYSIWYG editor, as long as:

- It can save files in plain text form.

- It gives you enough control over the location and content of scripts, tags, and macros.
- It doesn't have any features that interfere with the formatting of the HTML and Miva Script code.

Using a simple editor may be tedious if the files to be edited are large. However, a large Miva Script–based application will probably consist of many short files, rather than a few long ones; so a simple editor may be sufficient. You can often divide a long script into several short ones by defining functions (see Chapter 3).

As with HTML, Miva Script is mostly a free-format language. White space characters such as spaces, tabs, and extra blank lines can be used wherever you want, except in a few places such as inside variable names or string literals (see Chapter 2). The use of white space is also subject to HTML's usual rules: leaving space between tags and text may affect the display on the browser.

When creating and testing scripts, you can use Miva Mia in a single-user, offline environment. This allows you to develop and test everything without tying up your Web server. It also eliminates the need to place untested files on the World Wide Web, where a user might accidentally stumble into your testbed.

Miva Script has a number of features that support testing and debugging of scripts. The `<MIVA>` tag allows you to control Miva processing, which can help make programming errors easier to find. The `<MvCOMMENT>` tag allows you to put explanatory notes in your scripts. Both of these tags are described later in this chapter. Also, for every tag, there is an error variable which scripts can use to check for error conditions (see Chapter 2).

Running and Stopping Scripts

Web users usually start a script by clicking on a link or typing a URL into their browser. A Miva Script URL is very similar to one for a normal HTML document, except that Miva Script filenames usually end with `.mv`. On most servers, a typical URL will have the form

http://www.YourDomain.com/scriptname.mv?query

where `scriptname.mv` is the filename of the script to execute, and `?query` is optional text that may be used to pass data to the script. This type of URL is used with Miva Mia, and also with versions of Miva Empresa that use the Netscape API (NSAPI).

Some servers use the CGI version of Empresa. In that case, a URL will look more like:

http://www.YourDomain.com/cgi-bin/miva?scriptname.mv+query

In this case, `miva` is the filename of the (CGI) program, `scriptname.mv` is the first argument to the program, and `+query` is the optional text.

The exact interpretation of URLs will vary depending on how your domain and server are configured. For specifics, consult the administrator of your server. To ensure that your scripts are portable, you can use built-in variables such as `server_name` to write scripts that will accept either type of URL. For more information on using URLs to communicate with scripts, see Chapter 4.

The URL from the user's request is passed to a Web server, which identifies it as referring to a Miva Script file, and passes the file to the Miva engine. Once a script is started, it can execute other scripts by using the `<MvDO>` tag (See Chapter 3). This supports modular programming, since a large application can be divided into a number of smaller documents with less redundancy.

A script stops running when the Miva engine reaches the end of the file. A script can also terminate itself at any time with the `<MvEXIT>` tag. Also, the Miva engine will cause a *timeout* and force termination of a script if it runs too long without stopping. For more information on controlling scripts, see Chapter 3.

Anatomy of a Script

Before proceeding any further, we should define exactly what we mean by "script," since its meaning in Miva Script may be different from other scripting languages that you are familiar with. For instance, in client-side languages such as Javascript, a script is a clearly defined part of a document: it starts with a `<SCRIPT>` tag, and ends with `</SCRIPT>`. However, to the Miva engine, the entire document is a script. Miva Script tags and macros may be interspersed freely with HTML tags and regular text. Even a document with no Miva Script at all can be successfully processed by the Miva engine, although the "processing" would simply be a matter of passing the document unchanged to the output stream. Conversely, it is possible to write a valid script that accesses databases and does lots of useful work, but displays nothing at all on the user's browser. In this manual, then, the terms "script" and "document" are largely equivalent.

To learn how Miva Script is used, it is helpful to look at an extremely simple example, as shown in Listing 1-1.

Listing 1-1: A simple Miva Script example

```
1. <HTML>
2. <BODY>
3. <H1> Miva Script test </H1>
4. <MvASSIGN NAME="message" VALUE="{'Hello there'}">
```

```
5. Miva says &[message];. <P>
6. Louder: <MvEVAL EXPR="{toupper(message)}">!
7. </BODY>
8. </HTML>
```

Miva Script is used inside valid HTML documents. This document starts with the `<HTML>` and `<BODY>` tags, and ends with the corresponding `</BODY>` and `</HTML>`. After the `<BODY>` tag is a title for the document, which is displayed as a level-1 HTML heading because of the `<H1>` tag.

Miva Script uses tags and attributes in a manner much like HTML. Line 4 of this script uses the Miva Script tag named `<MvASSIGN>`. This tag has two attributes, `NAME` and `VALUE`. The tag creates a Miva Script variable named `message`, and puts the text `Hello there` in the variable. (In programming terminology, we say that the tag *assigns* the *value* `Hello there` to the variable.)

Line 5 of the script contains text that includes a Miva Script *macro*:

```
&[message];
```

A macro consists of the characters `&[` (ampersand and left square bracket) followed by a variable name and the characters `];` (right bracket and semicolon). A macro causes the contents of a variable to be placed in the output stream, so that it will be passed to the user as if it were part of the document. Since the variable `message` contains the text `Hello there`, line 5 causes the text "Miva says Hello there." to be displayed on the user's browser.

Line 6 contains the `<MvEVAL>` tag, which works similarly to the macro: it allows a script to insert text into the output stream. The text to insert is specified by the `EXPR` attribute. Instead of a variable name, this attribute can be a Miva Script *expression*, which may contain several variables and other types of symbols. Miva Script expressions are always enclosed by the brace or "curly bracket" characters, `{` and `}`. Expressions may be used as the value part of any attribute of any Miva Script tag.

The expression used here, `toupper(message)`, is a *call* to a *system function* named `toupper` that converts all the characters of `message` to upper case. In programming terminology, we say that the function *returns a value* consisting of all uppercase characters. So line 6 causes the text "Louder: HELLO THERE!" to be placed in the output stream.

Figure 1-3 shows what the browser screen might look like after loading the sample document. The following sections describe the parts of a script in more detail.

Figure 1-3:

Results of example script

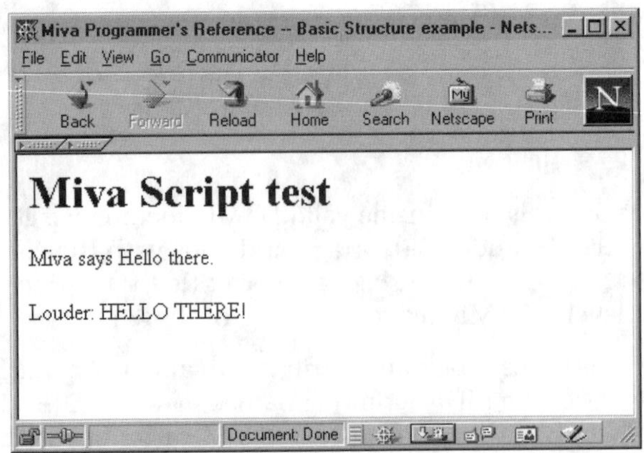

Tags and Attributes

As you have seen, Miva Script tags and attributes use the same syntax as HTML. Tag names are enclosed in angle brackets, < and >. Most Miva Script tag names start with the letters `Mv`. A tag may be a *container*, in which case it has a beginning and ending tag; for instance, `<MvIF>` must be used with a corresponding `</MvIF>`. Collectively, the two tags and the part of the document that they enclose are sometimes called a *block*. Tags that are not containers, known as *empty* tags, are used by themselves, such as the `<MvEVAL>` and `<MvASSIGN>` shown in the above example.

A tag may have one or more *attributes*, such as the `EXPR` attribute used with `<MvEVAL>` in the above example. Each attribute consists of a name and a value, separated by an equal sign.

In this manual, tag names and attributes are always shown in upper case, except for the lower case `v` in tag names that start with `Mv`. This is optional, as upper and lower case are equivalent in HTML, and also in Miva Script. Note, however, that in other places, particularly variable names and string literals, upper and lower case are **not** equivalent.

In Miva Script, as in HTML, attribute values do not need to be enclosed in quotes, unless they contain spaces or other special characters. However, it may be advisable to always use the quotes, for the sake of consistency, and to eliminate possible bugs in scripts. In this manual, all attribute values are shown enclosed in double quotes (`"`).

In HTML, either double quotes or single quotes (`'`) may be used to enclose attribute values; they are equivalent. In Miva Script, however, the two types of quotes have different meanings in some cases. Single quotes are required in some expressions, so it is advisable to always use double quotes around attribute values.

You can nest Miva Script tags inside HTML tags, and vice versa. You cannot nest one Miva Script tag inside another. However, you can often use a macro (see below) to achieve that effect, by placing the value of a variable into a tag's attribute.

The following sections describe two tags that are of general use to all Miva Script applications. Other tags are described in the following chapters.

<MIVA> tag

The `<MIVA>` tag allows you to control how the Miva engine processes your document. This can help with debugging scripts.

As seen by the Miva engine, a file consists of Miva tags, Miva macros, and "everything else." The `INTERPRET` attribute allows you to enable and disable the processing of Miva tags and/or macros. This has the effect of filtering the input to the Miva engine.

If you write `<MIVA INTERPRET="tags">`, Miva will stop processing macros; they will appear in the output stream unchanged, as an entity beginning with `&` and ending with `;`. If you write `INTERPRET="macros"`, Miva will process macros, but it will ignore tags; they will not appear in the output stream at all. Normal Miva processing is selected by `INTERPRET="tags,macros"`; this is the default condition. Giving `INTERPRET` a null value `""`, or any other value, will disable all Miva processing. If you are trying to debug a tricky application, temporarily disabling tag or macro processing may be a big help.

You can also control the output side of Miva processing. The output stream consists of HTML (tags and entities) and document text. The `STANDARDOUTPUTLEVEL` attribute allows you to enable and disable the output of HTML tags and/or document text. This has the effect of filtering the output of the Miva engine.

You can write `STANDARDOUTPUTLEVEL="text"` to suppress HTML code, and output only text, or `STANDARDOUTPUTLEVEL="html"` to suppress the text and pass the HTML. Normal Miva processing is selected by `STANDARDOUTPUTLEVEL="text,html"`; this is the default condition. Giving `STANDARDOUTPUTLEVEL` a null value `""`, or any other value, will disable all Miva output.

The `<MIVA>` tag also has a number of attributes that allow you to control error handling. For details, see the description of the tag in the Reference section of this manual.

<MvCOMMENT> tag

Programmers often include descriptive notes or other text in their files, and Miva Script provides the `<MvCOMMENT>` tag for this purpose. Everything between an `<MvCOMMENT>` and the corresponding `</MvCOMMENT>` is completely ignored by the Miva engine. It is not processed or included in the output stream.

Macros

As described above, a Miva Script macro consists of the characters `&[vvv];`, where *vvv* is a variable name. This is similar to an HTML *entity*. You may be familiar with other entities, such as `<` and `>` that are used instead of < and > to prevent confusion in HTML tag processing.

A macro causes the contents of the variable to be placed in the output stream. Note that macros can only by used with single variables. You can **not** put an expression, such as `{subtotal + tax}`, in a macro; you must use the `<MvEVAL>` tag for that.

One use of macros is to insert the values of Miva Script variables into tag attributes. For example, an HTML tag such as

```
<FONT COLOR="&[newcolor];">
```

will cause the browser to display text in the color specified by the Miva Script variable named `newcolor`.

Security and Encoding Macros

A possible security hazard exists if you use any macros whose values are provided by the user, perhaps by typing into a text box in a form. If, for instance, a malicious user types a Miva Script expression into the text box, and the text from the box is later placed in the output stream by a macro, it could have the effect of executing the expression that the user typed.

Caution: For security, do not use a variable in a macro unless its value is known. Don't use a macro for data entered by users or received from other external sources—or if you do, be sure to take precautions, as described below.

One way to provide security for macros is by writing script code to check for the presence of any Miva Script in the text the user enters. Another way is to specify *entity encoding* by adding a colon and the word `entities` to the macro, that is, `&[vvv:entities]` for a variable *vvv*. In this case, Miva examines the contents of the variable, and changes any special characters, such as < and >, to their entity equivalents before it passes the variable to the output stream. This will not affect how the output looks on the user's browser, but it will prevent tags and macros in the text from being processed. Entity encoding and decoding can also be performed by the `encodeentities()` and `decodeentities()` system functions (see Chapter 2).

Macros can also perform *attribute encoding*, which is useful for values that will be included in the query part of a URL, to download a new document or perform a transaction on a remote server. You specify attribute encoding by adding a colon and the word `attribute` to the macro, that is, `&[vvv:attribute]` for a variable *vvv*. In this case, Miva examines the contents of the variable, and changes any special characters to safe substitutes; for instance, an equal sign (=) is changed to `%3D`.

Functions

A Miva Script *function* is a part of a script, or a feature that is built in to the Miva engine, that is "packaged" so that it can be used, or *called*, within a script. The built-in features, called *system functions*, perform a variety of tasks for mathematics, text manipulation, and file and document processing. You can also create your own Miva Script functions with the `<MvFUNCTION>` tag, and call them with `<MvDO>`, as explained in Chapter 3.

Most functions accept one or more values, called *parameters* or *arguments*, that control their action or provide data for them to operate on. For example, the system function call `fdelete('myfile.dbf')` can be used to delete a file named by the argument, `'myfile.dbf'`.

A function can *return* a value to the script that called it, allowing it to act like a "smart variable" whose value depends on the arguments. For example, the system function `sqrt(x)` returns the square root of the value in the variable `x`. Functions written in Miva Script can return values by using the `<MvFUNCRETURN>` tag.

For More Information

For more detailed information on any of the tags and system functions discussed in this chapter, see the Reference section of this manual.

The script shown in Listing 1-1 is available online at this manual's companion Web site:

http://TopFloor.com/Miva/

2

Data and Expressions

Miva Script works with several types of data. Numbers, text, and other specialized data types can be used in expressions, assigned to variables, and passed to the output stream.

This chapter describes Miva Script's basic data objects:

- *Literals* have specific values but no name, such as the number `4` or the text `'Hello there.'`
- *Variables* have both a name and a value, such as `message` or `salestax`.
- *Function calls* can execute program functions and return result values, such as `toupper(message)` or `sin(theta)`.
- *Expressions* can use variables, literals, function calls, and symbols called *operators*, and return new values, such as `{toupper(message)}` or `{subtotal + shipping + tax}`.

Before reading this chapter, you may wish to type in the script for the Expression Calculator, which is shown in Figure 2-1; or you can download it from this manual's companion Web site. The Expression Calculator lets you type in values and expressions, and see the results by clicking a button. The calculator displays four text boxes into which you can type string or numeric values. The values are assigned to four variables named `a`, `b`, `c`, and `d`. Below the variables are four larger text boxes, into which you can type entire expressions. Each time you click the Recalculate button, Miva updates the variables, reevaluates the expressions, and displays the new results.

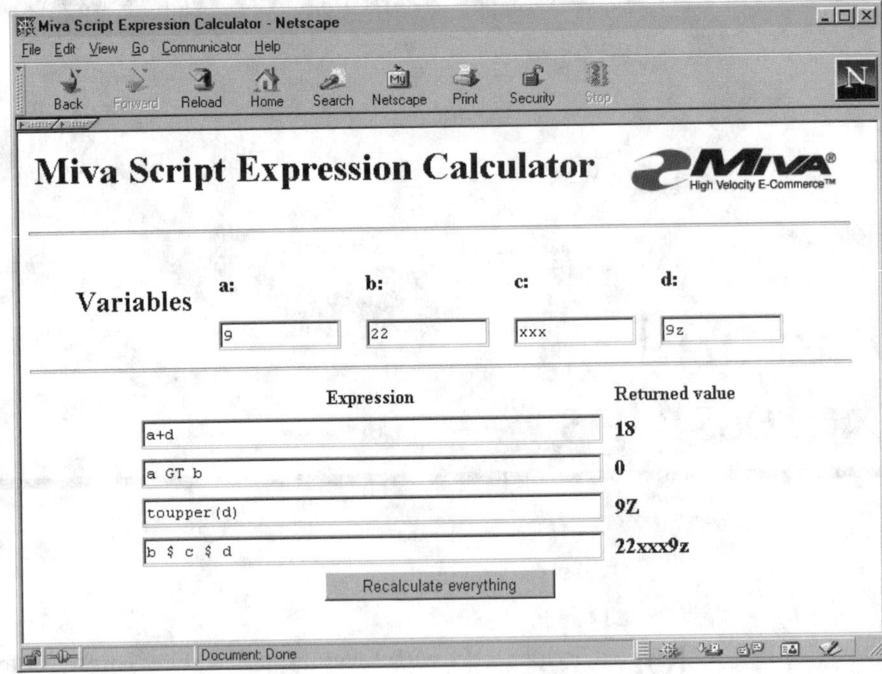

Figure 2-1: Using the Expression Calculator

Although the script uses some concepts that have not yet been explained, having the calculator running on your machine while you read this chapter can help you understand how Miva handles data. Basically, the script displays an HTML form into which you type values and expressions. Clicking the Recalculate button causes the script to rerun itself, and the values from the form fields are converted into variables that the script can use. (For complete information on using forms, see Chapter 4.)

Listing 2-1: Expression Calculator

```
<FORM ACTION="&[s.documenturl];" METHOD="POST">
<TABLE WIDTH="90%">
 <TR>
  <TD> <H2> Variables </H2> </TD>
  <TD> <H3> a: </H3> <INPUT TYPE="TEXT" NAME="a"
VALUE="&[a];" SIZE="12"> </TD>
  <TD> <H3> b: </H3> <INPUT TYPE="TEXT" NAME="b"
VALUE="&[b];" SIZE="12"> </TD>
  <TD> <H3> c: </H3> <INPUT TYPE="TEXT" NAME="c"
VALUE="&[c];" SIZE="12"> </TD>
```

```
  <TD> <H3> d: </H3> <INPUT TYPE="TEXT" NAME="d"
VALUE="&[d];" SIZE="12"> </TD>
 </TR>
</TABLE>
<HR>
<TABLE>
 <TR>
  <TH> Expression </TH>
  <TH> Returned value </TH>
 </TR>
 <TR>
  <TD> <INPUT TYPE="TEXT" NAME="expr1" VALUE="&[expr1];"
SIZE="48"> </TD>
  <TD> <MvIF EXPR="{expr1}"> <H3> <MvEVAL
EXPR="{&[expr1];}"> </MvIF> </TD>
 </TR>
 <TR>
  <TD> <INPUT TYPE="TEXT" NAME="expr2" VALUE="&[expr2];"
SIZE="48"> </TD>
  <TD> <MvIF EXPR="{expr2}"> <H3> <MvEVAL
EXPR="{&[expr2];}"> </MvIF> </TD>
 </TR>
 <TR>
  <TD> <INPUT TYPE="TEXT" NAME="expr3" VALUE="&[expr3];"
SIZE="48"> </TD>
  <TD> <MvIF EXPR="{expr3}"> <H3> <MvEVAL
EXPR="{&[expr3];}"> </MvIF> </TD>
 </TR>
 <TR>
  <TD> <INPUT TYPE="TEXT" NAME="expr4" VALUE="&[expr4];"
SIZE="48"> </TD>
  <TD> <MvIF EXPR="{expr4}"> <H3> <MvEVAL
EXPR="{&[expr4];}"> </MvIF> </TD>
 </TR>
```

```
</TABLE>

<INPUT TYPE="SUBMIT" VALUE="Recalculate everything">

</FORM>
```

Types of Data

A Miva Script *literal* is a part of a script that has a specific value and one of the following data types:

- Numbers.
- Text.
- Logical data (true or false).
- Bitwise data (binary numbers used for logical operations).
- Times and dates stored in Miva's universal format.

Miva can convert data from one type to another automatically. For instance, if you use the number 407 in a place where Miva expects a string, Miva will convert the number to the three-character string `'407'` and use that value for subsequent operations.

The following sections describe the types of data that Miva Script can use, and how to write them.

Numbers

Numbers are written in the usual way, as series of digits. A decimal point may be included. Unlike some languages, Miva Script usually does not make a distinction between *integers* (numbers without a decimal) and *real* or *floating-point* numbers (with a decimal). The only exception is for field variables in databases; for them, the number of digits and the position of the decimal point must be defined when the database is created. (For more details on databases, see Chapter 6).

Some examples of valid numbers are:

```
4

0.004

1234.567

-99
```

As the fourth example shows, you can write a negative number by placing a minus sign immediately before the first digit. Do not leave a space between the minus sign and the digit.

Miva Script provides a number of system functions for performing mathematical operations on numbers, as summarized below:

Function call	Returned value
`abs(x)`	absolute value of `x`
`acos(x)`	arccosine of `x`
`asin(x)`	arcsine of `x`
`atan(x)`	arctangent of `x`
`atan2(y, x)`	arctangent of quotient (`y / x`)
`ceil(x)`	"ceiling" (lowest greater integer) of `x`
`cos(x)`	cosine of `x`
`cosh(x)`	hyperbolic cosine of `x`
`exp(x)`	*e* to the power of `x`
`floor(x)`	"floor" (greatest lower integer) of `x`
`fmod(x, d)`	floating-point remainder of `x` divided by `d`
`int(x)`	integer part of `x`
`log(x)`	natural logarithm of `x`
`log10(x)`	base-10 logarithm of `x`
`power(x, p)`	`x` raised to the `p`'th power
`random(x)`	a random number no higher than `x`
`rnd(x, p)`	`x` rounded to `p` decimal places
`sin(x)`	sine of `x`
`sinh(x)`	hyperbolic sine of `x`
`sqrt(x)`	square root of `x`
`tan(x)`	tangent of `x`
`tanh(x)`	hyperbolic tangent of `x`

Text: Characters and Strings

Computer text is made of *characters*. A character can be one of the following:

- A normal, printable symbol, such as a letter, digit, or punctuation mark.
- *White space*, such as the space, tab, and Newline characters.
- *Control characters* are used for various specialized purposes; they may or may not be visible when sent to the browser as part of the output stream.

Most English-language applications use the ISO Latin-1 character set (see Appendix B for a complete listing). This manual will assume that this character set is being used for all examples.

The character set defines each character as a number. The system functions `asciichar()` and `asciivalue()` can be used to change numbers to characters, and vice versa. For example, `asciivalue('z')` returns 122, because the lowercase `z` is represented by the number 122.

A series of characters is often called a *string* in programming terminology. Generally, you write a string literal by enclosing the text in single-quote (apostrophe) characters (`'`). Some examples are:

Literal	Description
`'Hello there'`	This is the message from the example in Chapter 1.
`'The song is named "Maria."'`	This string contains double-quote characters.
`'It\'s my favorite.'`	Single quotes normally mark the beginning and end of a literal. To put one inside a literal, you must precede it with the backslash (\) character.
`'a'`	This string consists of a single character.
`''`	This string contains no characters at all, but it is valid nonetheless. It is called the *null* or *empty string*, and has a length of 0.

The number of characters in a string is called its *length*. You can determine the length of a string by using the `len()` system function. For example, `len(address)` returns the number of characters in a variable named `address`. Within a string, individual characters can be referred to by their position, with the first character numbered 1. For example, if the variable `s` contains the string `'abcdefghij'`, then the system function `substring(s, 3, 4)` returns `'cdef'`: a string of 4 characters, starting at the third character of `s`.

Miva Script provides a number of system functions for working with strings, as summarized below:

Function call	Returned value
`asciichar(n)`	Character whose numeric value is `n`
`asciivalue(c)`	Numeric value of the character in `c`
`decodeattribute(s)`	Copy of `s` with URL-encoded characters converted to normal text
`decodeentities(s)`	Copy of `s` with entity-encoded characters converted to normal text
`encodeattribute(s)`	Copy of `s` with special characters encoded for inclusion in URLs
`encodeentities(s)`	Copy of `s` with special characters encoded for inclusion in HTML
`gettoken(s, sep, n)`	`n`'th token in string `s`, with substring `sep` as divider between tokens
`glosub(s, old, new)`	Copy of `s` with all occurrences of substring `old` replaced by `new`
	True (1) if all characters in the string `s` are:
`isalnum(s)`	alphanumeric (letters or digits)
`isalpha(s)`	letters
`isascii(s)`	valid ASCII characters (values 0-127)
`iscntrl(s)`	control characters (values 0-31 or 127)
`isdigit(s)`	decimal digits
`isgraph(s)`	graphic characters (values 33-127)
`islower(s)`	lowercase letters
`isprint(s)`	printable characters (values 32-127)
`ispunct(s)`	punctuation symbols (graphic characters that are not letters or digits)
`isspace(s)`	white space: space (32), tab (9), vertical tab (11), Newline (10), or form feed (12)
`isupper(s)`	uppercase letters
`isxdigit(s)`	hexadecimal digits: decimal digits, or letters A-F (upper- or lowercase)
`len(s)`	Length of `s`
`ltrim(s)`	Copy of `s` with spaces removed from the left (front)

Function call	Returned value
`padl(s)`	Copy of `s` padded with fill characters at the left (beginning)
`padr(s)`	Copy of `s` padded with fill characters at the right (end)
`rtrim(s)`	Copy of `s` with spaces removed from the right side (end)
`substring(s, n, l)`	Part of `s`, starting at `n`'th character, with length `l`
`tolower(s)`	Copy of `s` with uppercase letters converted to lowercase
`toupper(s)`	Copy of `s` with lowercase letters converted to uppercase

Character Encoding

Miva Script provides two ways to modify strings by using substitutes for certain characters. *Entity encoding* is used for text that is being sent to a browser. In entity-encoded strings, characters are replaced with HTML entity equivalents; the most common ones are listed in the table below:

Character	Replacement
"	`"`
&	`&`
<	`<`
>	`>`

A complete list of entity codes can be found in Appendix B.

Scripts can also perform *attribute encoding*, which is useful for values that will be included in the query part of a URL, to download a new document or perform a transaction on a remote server. In attribute-encoded strings, spaces may be changed to + characters, and most punctuation and international characters are changed to a `%` followed by 2 hexadecimal digits (`0-9` or `A-F`); for instance, a slash character (/) is encoded as `%2F`.

Strings can be encoded by using the `encodeentities()` or `encodeattribute()` system function, or by using encoding macros as explained in Chapter 1. To decode an encoded string, i.e., to restore the original characters, use the `decodeentities()` or `decodeattribute()` system function.

Logical Data

Some Miva Script operations, such as making "either-or" selections with `<MvIF>` and `<MvELSE>`, use data whose only possible values are "true" and "false." These are called *logical* or *Boolean* operations.

Miva Script operations that produce a logical result use the value 1 for true, and 0 for false. For example, all databases have a variable called `eof` that will be equal to 1 if Miva has navigated beyond the last record of the database (`eof` stands for End Of File).

Miva Script operations that check a value to make a decision will consider it false if it is either 0 or the null string `''`. All other values will be considered true.

Bitwise Data

Miva Script provides some operations that treat numbers as *binary* values: groups of binary digits or *bits*, whose value is either 0 or 1. Miva Script has *bitwise* operators that perform logical operations on the individual bits (described later in this chapter). Bitwise operations are used with some system functions, such as `fchmod()` that sets file permission bits on Unix systems.

Times and Dates

Times and dates are useful for all kinds of business applications. Programming them can be difficult, because of the various conversions: seconds per minute, hours per day, various numbers of days in the month, etc. So Miva Script provides a number of features to ease this task.

Miva Script supports a *universal* format, also referred to as "`time_t` format" in some Miva documents. In this format, all the elements of a date and time are compressed into a single number representing the number of seconds since midnight, January 1, 1970, in universal time (also called Greenwich Mean Time or GMT). Miva Script provides system functions that read and write the various parts of the time and date. It also calculates time-zone adjustment in order to convert universal time to your local time.

Caution: When working with Miva Script time/date functions, keep the following points in mind:

1. Miva Script universal format only works for dates from January 1, 1970, through January 19, 2038.

2. Miva Script does **not** automatically adjust for Daylight Savings Time.

Miva provides a number of system variables that allow scripts to obtain time and date information, as listed in the table below. The static variables always contain the time when the script started; their values will not change while a script is executing. The dynamic variables always provide the current time and date; their values may change while the script is executing.

Static variable	Dynamic variable	Type	Value
time_t	dyn_time_t	Number	Number of seconds since January 1, 1970
tm_hour	dyn_tm_hour	Number	Current hour of the day, 0-23
tm_isdst	dyn_tm_isdst	Logical	True (1) if Daylight Savings Time is in effect
tm_mday	dyn_tm_mday	Number	Current day of the month, 1-31
tm_min	dyn_tm_min	Number	Current minute of the hour, 0-59
stm_mon	dyn_stm_mon	String	Current month, 3-letter abbreviation
tm_mon	dyn_tm_mon	Number	Current month, 1-12
tm_sec	dyn_tm_sec	Number	Current second of the minute, 0-59
tm_usec	dyn_tm_usec	Number	Current microsecond of the second, 0-999999. (This value may not be constantly updated. On Windows systems, it is advanced at 50-ms intervals.)
stm_wday	dyn_stm_wday	String	Current day of the week, 3-letter abbreviation
tm_wday	dyn_tm_wday	Number	Current day of the week: 1 = Sunday, 2 = Monday, etc.
tm_yday	dyn_tm_yday	Number	Current day of the year, 1-366
tm_year	dyn_tm_year	Number	Current year, 4 digits
stm_zone	dyn_stm_zone	String	Current time zone, complete string, e.g. `'Central Daylight Time'`

Using these variables in scripts may be simply a matter of displaying them with macros. For example, to display the current time, day of the week, and date, you could write

```
It is now &[tm_hour]; : &[tm_min]; : &[tm_sec];

on &[stm_wday];, &[stm_mon]; &[tm_mday];, &[tm_year];.
```

to produce a message such as

```
It is now 18 : 24 : 39 on Tue, Aug 31, 1999.
```

on the user's screen.

In addition to the system variables, Miva Script provides a number of system functions for working with times and dates, as summarized below:

Function call	Returned value
`mktime_t(yr, mo, dy, hr, min, sec, zone)`	Universal time/date value for specified year, month, day, hour, minute, second, and local time zone
`time_t_dayofmonth(t, z)`	Day of the month (from 1 to 31) from time value `t`, at local time zone `z`
`time_t_dayofweek(t, z)`	Day of the week (Sunday = 1, Monday = 2, etc.) from time value `t`, at local time zone `z`
`time_t_dayofyear(t, z)`	Day of the year (from 1 to 366) from time value `t`, at local time zone `z`
`time_t_hour(t, z)`	Hour (from 0 to 23) from time value `t`, at local time zone `z`
`time_t_min(t, z)`	Minute (from 0 to 59) from time value `t`, at local time zone `z`
`time_t_month(t, z)`	Month (from 1 to 12) from time value `t`, at local time zone `z`
`time_t_sec(t, z)`	Second (from 0 to 59) from time value `t`, at local time zone `z`
`time_t_year(t, z)`	Year (4 digits) from time value `t`, at local time zone `z`
`timezone()`	Number representing the local time zone for use with other time functions

Variables

A Miva Script variable is an object that has a name as well as a value. You can change its value by using the <MvASSIGN> tag to assign a new value to it; for example:

```
<MvASSIGN NAME="count" VALUE="{0}">
```

This sets the variable count to have a value of zero; this could be used to initialize the variable at the start of some series of transactions. Another example:

```
<MvASSIGN NAME="count" VALUE="{count + 1}">
```

This sets count to have the value count + 1, which has the effect of adding 1 to count. This could be used during a Web site user's session, to keep track of how many transactions have been performed.

In Miva Script, unlike some other languages, variables do not have a fixed type. A variable can hold a number one moment, and a string or any other type of data the next.

Variable names normally contain the letters A–Z, digits 0–9, and the underscore (_) character. Other characters can be used if they are preceded by a backslash (\). Upper- and lowercase letters are considered equivalent in variable names.

Names can start with any valid character; however, it is recommended that you not use names starting with a digit, unless it is required by the application. For example, to perform e-commerce transactions with UPS's QuickCost service, you must use the variable names that the server requires, some of which start with numbers (see Chapter 8). Some examples of names are:

```
x
zipcode
number_of_items_in_shopping_cart
```

When creating variables, you should generally give them names that describe the meaning or purpose of the data that they hold. Generally, names should be long enough to be descriptive; too much reliance on abbreviations can make your scripts hard to understand. However, if a variable is used a lot, giving it a short name can make your script more compact and easier to edit.

Some programming languages require you to explicitly define or declare the variables that you will use. In Miva Script, this is not necessary; you simply write the variable into your scripts wherever you need it. Of course, good programming practice generally requires that you do assign some value to a variable before you try to use it in calculations or display it to the user. When variables are created, their initial value is the null string ''.

Caution: Since Miva Script does not require you to declare variables, it is possible for typing errors to create new, unintended variables. For example, if you are using a variable named department, and you accidentally type departmebt somewhere in your script, Miva will not detect an error; it will simply regard departmebt as a new variable.

Variable Scope

Miva Script variables are grouped into regions or zones called *scopes.* Variables in different scopes are kept separate, even if they have the same name. This means that one name may refer to several different variables, depending on where it is used. To prevent any confusion, you can write a variable name with a prefix to specify the scope. The prefix consists of a single letter and a dot (`.`). The available scopes are summarized in the table below:

Name of scope	Prefix	Description
System	`s.`	System variables are built in to Miva, or are created automatically in response to actions by your script (see below).
Local	`l.`	Local variables are attached to a specific function that you create with the `<MvFUNCTION>` tag. They are only available when the function is running. (For details, see Chapter 3.)
Database	`d.` or *`dbname`*`.d.`	Database variables are associated with a specific database that your script has opened. If more than one database is open, you can distinguish between them by using the *`dbname`*`.d.` notation. (For details, see Chapter 6.)
Global	`g.`	Global variables are, everything not listed above: variables that are not assigned to any specific scope.

Of course, if several Web users visit your site at the same time, Miva provides each with a separate set of variables and scopes; multiple users will not read or modify each other's data.

Normally, there is no need to write the prefixes on variable names. Even if you use the same name in several places, Miva can distinguish between them according to its scoping rules. Specifically, as the Miva engine is reading your script, when it encounters a variable name, it searches the scopes in the same order in which they are shown in the table above: system, local, database, and global. So, for example, if you have a local variable and a global variable that are both named `count`, then any occurrences of the name `count` without a prefix will refer to the local one, because the local scope has precedence over the global one. If you need to explicitly reference the global one, you can write `g.count`.

System Variables

Miva Script system variables are those that are provided by the Miva engine, and are available to all scripts. Some of them are available whenever a script is running; for example, `documenturl` always contains a string specifying the URL that was used to call up the currently executing document. Other system variables are only available in certain situations. For example, the `<MvPOP>` tag causes Miva to create a number of system variables that are used for receiving e-mail. Scripts can only use these variables between an `<MvPOP>` and the corresponding `</MvPOP>` that marks the end of the loop (see Chapter 7).

There are two kinds of system variables. *Static* variables are those whose values are assigned by the Miva engine when a script starts executing, and which do not change while the script is executing. *Dynamic* variables are those whose values may change while the script is running. Most system variables are static, except for those that provide current time and date information (as described earlier).

The complete list of system variables, and the data that they contain, may vary depending on what platform and version of the Miva engine you are using. The table below lists most of the variables that are available. The Source column of the table tells where the variable's value is obtained: it may come from the Miva engine, the system environment, or the HTTP header of the document being processed. The Availability columns of the table tell which types of Miva engine provide the variable.

All the variables listed in the table are static except `dyn_time_remaining` and `recno`, which are marked as dynamic in the table. For more information on Miva Script URLs and APIs, see Chapter 4.

			Availability		
Name	**Source**	**Value**	**Empresa CGI**	**Empresa NSAPI**	**Miva Mia**
`apitype`	Miva	Platform: `'CGI'` (Empresa), `'NSAPI'` (Empresa), or `'Mia'`	•	•	•
`arg1, arg2, ...`	Miva	`arg1` returns the filename of the currently executing document, preceded by a slash (/) character. If this document was called by a URL that included a list of values separated by + characters, `arg2`, `arg3`, etc. will return the values from the list. If the document was called by a URL that included a list of name-and-value pairs separated by `&` characters, `arg2` will return the entire list as a single string.	•	•	•

Name	Source	Value	Availability Empresa CGI	Empresa NSAPI	Miva Mia
`auth_type`	Env.	Authentication method used by the server	•	•	
`callerid`	Miva	Each time a cookie-enabled browser accesses a Miva Script document, Miva creates a 32-character cookie that is unique to that browser and URL. The cookie lasts for one year after being set. Cookies can be turned off in Miva Empresa; contact your server administrator.	•	•	•
`content_length`	Env.	Length of any attached `(POST)` information	•		
`content_type`	Env.	Type of data for `POST`	•		
`documenturl`	Miva	Contains URL of the currently running Miva Script document. This URL also contains the character that separates the program name from the command line arguments (`?` for NSAPI and Miva Mia, and `+` for CGI).	•	•	•
`dyn_time_remaining`	Miva	Number of seconds remaining before the script times out (dynamic variable)	•	•	•
`gateway_interface`	Env.	Version of CGI used	•		
`globaltimeout`	Miva	Number of seconds that a script is allowed to execute before Miva will terminate it (timeout)	•	•	•
`http_accept`	HTTP	Comma-separated list of MIME types (type/subtype) that the browser will accept. This list is very incomplete on most browsers.	•	•	•
`http_accept_charset`	HTTP	Character sets preferred by the browser (other than the default ASCII or ISO Latin-1)	•	•	•
`http_accept_language`	HTTP	ISO codes for the languages preferred by the browser	•	•	•
`http_connection`	HTTP	String that browser sends to the server to preserve a TCP connection (also called a "keep-alive" string). Not supported by all browsers and servers.	•	•	•

Name	Source	Value	Availability: Empresa CGI	Empresa NSAPI	Miva Mia
`http_cookie`	HTTP	Contents of all the cookies set for the document	•	•	•
`http_host`	HTTP	Remote host name (usually same as `server_name`)	•	•	•
`http_pragma`	HTTP	Mode under which client is running	•		•
`http_referer`	HTTP	The document from which the current document was accessed	•		•
`http_user_agent`	HTTP	Browser name, platform, version, and library	•	•	•
`mivaversion`	Miva	Version of the Miva Script language preprocessor	•	•	•
`nargs`	Miva	If this document was called by a URL that included a list of values separated by + characters, `nargs` will return the number of values that were passed plus 1. If the document was called by a URL that included a list of name-and-value pairs separated by & characters, `nargs` will always return 2 (see `arg2`, `arg3`, etc. above).	•	•	•
`path_info`	Env.	Extra path information in the URL (a directory path that occurs immediately after the name of the CGI program in the URL)	•	•	
`path_translated`	Env.	`path_info`, translated to a physical location by prepending the server document directory to its value	•		
`process_id`	Miva	Currently running process number	•	•	•
`query_string`	Env.	Information passed after a URL and a ? via the `GET` method	•		
`recno`	Miva	Current record number in a file being read by `<MvIMPORT>`, or current record number in a database (dynamic variable)	•	•	•

Name	Source	Value	Availability		
			Empresa CGI	Empresa NSAPI	Miva Mia
`remote_addr`	Env.	IP address of remote host	•	•	•
`remote_host`	Env.	The domain name of the remote host	•	•	•
`remote_ident`	Env.	Remote username, from servers that support RFC 931 identification	•		
`remote_user`	Env.	Username associated with protected script, on servers that support user authentication	•	•	
`request_method`	Env.	`'GET'`, `'POST'`, or `'HEAD'`	•	•	•
`script_name`	Env.	Virtual path to CGI script; not mapped locally to actual path	•		
`server_hostname`	Env.	Name of the server	•	•	
`server_name`	Env.	Name of the server (same as `server_hostname`, if available)	•	•	•
`server_port`	Env.	Port on which server is running	•		•
`server_port_secure`	Env.	True (1) if the port is secure	•		
`server_protocol`	Env.	Name and revision of protocol used	•	•	•
`server_software`	Env.	HTTP server and version number that processed the request	•		•
`server_url`	Env.	`server_hostname`, in URL format	•	•	
`server_version`	Env.	Version of the server	•	•	
`user_agent`	HTTP	Same as `http_user_agent`		•	
`version`	Miva	Miva Empresa or Miva Mia version number	•	•	•

If you want to examine the names and contents of all the system variables in your current environment, the short script shown in Listing 2-2 will display them.

Listing 2-2: Reading system variables

```
<H1> Miva Script system variables </H1>


<MvASSIGN NAME="list" VALUE="{miva_getvarlist('s')}">
<MvASSIGN NAME="token" VALUE="dummy">
<MvASSIGN NAME="count" VALUE="1">


<MvWHILE EXPR="{gettoken(list, ',', count)}">
 <MvASSIGN NAME="token" VALUE="{gettoken(list, ',',
count)}">
 <MvASSIGN NAME="vval" VALUE="{&[token];}">


 &[count];. &[token]; = &[vval]; <BR>


 <MvASSIGN NAME="count" VALUE="{count + 1}">
</MvWHILE>
```

This script uses the system function `miva_getvarlist()` to obtain a single long string containing the names of all system variables, separated by commas. Then it uses a program loop, defined by `<MvWHILE>`, to extract each name from the string using the `gettoken()` system function. It uses macros to place the name and value in the output stream. The result of running the script will be similar to Figure 2-2. (The system functions and `<MvWHILE>` tag used in this script are explained later in this manual.)

Error Variables

Miva Script provides a set of variables that allow a script to check for error conditions. When the Miva engine detects an error while processing a tag, it normally displays a message in the output stream. However, these messages can be disabled by the `<MIVA>` tag. Whether the message is displayed or not, Miva always places the text of the message in a variable called `ttt_error`, where `ttt` is the name of a tag. For instance, if an error occurs while executing an `<MvOPEN>` tag, a message will be placed in the variable `MvOPEN_error`. Each Miva Script tag has a corresponding `_error` variable. All these variables are global (`g.` scope).

Figure 2-2:

Browser display of system variables

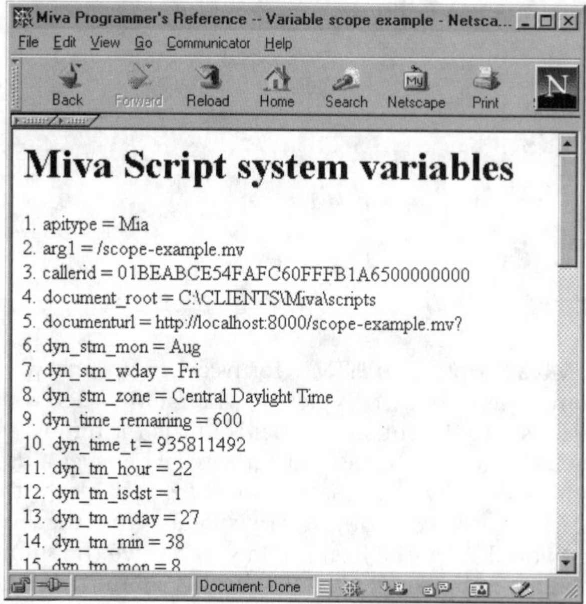

Site Variables

Site variables are those defined in a special source file that is available to the Miva engine. If a site variables file exists, any variables defined in it will be available to all scripts that the engine runs. Scripts can read and write them like other global variables. However, each script has its own local copies of these variables; so if one script changes a site variable's value, the change will not apply to other scripts.

For Miva Empresa, the creation and management of the site variables is handled by the system administrator. For your own copy of Miva Mia, you can create your own file, and specify it in the Miva Mia control panel. The content of the file is plain text; you can edit it with a simple Notepad-type editor, or with most word processing programs if you make sure to save it as plain text when you exit.

Each line of the file consists of a variable name and value, separated by an equal (=) sign. A line that starts with a pound (#) character is a comment that Miva ignores. If a variable name or value is too long to fit on one line, use the backslash (\) character to extend it to another line. The following text could be useful in a site variables file for a developer at a software corporation:

```
# Miva Script site variables for John P.

#

companyname=XYZZY Corporation
```

```
authorname=John Q. Programmer
authordept=Media Services
billingcode=1q23
copyrightnotice=Copyright © 2000 by XYZZY Corporation.\
All rights reserved.
```

Variables in Forms

In Miva Script, as in HTML, forms are the primary way of receiving information from a Web site user. Typically, when a Miva Script application provides a form for a user to fill out, all the fields in the form must be turned into variables for the script to use. To ease this process, whenever a user submits a form to a Miva Script URL, Miva automatically creates variables with names and values that match the contents of the form's fields. Note that this is a two-pass process—first you display the form, then you receive the submitted data—and the variables are not created until the form is submitted. The use of forms is described in more detail in Chapter 4.

Arrays

Most programming languages provide a way to create a single variable that can hold multiple values. Such a variable is usually called an *array*, and individual values called *elements* may be referenced by expressions such as `item[n]`, where `item` is the name of the variable, and `n` is a numeric value that specifies the element. Miva Script does not support array variables; however, you can achieve an equivalent result by using macros.

Miva Script macros allow you to write a script that creates a series of variables, as many as needed for your application. For instance, the tag

```
<MvASSIGN NAME="item&[count];" VALUE="{newitem}">
```

will assign a value to a variable named `item`*N*, where *N* is specified by the variable `count`. If your script initializes `count` to 1, and adds 1 to it each time it needs a new element, it will create variables named `item1`, `item2`, etc.

To read the value stored in an element, you can write `item&[n];`, where `n` is a variable that specifies the element. This notation can be used in expressions and tag attributes. For more information on using arrays, see Chapter 3.

Function Calls

A function call provides a way for a script to do either of the following:

- Execute another script (a user-defined function).
- Use some feature of the Miva engine (a system function).

In either case, a call consists of a function name followed by parentheses, and there may be one or more argument values inside the parentheses. If there is more than one argument, they are separated by commas. Note that the parentheses are required, even if there are no arguments.

A function call can return a value. For instance, in Chapter 1 we saw an example using the system function call `toupper(message)`, which returned a copy of the text from the variable `message` with all lowercase letters converted to uppercase. All system functions return a value. User-defined functions may or may not return a value, depending on how they are written.

Besides returning a value, functions may perform a variety of other tasks. They can assign new values to variables, call other functions, and read and write files or databases. For instance, the system function `fdelete(f)` is used to delete a file whose name is specified by the variable `f`. This function returns a value of true (1) or false (0) to indicate whether or not it succeeded in deleting the specified file.

In some cases, you may call a function in order to have it perform some task, and you may not care what the returned value is. In that case, you must execute the function call with `<MvASSIGN>`, and assign the returned value to a dummy variable. For example, if you want to use `fdelete()` to delete a file, and you don't care whether or not it succeeds, you should **not** write

```
<MvEVAL VALUE="{fdelete('myfile.dbf')}">
```

because it will place the returned value in the output stream, which could cause an unwanted 1 or 0 to appear on the browser screen. Instead, you can write:

```
<MvASSIGN NAME="unused_data" VALUE="{fdelete
('myfile.dbf')}">
```

"Parking" the returned value in a variable keeps it from disturbing your script. Functions and function calls are discussed in more detail in Chapter 3.

Expressions

Miva Script *expressions* are created by combining literals, variables, and function calls with one or more *operators*. Operators are symbols that designate operations to be performed on the data. They include the familiar + for addition and

- for subtraction, as well as many more symbols for other types of operations. When Miva reads an expression, it *evaluates* it; that is, it performs all the specified operations, so that the expression returns a single result value.

The simplest way to evaluate an expression is with the <MvEVAL> tag. For example, the tag

```
<MvEVAL EXPR="{2 + 3}">
```

will place the number 5 in the output stream. The expression is specified by the EXPR attribute of the tag.

Another way to use an expression is to assign its value to a variable, by putting it in the VALUE attribute of an <MvASSIGN> tag, as in:

```
<MvASSIGN NAME="total" VALUE="{subtotal + shipping + tax}">
```

This tag will add up the three variables named subtotal, shipping, and tax, and place the result in the variable named total. (It does not write the result to the output stream.)

The most common uses of expressions are in the VALUE attribute of <MvASSIGN>, and the EXPR attribute of <MvEVAL>, <MvIF>, and <MvWHILE>. However, you can use an expression as the value of **any** attribute in **any** Miva Script tag (but not in HTML tags).

Note that a Miva Script expression must be enclosed by the brace or "curly bracket" characters, { and }. The only exception is a shortcut that allows you to eliminate some typing when you write an expression that consists of a single string literal. In that case, you can omit the usual braces and single quotes. For example, the tag

```
<MvASSIGN NAME="color" VALUE="{'blue'}">
```

can be simplified to:

```
<MvASSIGN NAME="color" VALUE="blue">
```

The two forms are equivalent.

Operators

Most operators are represented by punctuation characters, but some have alphanumeric names. As with variables, operator names may be written in upper- or lowercase. In this manual, operators will be shown in uppercase, to help distinguish them from variables.

The values that an operator uses are called *operands*. Most operators in Miva Script are *binary*, meaning that they use two values. For example, in the expression {a + 1}, the variable a and the literal 1 are the operands.

A few Miva Script operators are *unary:* they use just one operand. The unary operators are the logical complement, NOT, and the bitwise complement,

BITOC. They are written before their operand, as in {NOT x}. The minus sign used to designate a negative number could be considered a unary operator, and it is in some other programming languages. However, in Miva Script, the unary minus is not a fully functional operator, since it can only be used as part of a literal: you can write -1, but not -x.

The following sections describe the various types of operators that Miva Script provides.

Mathematical Operators

Miva Script provides the usual arithmetic operations of addition, subtraction, multiplication, and division, as well as a few other useful operators. They are summarized in the table below.

Symbol	Meaning	Operation
+	Addition	{a + b} returns the sum of a and b.
-	Subtraction	{a - b} returns the difference of a and b.
*	Multiplication	{a * b} returns the product of a and b.
/	Division	{a / b} returns the quotient of a and b.
POW	Power	{a POW b} returns a raised to the power of b.
MOD	Remainder (modulus)	{a MOD b} returns the integer remainder when a is divided by b.
ROUND	Rounding	{a ROUND b} returns a rounded to have no more than b digits to the right of the decimal point.

String Operators

Miva Script provides several operators for manipulating strings, as well as the many system functions listed earlier.

Symbol	Meaning	Operation
$	Concatenation	{a $ b} returns a single string consisting of the characters of a followed by those of b.
IN CIN	Find substring (search from beginning)	{a IN b} returns a number representing the first position in b where a is found. CIN has the same function, but it ignores case: it considers upper- and lowercase letters to be equivalent. If a is not found, these operators return 0.

Symbol	Meaning	Operation
`EIN` `ECIN`	Find substring (search from end)	`{a EIN b}` returns a number representing the last position in `b` where `a` is found. `ECIN` has the same function, but it ignores case: it considers upper- and lowercase letters to be equivalent. If `a` is not found, these operators return 0.
`SUBSTR`	Extract substring	The second operand must be a string containing two numeric values (not variable names) separated by a comma. For example: `{a SUBSTR '7,2'}` returns a substring of `a`, starting at the 7th character, and having a length of 2. You may find the `substring()` system function more convenient in most cases.
`FMT`	Format a string	This operator has a number of features, which are detailed below.
`CRYPT`	Encrypt	This operator encrypts a string in a manner similar to the Unix `crypt` command. `{a CRYPT b}` returns a string created by encrypting `a` according to the key or "salt" value `b`. Only the first eight characters of `a` and the first two characters of `b` are used; others are ignored.

Formatting Strings with the FMT Operator

The `FMT` operator is used for reformatting strings. It has a powerful function that combines searching and editing operations. In the expression `{a FMT b}`, `a` is the string to be edited, called the *source*. `b` is a string that contains a *pattern*, which is a series of characters that instruct Miva how to process the source string.

In processing the `FMT` operation, Miva scans the source string from left to right, while applying instructions from the pattern. It continues as long as the source agrees with, or *matches*, the pattern. It stops scanning when it reaches either a nonmatching character or the end of the source. When processing is finished, Miva returns a value that may contain the matched characters, plus any additional characters added by instructions in the pattern.

A very simple example is the expression

```
{txt FMT '3.'}
```

which applies the pattern `'3.'` to the string in the source variable `txt`. The returned value will be the first 3 characters of `txt`, because the pattern `'3.'` means to match 3 characters. The number `3` is a count, and the `.` character is the pattern modifier that matches a character. The modifiers are listed below:

Character	Matches:	Additional action
`A`	A letter	Causes it to be displayed in uppercase in the returned value.
`a`	A letter	Causes it to be displayed in lowercase in the returned value.
`[Aa]`	A letter	This modifier passes the matched letters to the returned value without changing their case. (See `[]` below.)
`#`	A digit	
`P`	A digit	Causes "padding" with trailing zeroes if necessary to equal the count. For example, `{1 FMT '2P'}` returns `'10'`. Note that this type of padding is probably appropriate only for digits to the **right** of a decimal point.
`S`	A special character: anything except a letter or digit.	
`.`	Any character	
`[`*mmm*`]`	Any character that would match any of the modifiers *mmm*	

As mentioned above, a modifier can be preceded by a number; this causes `FMT` to match the specified number of characters. For example, `'3#'` matches 3 digits. A count of 0 has a special meaning: it causes Miva to accept any number of the specified character, including none. For example, `'0#'` matches any number of digits.

A modifier can also be preceded by an exclamation point (`!`) which has the effect of reversing the modifier. For example, `'!#'` matches a nondigit. One special case is `'!.'`, which has the effect of matching any character and discarding it, rather than including it in the returned value.

When combining a count with a reverse modifier, put the `!` first. For example, to match 3 nondigits, be sure to write `'!3#'`, **not** `'3!#'`.

Patterns have several other features that help reformat strings. An ampersand (`&`) followed by a number and a semicolon (`;`) allows you to insert any character in the returned value. The number, which may consist of up to 3 digits, is the character set value for the desired character (see Appendix B). This feature is very useful for formatting currency (money) values. The string `'&36;'` in a pattern will insert a dollar sign (`$`) into the returned value. Similarly, writing `'&163;'` will insert the British pound symbol (`£`).

Note: The &-notation cannot be used to add characters beyond the end of the source string.

Another useful feature of FMT is the ability to put separators into the returned value at regular intervals. For instance, to dispay a long number with commas between each group of 3 digits, use the pattern '3+,'. For instance, {12345678 FMT '3+,'} returns the string '12,345,678'. In the pattern, the digit before the + specifies the count of digits in each group, and the character after the + specifies the separator character to use. Note that when inserting separators, Miva counts from right to left, as is the usual practice.

We can combine these various features to create an expression that formats a number for output as a currency amount in standard form. The expression

```
{price FMT '&36;3+,0#S2P'}
```

will take the number in the variable price and format it with a dollar sign at the beginning, and two digits after the decimal point. The parts of the pattern are:

- &36; inserts the dollar sign.
- 3+, specifies commas between groups of 3 digits.
- 0# matches any series of digits.
- S matches a special character, presumably a decimal point.
- 2P matches up to 2 digits, adding a second zero if needed.

Comparison Operators

Miva Script provides operators that compare numbers or strings and return a logical (true or false) result value. When comparing strings, these operators use the numeric values of the individual characters (see Appendix B). This means that lowercase letters will have higher values than the corresponding uppercase.

Symbol	Meaning	Operation
GT	Greater-than	{a GT b} returns true (1) if a is greater than b, false (0) otherwise.
LT	Less-than	{a LT b} returns true (1) if a is less than b, false (0) otherwise.
EQ	Equal	{a EQ b} returns true (1) if a is equal to b, false (0) otherwise.
NE	Not-equal	{a NE b} returns true (1) if a is not equal to b, false (0) otherwise.

Symbol	Meaning	Operation
`GE`	Greater-or-equal	`{a GE b}` returns true (1) if `a` is greater than or equal to `b`, false (0) otherwise.
`LE`	Less-or-equal	`{a LE b}` returns true (1) if `a` is less than or equal to `b`, false (0) otherwise.

Logical Operators

Miva Script provides three logical operators that operate on entire values (as opposed to bitwise operations, which operate on individual bits within a number). These operators are often used with `<MvIF>` and `<MvELSE>` for decision making.

Miva considers an operand to be false if it contains the number 0 or the null string `''`; any other value is considered to be true. The result value returned by the operators will be 1 for true, or 0 for false.

Symbol	Meaning	Operation
`NOT`	Complement (opposite)	`{NOT a}` returns true if `a` is false; it returns false if `a` is true.
`AND`	Logical "And"	`{a AND b}` returns true if both `a` and `b` are true; it returns false if either operand is false.
`OR`	Logical "Or"	`{a OR b}` returns true if either `a` or `b` (or both) is true; it returns false if both `a` and `b` are false.

Bitwise Operators

Bitwise operations use numeric operands, which they treat as binary numbers. They perform logical operations on the individual bits. These operations are generally used only for operating-system-related functions and other types of technical programming where an understanding of binary arithmetic and logic might be required. For instance, Miva Script system functions such as `fchmod()` use individual bits within a number to specify the permission status of a file on a hard drive.

Symbol	Meaning	Operation
`BITAND`	Bitwise logical "And"	`{a BITAND b}` returns a number in which each bit is 1 if the corresponding bit in both `a` and `b` is 1.

Symbol	Meaning	Operation
BITOR	Bitwise logical "Or"	{a BITOR b} returns a number in which each bit is 1 if the corresponding bit in either a or b (or both) is 1.
BITXOR	Bitwise logical "Exclusive-Or"	{a BITXOR b} returns a number in which each bit is 1 if the corresponding bit in a or b (but not both) is 1.
BITOC	Bitwise logical complement	{BITOC a} returns a number in which each bit is the opposite of the corresponding bit in a.
BITSL	Bitwise shift left	{a BITSL b} returns the binary value of a, shifted b bits to the left.
BITSR	Bitwise shift right	{a BITSL b} returns the binary value of a, shifted b bits to the right.

Parentheses and Operator Precedence

When writing expressions with more than one operator, it is important to consider the order in which the operators are evaluated. Suppose a retail Web site has a script that evaluates the expression:

```
{subtotal + shipping + tax}
```

Three numbers will be added together; the order of the additions doesn't affect the result. It seems logical to just process the operators from left to right; and in fact, that is what Miva would do in this case.

But suppose the retailer has a special offer to pay half the shipping if the customer clicks the right link. Now the script needs to evaluate:

```
{subtotal + shipping / 2 + tax }
```

Now the picture is different. To get the correct result, Miva must do the division first. If it just goes from left to right, the customer will get 50% off on the merchandise, as well as the shipping cost.

There are several ways to avoid this sort of problem. One is to use parentheses, and change the expression to:

```
{subtotal + (shipping / 2) + tax}
```

When evaluating an expression, Miva always performs operations inside parentheses first. In a long expression, you may even have pairs of parentheses *nested* inside other parentheses. In these cases, Miva starts evaluating at the innermost nesting level, and proceeds outward.

Another way to control the order of evaluation is Miva Script's system of operator priorities, called *precedence*, that can eliminate the need for many parentheses. When evaluating an expression (or part of an expression) where there are no parentheses to specify the order, Miva evaluates the highest-precedence operators first, and then proceeds to the lowest. When two or more operators have the same precedence, Miva evaluates them from left to right.

The precedences of all Miva Script operators are listed below. Operators shown at the same level have equal precedence.

Precedence	Operator(s)
Highest	`NOT`
.	`FMT ROUND CRYPT MOD SUBSTR POW`
.	`/ *`
.	`+ - $ BITAND BITOR BITXOR BITOC BITSL BITSR`
.	`IN CIN EIN CIN EQ NE GE LE LT GT`
Lowest	`AND OR`

So, in Miva Script, the expression

```
{subtotal + shipping / 2 + tax }
```

will actually produce the intended result without parentheses. Division has a higher precedence than addition, so it is evaluated first.

Note that parentheses always override operator precedence in determining the order of evaluation. This means that, if you are writing an expression and you don't recall which operators have which precedence, you can always use parentheses to control how Miva should evaluate the expression. Some programmers like to use the parentheses, even when they are not required, to make their scripts easier to read and understand.

For More Information

For more detailed information on any of the tags and system functions discussed in this chapter, see the Reference section of this manual.

The scripts shown in the Listings are available online at this manual's companion Web site:

http://TopFloor.com/Miva/

See Appendix B for a complete list of the character set used by Miva Script.

For more information on HTTP protocols, see the World Wide Web Consortium's Web Site:

http://w3.org/

3

Program Control

Miva Script provides a number of features for controlling the flow of script execution:

- Conditional execution with <MvIF> and <MvELSE>.
- Program loops created with <MvWHILE>; also other tags that form loops.
- Stopping execution with <MvEXIT>, or when a script times out.
- Dividing a script into functions, and calling them from other scripts.

Each of these topics is discussed in this chapter.

Conditional Execution

A conditional block is a section of a script that may or may not be executed, depending on the conditions of certain variables or expressions. This provides a way for a script to "make decisions."

Miva Script provides conditional execution with the <MvIF> tag, which has a single attribute named EXPR. <MvIF> marks the start of a conditional block, which ends with the corresponding </MvIF>. In order to decide whether or not to execute the block, the Miva engine checks the value of the expression specified by EXPR. The expression is treated as a logical value: it is considered true if its value is anything except 0 or the null string ''. If the expression is true, Miva executes the contents of the block. If the expression is false, Miva skips the block, and continues execution at the point after the </MvIF>.

For example, suppose you are writing a script to be used as part of a retail shopping Web site. You know that people sometimes make typing errors, so you decide to set up your script to warn any user who tries to order more than $1000 worth of merchandise. You could write:

```
<MvIF EXPR="{total GT 1000}">

  <H2> Warning!  Your order's total value is over $1000.
</H2>

  Please check your order, then press Continue or Cancel
below.

</MvIF>
```

The EXPR attribute's value is the expression {total GT 1000}, so the text between <MvIF> and </MvIF> will only be executed if the variable total has a value greater than 1000. (Of course, this example would be used as part of a larger document that shows the user a list of the items ordered, plus the Continue and Cancel buttons.)

More advanced structures can be created with <MvELSE>. This tag, which takes no attributes, is used inside a conditional block: between <MvIF> and </MvIF>. It divides the block into a "true" part and a "false"part. Either part may be executed, depending on the value of EXPR, but not both.

As an example, suppose you are writing a script that displays a form letter or other message on the screen; and you want it to address the user as Mr. or Ms., depending on the user's gender. The user's name and gender were obtained from a database, or perhaps the user typed them into a form earlier in the session; they are stored in variables called lastname and gender. The gender variable consists of a single letter, 'M' or 'F'. To display the proper honorific, you could write:

```
Dear

<MvIF EXPR="{gender EQ 'M'}">

  Mr.

<MvELSE>

  Ms.

</MvIF>

&[lastname];, <P>
```

This script start with the word Dear that begins the message. Next, the <MvIF> tag checks the value of gender. If it contains 'M', the script puts the honorific

Mr. in the output stream. If gender contains 'F' (more precisely, if it contains anything other than 'M'), the script skips Mr. and inserts Ms. instead. Finally, a macro inserts the lastname variable in the display, followed by a comma and a paragraph break.

Multiple Conditions

There are several ways to use <MvIF> for more complex decision making. One is by using logical expressions in the EXPR attribute. For example, suppose you are creating a Web site that sells tickets to some event. The admission price is reduced for children under 12, and also for senior citizens age 65 or over. Assuming that the customer's age is already stored in a variable named age, you can write a script such as:

```
<MvIF EXPR="{age LT 12 OR age GE 65}">

  <Mv ASSIGN NAME="price" VALUE="{1.50}">

<MvELSE>

  <Mv ASSIGN NAME="price" VALUE="{3.50}">

</MvIF>

Your price is <MvEVAL EXPR="{price FMT '&36;3+,0#S2P'}">.
```

The EXPR specifies the expression {age LT 12 OR age GE 65}, which uses the logical OR operator. If the value of age is less than 12 or greater than or equal to 65, the expression will return 1 (true). So the variable price will be assigned either 1.50 or 3.50, depending on the age. The script ends with a line that displays the chosen price on the browser screen; the FMT operator is used to display it in conventional dollars-and-cents notation, as described in Chapter 2.

Logical expressions can include more than one variable. For instance, you might want to sell tickets to a women's health symposium that is only open to women over age 18. In that case, you could write a tag such as:

```
<MvIF EXPR="{age GE 18 AND gender EQ 'F'}>
```

This expression checks whether age is at least 18, and gender contains 'F'. It will only return true if both of these conditions are met.

Logical operators can be used with other types to make fairly complex decisions. If necessary, you can use parentheses to control the order in which the operators are evaluated. This was not necessary in the above examples, because the comparison operators have a higher precedence than the logical operators. Sometimes, you may include parentheses in a complex expression, simply to make it easier to read. (For more details on expressions and precedence, see Chapter 2.)

Caution: When making comparisons, be careful about the distinction between similar operators, such as GT and GE. This happens in ordinary conversation, as well as in computer language: "children under 12" is not the same as "children 12 and under." If you get one of these wrong, the result might be one unhappy client, or a whole lot of unhappy 12-year-olds.

Multiple Results

Sometimes, a script needs to make a decision that cannot be squeezed into a single expression. Suppose you want to sell tickets at a reduced price for seniors, but make them free for children. You only need to check one variable (age), but now you have three possible outcomes; and <MvIF> and <MvELSE> only provide for two choices.

There are several ways to make multiple-result decisions. One way is to *nest* one <MvIF> inside another, as in:

```
<MvIF EXPR="{age LT 12}">
  <MvASSIGN NAME="price" VALUE="{0}">
<MvELSE>
  <MvIF EXPR="{age GE 65}">
    <MvASSIGN NAME="price" VALUE="{1.50}">
  <MvELSE>
    <MvASSIGN NAME="price" VALUE="{3.50}">
  </MvIF>
</MvIF>
```

This script first checks if age is under 12, and if so, assigns a price of 0 (free). If age is not under 12, the script enters another <MvIF> which checks whether the value is at least 65. This combination of two <MvIF>'s allows you to make a three-way choice.

You can always use a set of "n" nested <MvIF>'s to make an "n+1" -way choice. But as "n" gets large, this becomes inconvenient. All those nested tags can be confusing to read, and they may be difficult to edit if you need to rearrange the various alternatives. In this case, you can use a series of nonnested <MvIF>'s; for instance, the above example can be rearranged into:

```
<MvIF EXPR="{age LT 12}">
  <MvASSIGN NAME="price" VALUE="{0}">
</MvIF>

<MvIF EXPR="{age GE 65}">
  <MvASSIGN NAME="price" VALUE="{1.50}">
</MvIF>

<MvIF EXPR="{age GE 12 AND age LT 65}">
  <MvASSIGN NAME="price" VALUE="{3.50}">
</MvIF>
```

This version produces the same result. It is a bit longer, and it will be a bit slower to execute, since the Miva engine must always process all three `<MvIF>`'s. However, these disadvantages may be offset by the fact that it is easier to read and rearrange, especially in a larger application with many possible results.

There is one shortcut that can be used with the above, to save a couple of lines. The script can start by assigning a default value, as in:

```
<MvASSIGN NAME="price" VALUE="{3.50}">

<MvIF EXPR="{age LT 12}">
  <MvASSIGN NAME="price" VALUE="{0}">
</MvIF>

<MvIF EXPR="{age GE 65}">
  <MvASSIGN NAME="price" VALUE="{1.50}">
</MvIF>
```

This script first assigns the full-price value; then it checks the two conditions that might require a different price. This produces the same result, with one less `<MvIF>`.

Multipass Scripts

Conducting an interactive session with a Web site user may require several documents, each of which accepts some data from the user and passes some results to the next step. This may force you to divide your application into a large number of short files. It may be more convenient to combine several steps into one document. You can write a script that calls itself one or more times, so that the Miva engine makes two or more *passes* through the script, producing different results each time.

Multipass scripts take advantage of the fact that, when a script is called for the first time, the values of all its variables are undefined. If one of these values is used in an `<MvIF>`, it will always produce a false result. Once the script has been executed, some variables can be assigned different values, and the script can pass these values to itself by submitting them as form data, or by other means such as adding them to the URL (see Chapter 4).

One example of a multipass script is the Expression Calculator shown in Chapter 2. This is a script that calls itself when the user clicks a button. It passes along the values of all its variables, and it uses these values to create the next display. However, this is a somewhat unusual case: a script that calls itself repeatedly, as many times as the user desires, and displays the same document each time. It's more common for an interactive application to consist of two or more distinct steps, with very different screen appearances. `<MvIF>` allows you to have one document with several "personalities."

A two-pass script is used in the Mail Sender applet that allows a user to send an e-mail message (described in detail in Chapter 7). This applet first displays a form where a user can enter information such as the destination address and message text, as shown in Figure 3-1.

The user fills in the form and clicks the Send button. Then the applet sends the message and displays an acknowledgement, as shown in Figure 3-2.

It would be simple to create this application as two separate documents: one to display the form, and another to take the submitted information and send the message. However, you can combine both steps into a two-pass script by using `<MvIF>`, as shown in Listing 3-1.

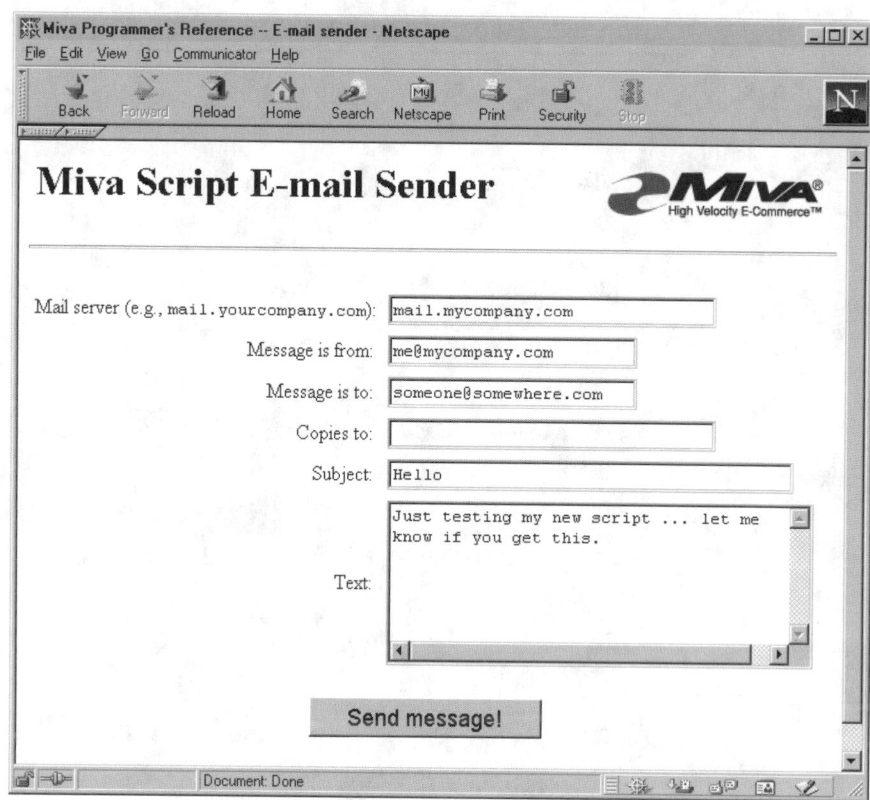

Figure 3-1: Mail Sender, pass 1

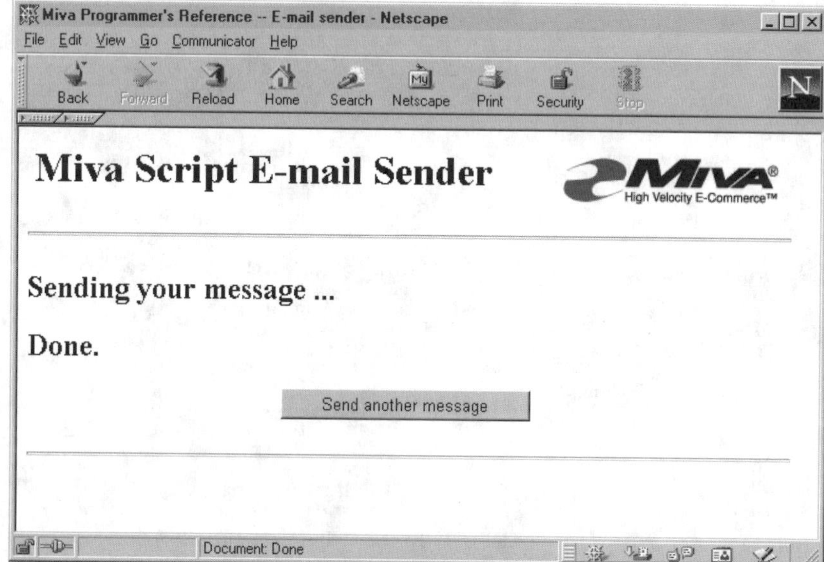

Figure 3-2: Mail Sender, pass 2

Listing 3-1: Two-pass script

```
<MvIF EXPR="{pass NE 2}">

 <!-- Pass 1:  display form -->

 <FORM ACTION="&[s.documenturl];" METHOD="POST">
 <TABLE>
  <TR>
   <TD ALIGN="RIGHT"> Mail server (e.g.,
<TT>mail.yourcompany.com</TT>):
   </TD>
   <TD> <INPUT TYPE="TEXT" NAME="mailserver" SIZE="32">
</TD>
  </TR>
  <TR>
   <TD ALIGN="RIGHT"> Message is from: </TD>
   <TD> <INPUT TYPE="TEXT" NAME="returnaddress" SIZE="24">
</TD>
  </TR>
  <TR>
   <TD ALIGN="RIGHT"> Message is to: </TD>
   <TD> <INPUT TYPE="TEXT" NAME="recipient" SIZE="24">
</TD>
  </TR>
  <TR>
   <TD ALIGN="RIGHT"> Copies to: </TD>
   <TD> <INPUT TYPE="TEXT" NAME="copyrecip" SIZE="32">
</TD>
  </TR>
  <TR>
   <TD ALIGN="RIGHT"> Subject: </TD>
   <TD> <INPUT TYPE="TEXT" NAME="subjectline" SIZE="40">
</TD>
```

```
  </TR>
  <TR>
   <TD ALIGN="RIGHT"> Text: </TD>
   <TD> <TEXTAREA NAME="messagetext" ROWS="6"
COLS="40"></TEXTAREA>
   </TD>
  </TR>
 </TABLE>
 <CENTER> <H2> <INPUT TYPE="SUBMIT" VALUE="Send message!">
</H2> </CENTER>
 <INPUT TYPE="HIDDEN" NAME="pass" VALUE="2">
 </FORM>

<MvELSE>

 <!-- Pass 2:  send message -->

 <H2> Sending your message ... </H2>

 <MvSMTP
 TO="&[recipient];"
 CC="&[copyrecip];"
 SUBJECT="&[subjectline];"
 MAILHOST="&[mailserver];"
 FROM="&[returnaddress];">

&[messagetext];

 </MvSMTP>

 <H2> Done. </H2>
```

```
<CENTER>
<FORM ACTION="&[s.documenturl];" METHOD="POST">
<INPUT TYPE="SUBMIT" VALUE="Send another message">
</FORM>
</CENTER>

</MvIF>
```

The Mail Sender script is controlled by the `<MvIF>` tag that checks the value of a variable named `pass`. The first time the script is run, this variable is undefined, which means that the expression `{pass NE 2}` will be true; so the `<MvIF>` will execute the "true" part of the block. So the script displays the form, which includes a hidden field named `pass` with a value of 2.

The form's `ACTION` attribute includes a macro using the system variable `documenturl`, which contains the URL that was used to call the script. So when the user submits the form, the script will rerun itself, and send along all the data from the form.

When the script is run for the second time, the variable `pass` is no longer undefined; it now has the value 2 that was submitted with the form. So this time, the `<MvIF>` will execute the "false" part of the block, which sends the e-mail message and displays an acknowledgement.

Multipass scripts are a very useful feature of Miva Script. They will be seen in many examples in the rest of this manual. The two-pass technique can be extended to three or more passes, using more `<MvIF>`'s as described above in the section on "Multiple Results."

Loops

Scripts, like programs in all languages, sometimes need to perform a certain function or series of steps repeatedly, two or more times in a row. The number of repetitions may be known in advance, or it may depend on the user's activities or other conditions that are determined while the script is executing. A repeating structure in a program is called a *loop.* Miva Script provides the `<MvWHILE>` tag for writing loops, and there are a number of other tags that have built-in looping.

Looping with <MvWHILE>

The <MvWHILE> tag creates a loop that is controlled by the expression specified by the EXPR attribute. The *body* of the loop is everything between an <MvWHILE> and the corresponding </MvWHILE>. Miva executes the loop body repeatedly as long as the expression specified by EXPR is true. Note that if the expression is initially false, the loop body will not be executed at all. Also, if the expression becomes true and remains true, you have created an *infinite loop:* it will execute continuously until your script times out (see "Stopping Scripts" later in this chapter).

A common way to use a loop is to cause your script to execute some action a specific number of times. In that case, you need to use a variable as a *counter* to control the loop. Listing 2-2 shows a loop that displays all the characters in the character set (see Chapter 2). This could be useful if you need to find out the shapes of all the characters that are available with your computer and browser. The script displays a table with one column showing numeric values from 32 to 255, and another column showing the corresponding character for each value.

Listing 3-2: Loop using <MvWHILE>

```
<TABLE>
 <TR>
  <TH> Number <TH> Character
<MvASSIGN NAME="n" VALUE="32">


<MvWHILE EXPR="{n LE 255}">
 <TR>
  <TD ALIGN="CENTER"> &[n];
  <TD ALIGN="CENTER"> <MvEVAL EXPR="{asciichar(n)}">
 <MvASSIGN NAME="n" VALUE="{n + 1}">
</MvWHILE>


</TABLE>
```

The script starts by using tags to create an HTML table and define two column headers. Then it creates a variable named n to use as a counter, and assigns it an intial value of 32. (Values from 0 to 31 are generally not used for displayable characters.)

Next is the <MvWHILE> that defines the loop. The expression {n LE 255} means that the loop will continue to repeat as long as the value of n is less than or equal to 255.

In the loop body are HTML tags that create one row of the table. A macro is used to put the value of n into the first column, and the expression asciichar(n) generates the corresponding character in the second column.

The last tag before the closing </MvWHILE> is an <MvASSIGN> that is used to increase the value of n by adding 1 to it. This is important: for a loop of this type, you must put something in the loop body to advance the counter. Otherwise, you will have created an infinite loop.

The final <TABLE> tag closes the HTML table. A portion of this script's output is shown in Figure 3-3.

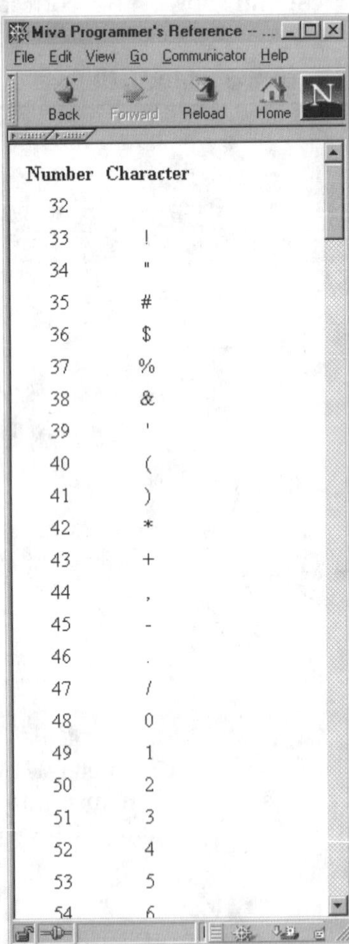

Figure 3-3: Character set display

Terminating Loops with <MvWHILESTOP>

Sometimes, a loop must be interrupted before the <MvWHILE> expression becomes false. You can use the <MvWHILESTOP> tag inside the loop body to stop a loop at any time. After executing this tag, execution of your script continues at the point just after the <MvWHILE>, as it would if the loop had terminated normally. <MvWHILESTOP> is only used in a loop body, i.e., between <MvWHILE> and the corresponding </MvWHILE>.

<MvWHILESTOP> is generally enclosed in an <MvIF> block that detects the condition that causes the interruption. For instance, suppose you have a script that is reading a series of records from a database. You want it to stop after reading 25 records, in order to display data to the user in page-size segments; but you also want it to stop if it reaches the end of the database in mid-page. Listing 3-3 shows a way to do this.

Listing 3-3: Terminating a loop

```
<MvASSIGN NAME="n" VALUE="1">
<MvWHILE EXPR="{n LE 25}">

 Record &[n]; :      
 #<MvEVAL EXPR="{d.itemnum}">,
 <MvEVAL EXPR="{d.itemname}">,
 $<MvEVAL EXPR="{d.price}">,
 <MvEVAL EXPR="{d.weight}">lb.
 <BR>

 <MvASSIGN NAME="n" VALUE="{n + 1}">
 <MvSKIP ROWS="1">

 <MvIF EXPR="{d.eof}">
  <MvWHILESTOP>
 </MvIF>

</MvWHILE>
<P> End of display. <P>
```

This script is intended to be used with a database of retail merchandise. Assume that the database has already been opened; the variables `itemnum`, `itemname`, `price`, and `weight` are used to read the database records. (Databases are explained in detail in Chapter 6; but you should be able to follow this simple example without studying it.)

The script starts, like the previous example, by assigning the counter variable `n` an initial value of 1. The `<MvWHILE>` expression, `{n LE 25}`, should cause the loop to execute 25 times. This is followed by text, tags, and macros to display the contents of one database record. Next comes a tag to advance the counter, as used in the previous example. This is followed by an `<MvSKIP>` tag that advances to the next database record.

A possible problem with the loop is that if the database does not have 25 records left to display, the last one will be displayed over and over again. To prevent that, we use an `<MvWHILESTOP>`. It is placed inside an `<MvIF>` that tests the database variable `d.eof`, which becomes true when the end of the database is reached. So, after the last database record has been displayed, the script will break out of the loop, and proceed to show the `End of display` message.

Other Loops

Some Miva Script operations, such as reading records from a file, are very often used in loops. As a programming shortcut for these operations, there are several tags that automatically form loops. All of these are container tags; the loop body is everything contained between the matching tags, such as `<MvCALL>` and `</MvCALL>`. For each of these loops, there is a corresponding `-STOP` tag that functions like `<MvWHILESTOP>`, to break out of a loop before its normal termination occurs. All the looping tags are described in the table below.

Tag	Loops once for...	Terminating tag	For details, see Chapter:
`<MvCALL>`	Each object (text or HTML tag) that it retrieves from the document or server	`<MvCALLSTOP>`	5
`<MvIMPORT>`	Each record of the file that it is reading	`<MvIMPORTSTOP>`	5
`<MvPOP>`	Each e-mail message that it retrieves	`<MvPOPSTOP>`	7
`<MvCOMMERCE>`	Each set of results, if necessary	`<MvCOMMERCESTOP>`	8

Programming Arrays

Most programming languages provide some way to store a series of values in one variable, with a notation such as `item(3)` or `transaction[next]`. These variables are called *arrays*, and the individual values are called ***elements***. Miva Script provides a pseudoarray functionality with macros. You can easily create and manipulate a series of variables with similar names, such as `item1`, `item2`, `item3`, etc.

To create one of these pseudoarray variables, you write a name followed by a macro, with no intervening space, such as:

```
<MvASSIGN NAME="item&[count];" VALUE="something">
```

This tag assigns a value to a variable named `itemN`, where *N* is specified by the variable `count`. If your script initializes `count` to 1, and adds 1 to it each time it needs a new element, it can create variables named `item1`, `item2`, `item3`, etc.

To read the value stored in an element, you can write `item&[n];` in any Miva Script expression, where `n` is a variable that specifies the element.

Caution: Remember that in an array variable, there must be **no** space between the variable name and the macro.

To illustrate the use of Miva Script arrays, Figure 3-4 shows a Shopping Cart Simulator that represents part of a functioning e-commerce Web site. This simple simulator allows you to type in the quantity, name, and other information for each "product" that you wish to "order."

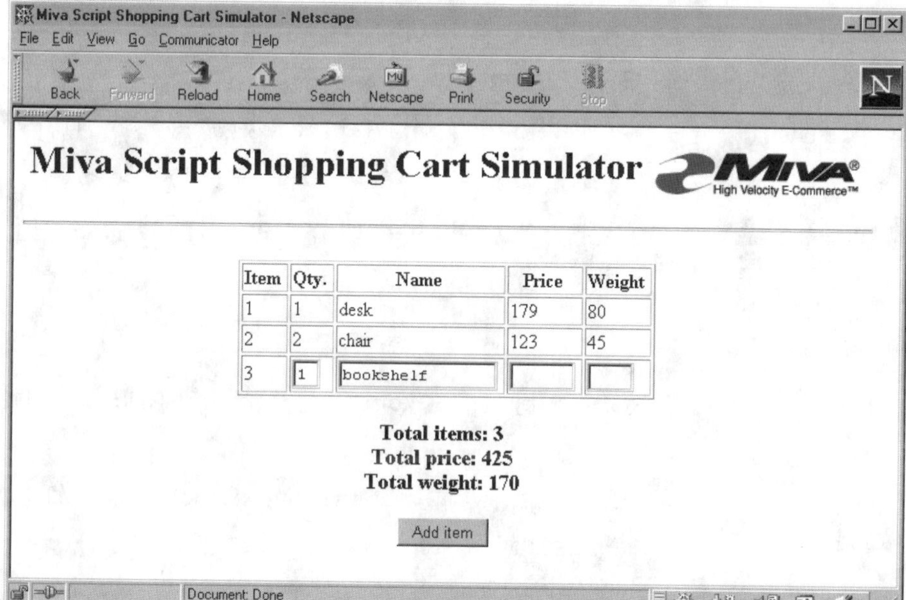

Figure 3-4: Shopping Cart Simulator

The Simulator script is shown in Listing 3-4. It is a multipass script using an HTML form. Each time you submit the form, it adds another item to the shopping cart, and the script reruns itself. All the information about the ordered items is stored in arrays. The information for the first item is stored in variables named `qty1`, `name1`, `price1`, and `weight1`. The next item's data is stored in `qty2`, `name2`, `price2`, and `weight2`; and so forth. The script uses an `<MvWHILE>` loop to display and manage the information from the arrays.

Listing 3-4: Shopping Cart Simulator

```
<FORM ACTION="&[s.documenturl];"
 METHOD="GET"
 ENCTYPE="multipart/form-data">

<TABLE BORDER="1">
 <TR>
  <TH> Item <TH> Qty. <TH> Name <TH> Price <TH> Weight
 </TR>
 <MvASSIGN NAME="n" VALUE="1">
 <MvWHILE EXPR="{n LE itemcount}">

  <TR>
   <TD> &[n]; </TD>
   <TD> <MvEVAL EXPR="{qty&[n];}"> </TD>
   <TD> <MvEVAL EXPR="{name&[n];}"> </TD>
   <TD> <MvEVAL EXPR="{price&[n];}"> </TD>
   <TD> <MvEVAL EXPR="{weight&[n];}"> </TD>
  </TR>

  <MvHIDE
FIELDS="qty&[n];,name&[n];,price&[n];,weight&[n];">

  <MvASSIGN NAME="totalqty" VALUE="{totalqty + qty&[n];}">
  <MvASSIGN NAME="totalprice" VALUE="{totalprice +
(qty&[n]; * price&[n];)}">
```

```
  <MvASSIGN NAME="totalweight" VALUE="{totalweight +
(qty&[n]; * weight&[n];)}">

  <MvASSIGN NAME="n" VALUE="{n + 1}">
  </MvWHILE>

 <TR>
  <TD> &[n];
  <TD> <INPUT TYPE="TEXT" NAME="qty&[n];" SIZE="2">
  <TD> <INPUT TYPE="TEXT" NAME="name&[n];" SIZE="16">
  <TD> <INPUT TYPE="TEXT" NAME="price&[n];" SIZE="6">
  <TD> <INPUT TYPE="TEXT" NAME="weight&[n];" SIZE="4">
 </TR>

</TABLE>

<MvASSIGN NAME="itemcount" VALUE="{itemcount + 1}">
<MvHIDE FIELDS="itemcount">

<H3>
Total items: &[totalqty]; <BR>
Total price: &[totalprice]; <BR>
Total weight: &[totalweight]; <BR>
</H3>

<INPUT TYPE="SUBMIT" VALUE="Add item">
</FORM>
```

The script starts by opening an HTML form and starting a table to display the order information. Once again, the variable `n` is used as a counter for the `<MvWHILE>` loop, and is initialized to 1. The variable `itemcount` holds the number of items ordered. It is initially undefined, which means that it will return zero when used in numeric operations. Its value is increased by 1 each time an item is added to the shopping cart.

Next, an <MvWHILE> tag creates a loop that processes all the data in the arrays, using the variable n to count from 1 to the current value of itemcount. Since itemcount is initially zero (nothing has been ordered yet), the loop will not execute at all the first time the script is executed. Once some items have been entered, the loop begins to function. It displays the information about the items as rows of the table.

Then the loop uses an <MvHIDE> to store the array variables in the form, so that they will be passed along each time the script reruns itself. An <MvASSIGN> tag adds up the total number of items ordered; and two similar tags compute the total price and weight of all items. Some additional arithmetic is required for the last two, since to compute the total, each item's price and weight must be multiplied by the quantity ordered. The last thing in the loop is the familiar tag that adds 1 to n.

After the end of the loop, the script creates one more table row containing text boxes in which the user enters information about each item. Then comes a tag that adds 1 to itemcount, and an <MvHIDE> to pass the new itemcount value along when the script reruns itself. Finally the script shows the total count, price, and weight, which are followed by the button to submit the form.

Miva Script Functions

Miva Script provides two kinds of functions: system and user-defined. System functions are built-in features of Miva, including mathematical functions such as sin(x), text operations such as substring(str, pos, len), and file operations such as fdelete('tempfile.dat'). Some of these have been discussed in earlier chapters. They are written with a function name followed by parentheses that may contain one or more values called *parameters* or *arguments*. They generally return some result value that is used by the script that called the function.

You can define your own functions with the <MvFUNCTION> tag. Functions that you create can be used in expressions, just like system functions. They are useful whenever you have a series of tags or a segment of HTML that occurs in several places in your application. Instead of writing the same code several times, you can write the function once, and call it in each place where it is needed. This reduces the size of your script, and also simplifies the work of editing it: if a change needs to be made, you only have to make it in one place.

For instance, to convert a number to a dollars-and-cents string with the proper punctuation, you can use the FMT operator in an expression such as:

```
{price FMT '&36;3+,0#S2P'}
```

This expression is cryptic-looking: hard to read and remember. But you can package it in a function:

```
<MvFUNCTION
  NAME="money"
  PARAMETERS="amount"
>
  <MvFUNCRETURN VALUE="{amount FMT '&36;3+,0#S2P'}">
</MvFUNCTION>
```

With this definition in use, you can write `money(price)` instead of `price FMT '&36;3+,0#S2P'`; and you can also write `money(tax)`, `money(total)`, etc. anywhere in your script. Using the function makes your scripts easier to read, and eliminates the need to for you to memorize or look up the correct value for the complex `FMT` expression.

The `<MvFUNCTION>` tag above has two attributes. `NAME` specifies the name of the function, and `PARAMETERS` specifies the names of any variables that are used to pass parameters to the function. Everything between the `<MvFUNCTION>` and the matching `</MvFUNCTION>` is the *body* of the function: the text or tags that are executed when you call the function.

Note that the parameter variables are used in the function definition; different names may be used when the function is called. In the above example, the function's single parameter is called `amount`. But when you call the function, you can write `money(x)`, `money(y)`, `money(totalprice + salestax)`, etc. Parameters are *local* variables; they can only be used inside the `<MvFUNCTION>` block. You can create additional local variables by writing the `l.` prefix on their names. (For more on local variables, see "Variable Scope" in Chapter 2.)

It is possible to write a function that needs no parameters. However, when calling the function, you must still write the parentheses after the function name, even though there are no values inside them.

`<MvFUNCTION>` accepts two other attributes, which are not shown in the example. `STANDARDOUTPUTLEVEL` controls how Miva processes the function body; and `ERROROUTPUTLEVEL` controls error handling. These two attributes are described in detail in the Reference section of this manual.

A function can use the `<MvFUNCRETURN>` tag to return a result value to the expression that called the function. The `VALUE` attribute specifies the variable or other expression whose value will be returned. See "Returning Values" below for more details on this.

A function can be used anywhere in a script. In Miva Script, unlike some languages, a function does **not** need to be defined before it is used. A function may be defined in one file and called in another (see below). Miva Script also supports *recursive* functions: those that call themselves.

Below is a more complex example of a function. It might be useful in an online shopping application, to figure the cost of a purchase. Assume that this retailer offers free shipping for items up to 5 pounds, and 50 cents for each pound over 5.

```
<MvFUNCTION NAME="itemcost"
 PARAMETERS="qty,price,weight,tax"
>
 <MvASSIGN NAME="l.cost" VALUE="{qty * price * (tax +
1)}">
 <MvIF EXPR="{qty * weight GT 5}">
  <MvASSIGN NAME="l.cost" VALUE="{l.cost + (weight - 5) *
0.5}">
 </MvIF>
 <MvFUNCRETURN VALUE="{l.cost}">
</MvFUNCTION>
```

The <MvFUNCTION> tag specifies the function's name is `itemcost`. It takes four parameters that specify the quantity ordered, single-unit price and weight, and sales tax rate (e.g. 0.05 for 5%).

The first thing the function does is create a local variable named `cost`. It is written as `l.cost` to specify that it is local; this prevents it from being confused with any other variable named `cost` that your application might use. `l.cost` is assigned an initial value that accounts for the quantity, item price, and tax.

Next the function uses an <MvIF> to check if the total weight (item weight times quantity) is more than 5. If it is, the script adds an additional amount to `l.cost`. Finally, the function uses <MvFUNCRETURN> to pass the final value back to the expression that called it.

When this function definition is in use, you can write an expression such as

```
{itemcost(q, p, w, t)}
```

where `q`, `p`, `w`, and `t` can be any variables in your application. They could come from a text file, a database, or from an HTML form that was submitted by a customer.

Returning Values

As the above examples illustrate, the <MvFUNCRETURN> tag allows a function to return a value to the expression that called it. This is optional; some functions can do what they need to do without returning a value. Bear in mind, though, that if a function returns a value, the calling script must do something with it. Otherwise, it will either appear in the output stream, or interfere with the processing of an expression and cause an error. Sometimes it is necessary to use <MvASSIGN> to place a returned value into a dummy variable.

The processing of values returned from functions that you create is the same as for system functions. For more information on using functions, see "Function Calls" in Chapter 2.

Calling Functions in Other Files

The simplest way to use a function is to write its definition in the document where it will be used. However, in the process of creating a large application, it is common to develop a "library" of functions, some of which may be used in dozens of documents. It is inefficient to have to copy one function definition into many files. To eliminate this redundancy, Miva Script allows a script in one document to call a function in another one by using <MvDO>.

For example, suppose that the money() function defined above was placed in a library file called funclib.mv. To call the function, you would write a tag such as:

```
<MvDO
 FILE="funclib.mv"
 NAME="dollars"
 VALUE="{money(totalcost)}"
>
```

This tag causes Miva to look in the file specified by the FILE attribute. The VALUE attribute specifies the function call and parameters. Miva will try to find an <MvFUNCTION> tag that defines the function with the specified name; if it is found, Miva executes the function. If the function returns a value, Miva places it in the variable specified by the NAME attribute. The above example causes Miva to look in the file funclib.mv for a function named money. Assuming it is found, Miva will evaluate money(totalcost), and place the result in the variable dollars.

The <MvDO> tag is also used to include entire files in the output stream (server-side includes). For more on this, see Chapter 5.

Stopping Scripts

Normally, when Miva executes a script, it continues until it reaches the end of the file. However, there may be times when you want to allow a script to stop executing before it reaches the end—for example, in case some error condition is detected that requires an immediate stop. You can do this with the <MvEXIT> tag. When it is executed, it immediately stops the script's execution. It "flushes" the output stream to ensure that all text and tags are passed to the browser, regardless of any delays caused by network traffic, slow modems, etc.

If <MvEXIT> is used in a script that was called by <MvDO>, the calling script is also terminated, as are any additional nested calls. (To return from a function called by <MvDO> and resume execution of the calling script, use <MvFUNCRETURN>.)

A script may also be stopped by a *timeout*. To protect against infinite loops, the Miva engine automatically stops a script if its execution continues beyond a specified time limit. The time limit is set by your server's system manager. A script can read this limit (in seconds) in the system variable `globaltimeout`. Also, a script can read the system variable `dyn_time_remaining` at any time, to find the number of seconds left before it will time out.

For More Information

For more detailed information on any of the tags and system functions discussed in this chapter, see the Reference section of this manual.

The scripts shown in the Listings are available online at this manual's companion Web site:

http://TopFloor.com/Miva/

4

Interaction and Communication

Interaction with users is an essential feature of Web sites today; there is much more on the Web than just passive collections of text and images. This chapter discusses Miva Script features that allow scripts to receive information from users. Some of these techniques can also allow scripts to exchange data with other scripts, creating powerful multidocument applications.

If you're experienced with client-side scripting languages such as Javascript, you will need to shift your thinking somewhat. In Javascript, you can write a single script that displays some text, waits for input from the user, and then continues execution to process the input. In Miva Script, however, the processing is done on the server side, so a single script cannot be truly interactive. It starts up, does its work, and shuts down while the document is being written to the browser. It has no opportunity to pause and receive input from the user while it is running.

So in Miva Script, an interactive application consists of a series of documents, one for each step in the user's session. Typically, the user accesses your application's start page, and then submits some data with an HTML form. This runs a script that processes the data from the form, and displays a new document. The user may submit more data, and run another script, and so on, for as many steps as needed to complete the session.

Besides using forms, another way that the user can send data to a script is by simply clicking on a link. The link's URL may include a query portion, usually consisting of a question mark (?) followed by keywords or other text. The Miva engine receives any data passed in this way, and places it in variables that the script can use.

Miva Script and Forms

Forms are the primary way for users to enter all kinds of information, and Miva Script supports them in a way that makes the data very easy to use. To write a form that submits data to a script, place the URL of the script in the form's `ACTION` attribute. For instance:

```
<FORM
 ACTION="http://www.myWebSite.com/accept.mv"
 METHOD="POST"
>
 Name: <INPUT TYPE="TEXT" NAME="username"> <BR>
 Gender: <SELECT NAME="gender">
  <OPTION VALUE="M"> Male
  <OPTION VALUE="F"> Female
 </SELECT> <BR>
 <INPUT TYPE="SUBMIT">
</FORM>
```

This simple form consists of one text box, one select box (pull-down menu), and a Submit button. Its appearance on the screen will be similar to Figure 4-1.

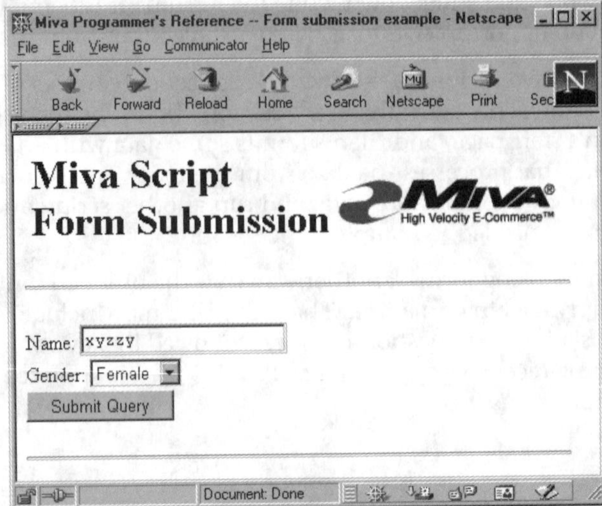

Figure 4-1: Typical form

The <FORM> tag's METHOD attribute is POST, as is usual for forms. The ACTION attribute specifies the script, accept.mv, that will receive the submitted data. Although this example shows a complete URL, you will usually use system variables here to make your script portable (as described in "Portability" later in this chapter).

Receiving data from a form is trivial. When the script accept.mv starts running, all the fields from the submitted form are available to it in variables. The variable names are the same as those specified by the NAME attributes of the <INPUT> tags. For example, to display the submitted data, accept.mv can simply use macros:

```
Username: &[username:entities]; <BR>
Gender: &[gender]; <BR>
```

Here, macros are used to show the variables' contents; the result will be similar to Figure 4-2. Note that the macro for the username variable is entity-encoded, to ensure that the user is not able to type in something that might be interpreted as part of the script.

Caution: To avoid security hazards, always take precautions with macros containing variables whose values are provided from Web users or other unknown sources. For more on security hazards of macros, see "Security and Encoding Macros" in Chapter 1.

For the sake of simplicity and clarity, security features are **not** shown in most of the examples in this manual.

Figure 4-2:

Display of received form data

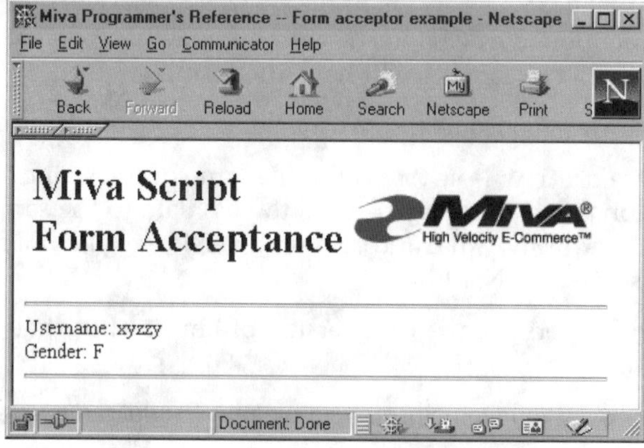

Hidden Data in Forms

Often, an interactive application uses a number of variables to collect information about the user's session. These variables must be passed along from one script to the next as the user proceeds; you don't want the user to have to retype them, and you may not want them to be visible on the screen. One solution is to use hidden form fields. For example, a statement such as

```
<INPUT TYPE="hidden" NAME="zipcode" VALUE="&[zipcode];">
```

could be used to create a hidden form field to carry the value of the `zipcode` variable from one script to the next. Because this is a common technique, Miva Script provides a shortcut with the `<MvHIDE>` tag. This tag is only used inside forms, i.e., between a `<FORM>` and the corresponding `</FORM>`.

`<MvHIDE>` has a single attribute, `FIELDS`, whose value is a list of variable names separated by commas. Miva generates a hidden field for each variable, so that their names and values will be passed to the script—or any HTML document or server—when the form is submitted. For example, a tag such as

```
<MvHIDE FIELDS="lastname,firstname,address,city,state,
zipcode,phone">
```

could be used to pass along a customer's contact information.

Miva Script URLs

As mentioned above, a user can pass data to a script by clicking on a link, if the link's URL includes a query portion. Miva places the query data into variables that the script can read.

As mentioned in Chapter 1, the URL may have one of two formats. On most servers, a typical URL will have the form

http://www.YourDomain.com/scriptname.mv?query

where `scriptname.mv` is the filename of the script to execute, and `?query` is optional text that may be used to pass data to the script. This type of URL is used with Miva Mia, and also with versions of Miva Empresa that have the Netscape API (NSAPI).

Some servers use the CGI version of Empresa. In that case, a URL will look more like:

http://www.YourDomain.com/cgi-bin/miva?scriptname.mv+query

In this case, `miva` is the filename of the (CGI) program, `scriptname.mv` is the first argument, and `+query` is the optional text.

In either case, the Miva engine reads the query data, and passes it to the script in variables. The variables will contain the same values for any query, regardless of which URL format is used. This makes it easy to move scripts from one server to another. (For more on this, see "Portability" below.)

Types of Queries

The *query* text itself may also be in one of two different formats: list of values, or name/value pairs. The choice of which type to use is up to you, and can vary for each URL in your application. However, to simplify debugging, it is recommended that you choose one format, and use it consistently throughout your application. Each format is described in detail below.

Before proceeding, you may want to type in the URL Inspector script shown in Listing 4-1. This script lets you experiment with queries by typing them into your browser, as shown in Figures 4-3 and 4-4.

List of Values

A list-of-values query consists of one or more data fields, sometimes called *arguments*, separated by plus (+) signs, such as:

http://www.YourDomain.com/order.mv?shirt4351+med+1

When the script `order.mv` is called, it receives the argument values as strings in system variables. The variable `arg2` will contain `'shirt4351'`; `arg3` will contain `'med'`; and `arg4` will contain `'1'`. You may be wondering what happened to `arg1`. It contains the script pathname itself: `'/order.mv'` for the above example.

One other variable, `nargs`, will contain the number of arguments: 4 for this example. Note that `nargs` will always be at least 1, and the `arg1` variable will always be present for all scripts, even ones that are not called with a list-of-values query.

If a query contains a null argument, it is ignored. For example, `myscript.mv?a+b++c` will result in `nargs` being set to 4, not 5; the Miva engine ignores the empty argument implied by the `++`.

Name/Value Pairs

A name/value query uses a more complex format, in which each argument consists of a name and a value separated by an equal (=) sign, and the arguments are separated by ampersands (&):

http://www.YourDomain.com/order.mv?item=shirt4351&size=med&qty=1

In this case, since each argument includes its own name, Miva simply creates variables with the specified names and values. So `item` will contain `'shirt4351'`, `size` will contain `'med'`, and `qty` will contain `'1'`.

When processing a script with a name/value query, the system variable `nargs` always contains 2, and `arg2` contains the entire text of the query (`'item=shirt4351&size=med&qty=1'` for the above example.)

If there is an argument with no = sign in a name/value query, Miva will set the variable's value to be the same as the name. So for example, the URL `myscript.mv?a&b` creates a variable named `a` that contains the string `'a'`, and another named `b` that contains `'b'`.

What happens when the query consists of a single text field with no + or & separators? The Miva engine makes it easy for you by processing it both ways. The URL `myscript.mv?xyz` sets `nargs` to 2, and sets `arg2` to `xyz`; and it also creates a variable `xyz` and sets its value to the string `'xyz'`.

The name/value format makes programming simpler for the script that processes the query. It also has advantages for the script that calls the URL:

- It allows the arguments to be in any order.
- It makes it easy to omit any unneeded arguments (uninitialized variables will contain the null string).
- It makes it easier to filter out reserved characters (see "Special Characters in Queries" below).

There is one possible disadvantage to name/value queries, which should be highlighted:

Caution: Processing name/value queries causes the Miva engine to create and initialize new global variables. If a script receives an argument whose name is the same as a variable used by the script, there could be conflict that would cause an error.

If you are using name/value URLs in a large application, take care to keep track of the names used for program arguments, and make sure they do not conflict with variables created by programmers.

Working with Query Data

The URL Inspector script in Listing 4-1 gives some examples of how to read query data, and allows you to try various queries yourself. The script simply displays the contents of all the related variables, so you can see exactly how a query is interpreted.

Listing 4-1: URL Inspector

```
Server: &[server_name]; : &[server_port]; <BR>
Document: &[documenturl];
<HR>
nargs: &[nargs]; <BR>
arg1: &[arg1]; <BR>
<MvASSIGN NAME="n" VALUE="{2}">
<MvWHILE EXPR="{n LE nargs}">
 arg&[n];: <MvEVAL EXPR="{arg&[n];}"> <BR>
 <MvASSIGN NAME="n" VALUE="{n + 1}">
</MvWHILE>
<P>

<MvASSIGN NAME="list" VALUE="{miva_getvarlist('g')}">
<MvASSIGN NAME="token" VALUE="dummy">
<MvASSIGN NAME="n" VALUE="1">
<TABLE BORDER>
 <TR>
  <TH> Name </TH>
  <TH> Value </TH>
 </TR>
<MvWHILE EXPR="{gettoken(list, ',', n)}">
 <MvASSIGN NAME="token" VALUE="{gettoken(list, ',', n)}">
 <MvIF EXPR="{NOT (' ' IN token)}">
  <MvASSIGN NAME="vval" VALUE="{&[token];}">
 <TR>
  <TD> &[token]; </TD>
  <TD> &[vval];   </TD>
 </TR>
```

```
  </MvIF>
  <MvASSIGN NAME="n" VALUE="{n + 1}">
</MvWHILE>
</TABLE>
```

The display produced by this script is shown in Figures 4-3 and 4-4. The script starts by displaying some system variables that specify the server and document (more on these in "Portability" below). Next it displays the system variables `nargs` and `arg1`, which are always present as explained above. Then it uses an `<MvWHILE>` loop (see Chapter 3) to display any additional `argN` variables. This part of the display shows all the variables used in processing a list-of-values query.

Next the script creates an HTML table, and uses the system function `miva_getvarlist()` to obtain a list of all the global variables in the program (see Chapter 2). It uses one row of the table to display each variable's name and value. This part of the display is just a bit confusing, because it contains some data that is not really relevant to the query: miscellaneous global variables such as `n`, and a few that are automatically created by the Miva engine, such as `MvWHILE_ERROR`. However, if you look at Figure 4-4, you can see that the table includes the variables `item`, `size`, and `qty` that were specified in the URL seen in the Location box at the top of the browser screen.

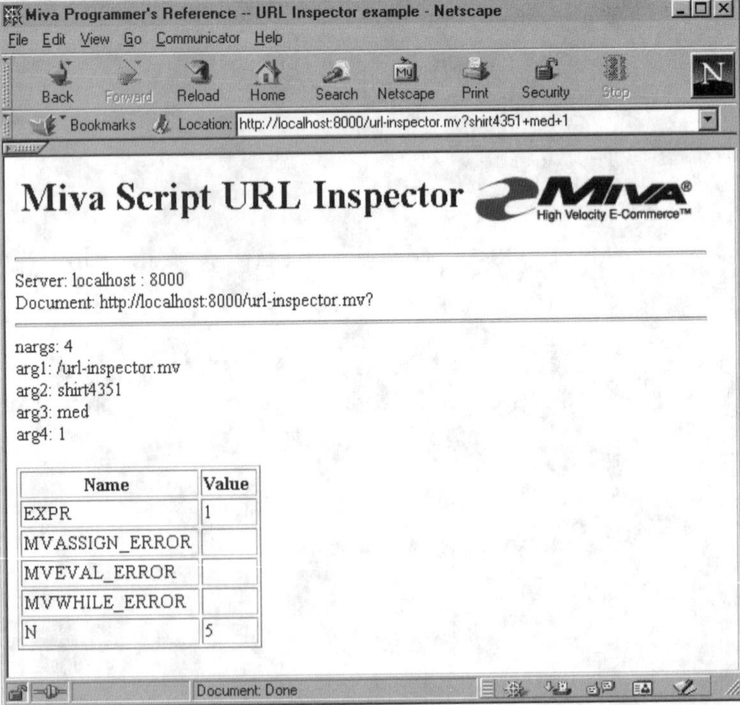

Figure 4-3: List-of-values query

Figure 4-4:

Name/value query

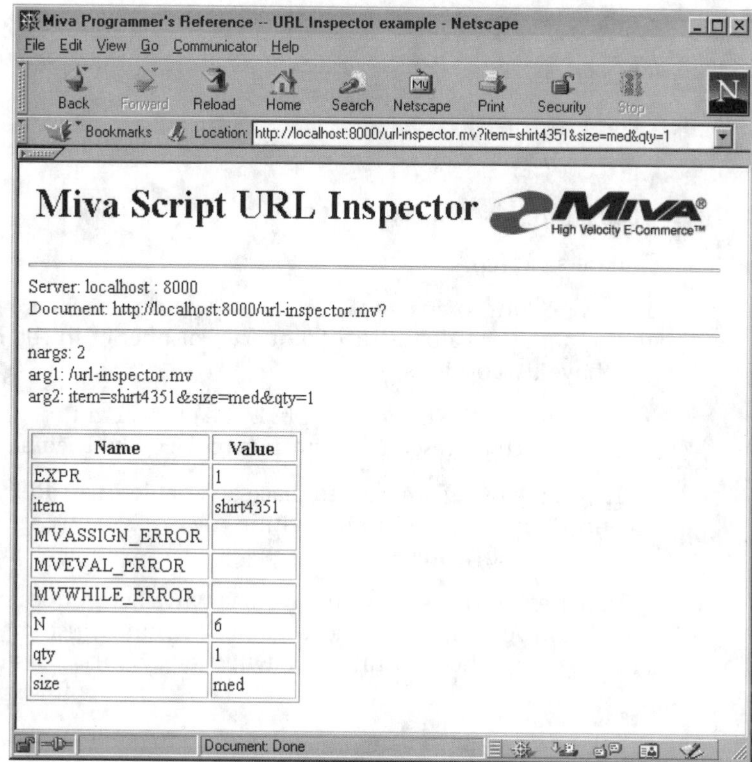

Special Characters in Queries

As mentioned above, some characters, such as space, +, &, and = have special meanings in queries. So if these characters appear in the names or values of any query, you must make substitutions. Which characters are reserved depends on the type of query. In list-of-values queries, the following characters are reserved:

Character	Substitute
Space ( )	%20
Plus (+)	%2B
Minus/hyphen (-)	%2D
Tilde (~)	%7E

In name/value queries, the set of reserved characters, and the values to substitute for them, are somewhat different:

Character	Substitute
Space ( )	Plus (+)
Plus (+)	`%2B`
Percent (%)	`%2F`
Equal (=)	`%3D`
Ampersand (&)	`%26`

It is important to ensure that the reserved characters are not accidentally used in the name or value parts of a query. For queries in the name/value format, you have two options.

- You can use the `encodeattribute()` system function to create a copy of a string with all reserved characters replaced by their substitutes.
- If you are using a macro to place a variable in a URL, you can cause attribute encoding in the macro by writing the `:attribute` suffix after the variable name (see Chapter 1).

For queries in the list-of-values format, Miva Script does not provide these shortcuts. However, you can achieve a similar result by using `encodeattribute()` after making other substitutions with the `glosub()` system function.

Cookies

Browser cookies are used to store small amounts of information in the Web user's computer. Miva Script provides a system variable, `http_cookie`, that contains the names and values of all cookies associated with a document. Your scripts can read this variable, but they have no direct way to modify the actual cookies. Scripts can create cookies by using the HTML `<META>` tag. This tag works the same with Miva Script as it does in normal HTML documents.

When a script is run, the Miva engine creates a cookie for it named `hts-callerid`. Its value is a unique 32-character ID, and it is set to last one year before expiring. This value can be used by scripts to identify the user, in order to display a "Welcome Back, Chris" message, access a customer's purchase history, etc. The value of the unique ID is also available to scripts as the `callerid` system variable. Creation of Miva cookies can be turned on or off by the server administrator.

For more information about cookies, see the online reference at:

http://www.netscape.com/newsref/std/cookie_spec.html

Programming Techniques and Considerations

This section lists some other techniques and ideas that will be helpful in designing interactive scripts and applications.

Multipass Scripts

Although an interactive session consists of many steps, it is possible to combine two or more steps into a single "multipass" document. The technique for this uses the `<MvIF>` tag; it is discussed in detail in Chapter 3.

Accessing Other Documents

Scripts can interact with other scripts without waiting for the user to click something.The `<MvCALL>` tag allows a script to simulate a browser, performing HTTP requests and retrieving data, while it is processing a script. It can access other documents anywhere on the Internet, using URLs with queries. It can also simulate the submitting of a form. The results of these requests can be processed like any other text: displayed to the user, stored in databases, etc. `<MvCALL>` is described in more detail in Chapter 5.

Portability

Since a large application consists of many scripts, it is common for one script to contain URLs that reference another. For instance, the script that displays the opening page might contain a reference to:

http://yourDomain.com/page2.mv

The problem with writing the URL directly into your script is that it is not portable. If you develop your scripts on Miva Mia, you will need to edit a number of URLs when you install it on your server. If you move it from a CGI-type server to an NSAPI-type, you will need to change them again.

To eliminate the need for all this editing, you can use several system variables as part of the URL. The variable `server_name` contains the name of the HTTP server on which a script is currently running. This will usually be the same for all scripts that are part of one application. So the above URL could be made portable by rewriting it as:

http://&[server_name]/page2.mv

For completeness, you should also include the variable `server_port`, which contains the HTTP server port number, making the URL look like:

http://&[server_name]:[server_port]/page2.mv

Another variable that can help you write portable scripts is `documenturl`, which contains the complete URL that was used to call the script. It starts with the initial `http:` and continues through the `?` or `+` that marks the beginning of the query, but not the query data itself. If there is no query data, the Miva engine adds the `+` or `?`, depending on whether it uses NSAPI or CGI URLs. `documenturl` can be useful in various situations:

- It allows a script to pass its own URL to other scripts that may need to call it.
- It allows a multipass script to call itself (see Chapter 3).
- It can be displayed on the browser screen, perhaps in small text at the bottom of the page, for tracking or debugging purposes.

All three of these system variables are displayed by the URL Inspector script described earlier, so it can help you learn how they work. These variables will also be seen in other examples in later chapters of this manual.

Multiuser Applications

Since Web sites can be accessed by many users at once, your application may need a way to keep track of them. For instance, if several users are shopping at a retail site, the shopping-cart data for all of them may be kept in a single database file; so you need a way to assign a unique ID to each customer as soon as they "arrive." The system function `makesessionid()` can be helpful for this. It returns a single large number that is guaranteed to be unique.

Security

When processing credit card numbers and other private data, it is very important to ensure that all data are protected. Use secure protocols whenever possible. Keep data about customers in databases; do not place it in hidden form fields, cookies, or other places where a malicious user might be able to see or modify it. Use passwords when appropriate. Keep critical scripts off the World Wide Web altogether: publish them on corporate intranets, or run them offline using Miva Mia.

User-Friendliness

If your Web site is going to be used by the general public, you may need to give extra attention to how it interacts with the users. Many of them will not be computer-literate, so you must make everything easy to use, and also protect against user errors. Of course, you must also safeguard against the possibility of an attempt by malicious users to steal or damage your data. Whole books have been written about these subjects: the skills involved are quite different from those used in other kinds of programming work. To some extent, user-interface design is as much an art as a science. Here are some general points that will help make your application easy to use.

- Remember the "ten-second rule" described by Ted Nelson, the visionary who invented the term "hypertext." He took note of arcade video games, which never have more than about three buttons and one paragraph of instructions. The designers of these games know that if typical 9-year-olds can't learn the whole game in ten seconds of study, they will spend their quarters somewhere else.

  Your users may be more patient and intelligent than 9-year-olds, but don't count on it. After years of working with complex systems, most programmers no longer realize that a fairly "simple" program can be daunting to novices. Always test your applications with typical users before publishing them.

- Assume that users can and will make any possible kind of error. Just because a text box is labelled "ZIP Code" doesn't mean that a user won't accidentally type in letters instead of digits. Will that crash your program?

  Every piece of data provided by a user must be checked for validity. If some invalid data is provided, your application must notify the user and allow him or her to correct it. (Be especially careful with macros, since they are a possible security hazard, as discussed in Chapter 1.) When possible, use buttons or drop-down menus instead of text boxes.

- Keep screen layouts clear and simple. Don't display too much information at one time. If you need to collect a lot of information in forms, use several short ones instead of one long one. Try to keep documents short enough that the user doesn't need to do a lot of scrolling.

For More Information

For more detailed information on any of the tags and system functions discussed in this chapter, see the Reference section of this manual.

The scripts shown in the Listings are available online at this manual's companion Web site:

http://TopFloor.com/Miva/

5

Working with Files and Documents

Miva Script provides a variety of ways to manipulate HTML documents and other types of files. Scripts can perform operations such as:

- Reading an HTML document or text file and passing it to the output stream (server-side include).
- Reading and writing text files on the server.
- Reading an HTML document and separating tags, attributes, and text, so that scripts can read or edit the information.
- Uploading a file from the Web site user's computer, and storing it on the server or performing other operations on the uploaded data.
- Locking and unlocking files to allow multiuser access.
- Standard file system operations such as deleting a file, renaming it, checking its size, etc.

Each of these topics is discussed in this chapter. Miva Script also provides two other types of file-related operations that are not covered in this chapter. Browser cookies are discussed in Chapter 4, and database operations are described in Chapter 6.

Scripts can access documents all over the Internet by using URLs, but some operations can only be used on files stored on the server. The Miva engine uses two standard directories for these files:

- The *standard scripts directory* holds Miva Script and HTML documents.
- The *standard data directory* holds all other types of files: text-based "flat files," databases, retrieved e-mail messages, etc.

Each of these standard directories can be divided into subdirectories to help you organize your files and documents.

The exact location (path) of these directories may vary depending on your platform and system configuration. If necessary, ask your server administrator how to access them.

Server-Side Includes

A *server-side include* is a way for the server to include the contents of one HTML document inside another. This can be useful, for instance, in a large Web site where each page needs to have a standard header containing the company name and logo. In plain HTML, the page header would have to be duplicated in each document; and a change to the header would require editing all the documents.

Using server-side includes, the page header can be placed in a separate document, and the server can include it in each Web page when a user views it. In Miva Script, this function is provided by the `<MvDO>` tag. For example, if the header is in a file called `page_header.mv`, then the tag

```
<MvDO FILE="page_header.mv">
```

will insert the contents of the header file into a document. The `FILE` attribute specifies the pathname of the file to include. The file must be in the standard scripts directory, or a subdirectory of it. `<MvDO>` can also be used with other attributes to call a function defined in the included files, as described in Chapter 3. However, when using `<MvDO>` to include the entire contents of a file, you should specify only the `FILE` attribute.

A basic page header might include a simple "letterhead" with a name, logo image, and a horizontal bar to separate it from the body of the page, such as:

```
<H2> XYZZY Company

<IMG src="xyzzy_logo.gif"

</H2>

<HR>
```

If there are any Miva Script tags or macros in the included file, they will also be processed. For instance, the above example could be enhanced with Miva Script macros to include the current date:

```
<H2> Company Name

<IMG src="logo.gif"

</H2>
```

```
<CENTER> Today is &[stm_mon];. &[tm_mday];, &[tm_year].
</CENTER>

<HR>
```

If the included file contains additional <MvDO> tags, it can include additional files in a nested fashion.

Reading and Writing Text Files

Miva Script has an <MvIMPORT> tag that reads from files, and an <MvEXPORT> tag that writes to them. The files must be in the Miva data directory or its subdirectories.

For both reading and writing, the file format is the same. These files are sometimes called *flat files*, to distinguish them from databases that have a more complex record structure. Each file must consist of lines of text , sometimes called *records*, each of which ends with a Newline character (`asciichar(10)`). Each record contains data sections called *fields*, which are divided by separator strings called *delimiters*. Each record should have the same number of fields. This format is flexible enough that it can be used for many common types of text-based files, such as the CSV format for which examples are shown below.

The <MvIMPORT> tag reads data from flat files, and places it in variables that a script can use. Conversely, the <MvEXPORT> tag accepts data from variables, and writes it to a flat file. The following sections describe each of these tags in detail.

Reading Files with <MvIMPORT>

To read a file, you write an <MvIMPORT> tag, and a corresponding </MvIMPORT>. These two tags form a loop: everything between them is executed repeatedly, once for each record in the file. The `FILE` attribute of <MvIMPORT> specifies the pathname of the file to read. The `FIELDS` attribute lists one or more variables to hold the data from the fields; and the `DELIMITER` attribute specifies the string that separates the fields.

As an example, suppose you want to read some data from a CSV file. CSV, which stands for comma-separated values, is a format that is often produced by database and spreadsheet programs. In a CSV file, each field is enclosed by quote (`"`) characters, and there are commas between them. So an employee data file in CSV format might have records that look like this:

```
"1001","Smith","John","M","12345"

"1003","Bizzy","Bee","F","44444"

"1005","Zyvith","Yvonne","F","12346"
```

Miva Script can read this file by specifying the string `","` (quote, comma, quote) as the `DELIMITER` attribute, since it occurs between adjacent fields. This would still leave one quote character at the beginning of the first field, and another at the end of the last field; but it's easy enough to remove them with the `substring()` system function.

Listing 5-1 shows a script that uses `<MvIMPORT>` to read the employee file shown above, and display its contents on the browser screen.

Listing 5-1: Reading a CSV file with <MvIMPORT>

```
<TABLE>
 <TR>
  <TH> ID number </TH>
  <TH> Name </TH>
  <TH> Gender </TH>
  <TH> ZIP code </TH>
 </TR>

<MvIMPORT
 FILE="employees.csv"
 FIELDS="num,lastname,firstname,gender,zipcode"
 DELIMITER="\",\""
>

 <TR>
  <TD> <MvEVAL EXPR="{substring(num, 2, len(num) - 1)}">
</TD>
  <TD> &[firstname]; &[lastname]; </TD>
  <TD> &[gender]; </TD>
  <TD> <MvEVAL EXPR="{substring(zipcode, 1,
len(zipcode) - 1)}"> </TD>
 </TR>

</MvIMPORT>
</TABLE>
```

The script starts by setting up an HTML table to display the data from the file. Then it executes `<MvIMPORT>` to open the file, which in this case is named `employees.csv`. The tag also defines five field variables, and specifies the `DELIMITER` string `","` described above; note the use of the backslash character (\) to insert quote characters in the attribute value. Between the `<MvIMPORT>` and `</MvIMPORT>` is a loop that adds rows to the table by using `<TR>`, and creates cells in the row by using `<TD>`.

The first field variable, `num`, is inserted in the table with an `<MvEVAL>` tag. The expression in this tag,

```
{substring(num, 2, len(num) - 1)}
```

has the effect of removing the first character from the string: this removes the quote character at the beginning of the record. A slightly different expression,

```
{substring(zipcode, 1, len(zipcode) - 1)}
```

removes the other quote from the end of the last field, `zipcode`.

The values from the other field variables are inserted into the table by macros. Note that `firstname` and `lastname` are included in a single table cell.

The tags and text inside the `<MvIMPORT> ... </MvIMPORT>` loop will be executed once for each record in the file. After all records have been read and displayed, the loop terminates, and the `</TABLE>` tag finishes the table. The display generated by this script is shown in Figure 5-1.

Figure 5-1: CSV file display

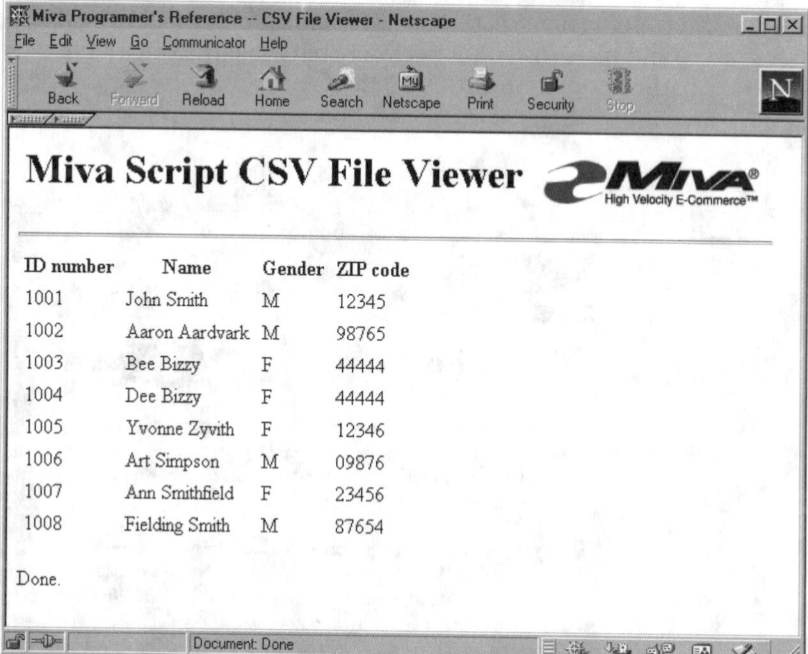

Reading Plain Text

You may sometimes need to use <MvIMPORT> to read files in which the number of fields per record is not constant, or the exact format is not known in advance. One example of this would be an ordinary text file, such as an e-mail message typed by a user. If you can choose a DELIMITER string that you are certain will not appear in the file, then <MvIMPORT> will read each line of text (record) into a single field variable as a single long string. An easy way to do this is to specify a null DELIMITER. Listing 5-2 shows a simple script that can read a plain text file and display it on the browser.

Listing 5-2: Reading a text message

```
<MvIMPORT
 FILE="message.txt"
 FIELDS="line"
 DELIMITER=""
>
 &[line]; <BR>
</MvIMPORT>
```

The <MvIMPORT> tag defines a single field variable, line, to receive each line of text. The body of the loop consists of a macro that places line in the output stream, along with a <BR> tag to force a new line on the browser screen. The <BR> is not strictly necessary, but it helps make the formatting, such as margins and blank lines, more closely resemble the original text. A typical display from this script is shown in Figure 5-2.

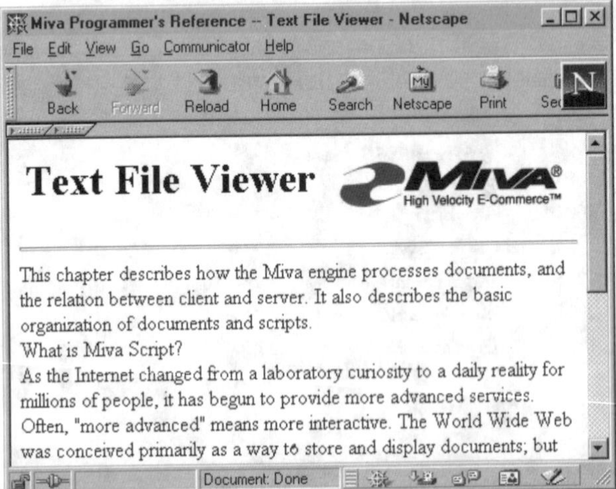

Figure 5-2: Viewing a text file

Filtering Input

To help with finding particular records in a file, the <MvIMPORT> tag has an optional FILTER attribute. The value of this attribute is a Miva Script expression that contains at least one field variable. Miva evaluates this expression after reading each record. If the expression returns a false value (either 0 or the null string ''), Miva skips processing the record, and immediately reads the next one. This has the effect of filtering the file, so that your script only retrieves records for which the filter expression is true. For instance, in the CSV File Viewer shown in Figure 5-1, if you wanted to display only the records for male employees, you could add the attribute

```
FILTER="{gender EQ 'M'}"
```

to the <MvIMPORT> tag. This has the effect of suppressing any records that do not have 'M' in their gender field.

Note that searching a text file is a relatively slow operation. If your file is large, you should probably convert it to a database for faster access (see Chapter 6).

Record Number

Miva creates a variable named recno that is used to count the records read by <MvIMPORT>. Although it is a global variable, it can only be used inside an <MvIMPORT> ... </MvIMPORT> loop. The value of recno starts at 1, and is increased by 1 each time another record is read. Records that are rejected by the use of a FILTER attribute are not counted.

Note that if you have any open databases, you will also have a variable named recno in the database scope. In this case, you will need to write g.recno to explicitly reference the recno for the text file. (Variable scopes are explained in Chapter 2).

Stopping Input

If you need to interrupt an <MvIMPORT> loop before it reaches the end of the text file, you can use <MvIMPORTSTOP>. This tag, which must be placed somewhere inside the loop, causes Miva to stop reading records, and to continue execution of the script at the point just after the </MvIMPORT> tag.

This tag is usually placed inside an <MvIF> block. For instance, to cause a script to read just ten records, you could place the tags

```
<MvIF EXPR="{recno EQ 10}">
 <MvIMPORTSTOP>
</MvIF>
```

inside the loop, just before the </MvIMPORT>.

Writing Files with <MvEXPORT>

The <MvEXPORT> tag is used to write data to a text file. Its action is complementary to <MvIMPORT>, but it operates differently. This tag does not create a loop; there is no ending "/MvEXPORT" tag. It writes a single record each time it is executed. To write a series of records, you can create a loop with tags such as <MvWHILE>, and place <MvEXPORT> inside the loop. However, there may be times when writing a single record is sufficient to store a small amount of data; in that case, no loop is required.

<MvEXPORT> has three attributes, whose functions are the same as for <MvIMPORT>:

- FILE specifies the pathname of the file to write, starting in the standard Miva data directory.
- FIELDS specifies the names of variables to write.
- DELIMITER specifies the separator characters to place between the fields.

(There is no FILTER attribute for this tag.)

If the specified file already exists, <MvEXPORT> adds the new data at the end of the file. This is convenient when using <MvEXPORT> to keep a log of Web site activity, a guest book, or other archival types of information. However, if you need to make sure that a new file is created, and any old data deleted, you can use the fdelete() system function to delete any existing file; then <MvEXPORT> will create a new file.

The Miva Script function shown below can be used to create a log file:

```
<MvFUNCTION NAME="write_log" PARAMETERS="filename">


<MvASSIGN NAME="l.current_date"
 VALUE="{stm_mon $ ' ' $ tm_mday $ ', ' $ tm_year}">
<MvASSIGN NAME="l.current_time"
 VALUE="{tm_hour $ ':' $ tm_min $ ':' $ tm_sec}">


<MvEXPORT
 FILE="&[filename];"
 FIELDS="current_date,current_time,documenturl"
 DELIMITER="  "
>


</MvFUNCTION>
```

The function, named `write_log()`, accepts a single argument that specifies the name of the log file. It starts by assigning two local variables, `current_date` and `current_time`, to contain the date and time in forms that are easy to read. Next, the `<MvEXPORT>` tag writes the date and time values to the specified log file, followed by the system variable `documenturl` that contains the URL of the current document. The macro in the `FILE` attribute inserts the filename specified when the function is called; this allows the function to write to many different log files. However, since each log entry contains the URL of the document from which it is written, it is possible for many documents to share a single log file: when you read the file, you will be able to tell which document created each entry.

This function can be called by a tag such as

```
<MvDO
 FILE="logger.mv"
 NAME="dummy"
 VALUE="{write_log('Weblog.txt')}"
>
```

where `logger.mv` is the name of the script file containing the `write_log()` function, and `Weblog.txt` is the name for the log file.

Sending HTTP Requests

For advanced processing of HTML documents, Miva Script provides the `<MvCALL>` tag, which allows Miva to send many types of HTTP requests, much like a Web browser, such as:

- Sending `GET` or `POST` requests to a server.
- Adding additional data to the request, as if posting from an HTML form.
- Uploading entire files to the server.

It can also analyze a received HTML document, and separate the tags and attributes from the normal text.

`<MvCALL>` has four attributes:

- `ACTION` specifies the URL of a document or server transaction.
- `METHOD` may be either `GET` or `POST`; as for HTML forms, it specifies the type of request to make.
- `FIELDS` specifies any variables that you wish to send along with the request.

- `FILES` specifies variables whose values are the names of any files that you wish to upload along with the request.

The `ACTION` and `METHOD` attributes are required. `FIELDS` and `FILES` are optional, and may only be used with `METHOD="POST"`.

Reading Documents

After executing <MvCALL>, a script will generally receive some sort of document as a response to the HTTP request. Even if the main purpose of the request is to submit some data to a server, there is usually an acknowledgement document that is returned to the user.

To process the received document, <MvCALL> and the corresponding </MvCALL> form a program loop. The loop is executed once for each object in the incoming document. Each object is either an HTML tag or a segment of plain text. Inside the <MvCALL> ... </MvCALL> loop, a number of variables are available to provide information about each object:

`callobjecttype`	Contains `'text'` or `'tag'` to specify the type of the object.
`callvalue`	Contains the actual text of the entire object. If the object is text, `callvalue` includes all white space. If the object is a tag, `callvalue` includes all attributes, values, and punctuation, including the opening and closing angle brackets.

If the object is a tag, a number of additional variables are available that describe it:

`callobjectelement`	The tag name, without angle brackets, e.g. `'IMG'` or `'/TABLE'`
`callobjectnumattributes`	The number of attributes for the tag.
`callobjectattribute`*N*	(where *N* is 1, 2, ...) The name of tag attribute number *N*.
`callobjectvalue`*N*	(where *N* is 1, 2, ...) The value assigned to tag attribute number *N*.

In addition, a number of variables provide information about the HTTP headers that Miva received with the document:

`callnumberofheaders`	The number of headers received.
`callreturnheader`*N*	(where *N* is 1, 2, ...) The text of header number *N*.

With all this information, a script can perform fairly advanced filtering of HTML documents: it can remove tags, change their attributes, or add additional text or tags at various points. As a simple example, the following script reads a document and removes all tags, passing only the text to the output stream:

```
<MvCALL
 ACTION="http://mydomain.com/somedocument.htm"
 METHOD="GET">
 <MvIF EXPR="{callobjecttype EQ 'text'}">
  <MvEVAL EXPR="{callvalue}">
 </MvIF>
</MvCALL>
```

The body of the loop uses an `<MvIF>` tag to check if each retrieved object is text. If it is, the `<MvEVAL>` is used to place it in the output stream. This has the effect of discarding all the tags.

Sending Data with a Request

When using `METHOD="POST"`, you can submit additional data along with a request by specifying the names of one or more variables in the `FIELDS` attribute. When the `<MvCALL>` is executed, the names and values of these variables are passed to the HTTP server as part of the request. To the server, the effect is the same as if the variables had been fields in an HTML form that a user submitted. For instance, to request a private document with password protection, you could use a script such as

```
<MvCALL
 ACTION="http://www.privatedocuments.com/restricted.htm"
 METHOD="POST"
 FIELDS="username,password"
>
```

where `username` and `password` are two variables containing the necessary values to access the restricted document.

With either `GET` or `POST`, you can also pass additional data to the server by adding it to the URL, as when calling a search engine with a tag such as:

```
<MvCALL

ACTION="http://www.search.com/results.htm?keyword=fran&numb
er=30
```

```
METHOD="GET"
>
```

When using POST, you can combine both ways of submitting data, as in:

```
<MvCALL
ACTION="http://www.privatedocuments.com/restricted.htm?chapter=5"
 METHOD="POST"
 FIELDS="username,password"
>
```

This example uses the FIELDS attribute to pass the username and password, as in the earlier example. However, this one also adds data to the URL, to request a single chapter of the restricted document.

Ways of passing data in URLs are discussed in more detail in Chapter 4.

Uploading Files

When using <MvCALL> with METHOD="POST", you can upload files to the server by specifying the names of one or more variables in the FILES attribute. Note that these are the names of the **variables**, not the actual files. The values of the variables should be the pathnames of the files. For example:

```
<MvASSIGN NAME="datafile" VALUE="employees.txt">
<MvCALL
 ACTION="http://yourcompany.com/cgi-bin/receiver.cgi"
 METHOD="POST"
 FILES="datafile"
>
  <MvEVAL EXPR="{callvalue}">
</MvCALL>
```

This example will upload the file named employees.txt to a CGI script named receiver.cgi. The <MvEVAL> inside the <MvCALL> ... </MvCALL> block may not be necessary: its purpose is to receive and display any response that receiver.cgi sends back to the browser after receiving the uploaded file.

Of course, it is possible to upload a file without using Miva Script, by having the user select it with a file browser box on a form. This can be done with ordinary HTML tags such as:

```
<FORM
 ACTION="http://yourcompany.com/cgi-bin/receiver.cgi"
 METHOD="POST"
 ENCTYPE="multipart/form-data"
>

<INPUT TYPE="FILE" NAME="FILEBOX">
<P>
<INPUT TYPE="SUBMIT" VALUE="Send the file">

</FORM>
```

This HTML code generates a form containing a file browser box and a Submit button. Note that in the `<FORM>` tag, the `METHOD` must be `POST`, and the `ENCTYPE="multipart/form-data"` attribute must be included. The file browser box can, of course, be used in a larger form with other text fields, buttons, etc.

The above examples both use URLs that send the uploaded file to a CGI program. However, it is entirely possible to upload a file to a Miva Script URL, and process it with another script, as described in the next section.

Receiving Uploaded Files

For a script to receive an uploaded file, it must contain two functions, defined with `<MvFUNCTION>`, to process the file. Note that, although you need to define these functions, you do **not** write any tags that call them. Instead, the Miva engine will call these functions automatically when the script receives an uploaded file.

One function must be named `Miva_ValidateFileUpload`: its purpose will be to examine some information about the uploaded file, and decide whether or not to accept it. The other function must be named `Miva_ProcessFileUpload`: its job is to actually process the data from the file. (The use of uppercase letters is optional. Miva considers upper- and lowercase to be equivalent in variable and function names.)

Note that if a script receives any uploaded files, both of these functions will be called immediately when the script starts to execute. So if you want to have a header or other text that appears at the top of the page, or Miva Script tags that are executed as soon as the script starts, this material will have to be placed inside the `Miva_ValidateFileUpload` function.

Validating an Upload

When your script receives an uploaded file, the Miva engine will call your `Miva_ValidateFileUpload` function, which may be defined by a tag such as:

```
<MvFUNCTION
 NAME="Miva_ValidateFileUpload"
 PARAMETERS="fieldvar,filename,mime_type"
>
```

(This must be followed by a function body and closing `</MvFUNCTION>`, of course.) You may choose your own names for the variables defined in the `PARAMETERS` attribute; however there must be three of them. When the Miva engine calls your function, the three variables will provide information to your script:

- `fieldvar` (or whatever you name it) will contain a string that specifies the name of the field variable that was used to pass the filename.
- `filename` will contain a string that specifies the pathname of the uploaded file on the computer that sent it.
- `mime_type` will contain a string that specifies the MIME data type of the uploaded file.

Your function may use these values (and any other variables, functions, or tags that you design) to decide how to handle the file. The function must end with an `<MvFUNCRETURN>` that returns a value to the Miva engine:

- A value of -1 tells Miva to discard this file: do nothing with the uploaded data.
- A value of 0 tells Miva to accept the entire file.
- Any positive number tells Miva to accept data from the file up to the specified number of bytes. This gives you some protection against users who try to upload extremely large files.

Processing an Upload

After the validation function, the Miva engine will call your `Miva_ProcessFileUpload` function. This function may be defined by a tag such as:

```
<MvFUNCTION
 NAME="Miva_ProcessFileUpload"
```

```
 PARAMETERS="fieldvar,filename,status,tempfile,mime_type,
size"

>
```

(This must be followed by a function body and closing `</MvFUNCTION>`, of course). You may choose your own names for the variables defined in the `PARAMETERS` attribute; however there must be six of them. When the Miva engine calls your function, these variables will provide information to your script:

- `fieldvar` will contain a string that specifies the name of the field variable that was used to pass the filename.
- `filename` will contain a string that specifies the pathname of the uploaded file on the computer that sent it.
- `status` will contain `'SKIPPED'`, `'COMPLETE'`, or `'PARTIAL'`, depending on the value that your `Miva_ValidateFileUpload` function returned.
- `tempfile` will contain a string that specifies the name of a temporary file where the uploaded data is stored. (See Listing 5-4.)
- `mime_type` will contain a string that specifies the MIME data type of the uploaded file.
- `size` will contain a number that tells the size of the file. Note that if your script selected a partial upload, this variable will still specify the size of the **entire** file.

Your function may use these values (and any other variables, functions, or tags) to process the file.

Listings 5-3 and 5-4 demonstrate sending and receiving a file. Listing 5-3, the File Uploader, displays a form that allows the user to choose and send a file. Listing 5-4, the Upload Viewer, receives the uploaded file and displays it on the browser. (If you try this, be sure to upload only files containing HTML or other browser-compatible text.)

Listing 5-3: File Uploader

```
<FORM

 ACTION="http://&[server_name];:&[server_port];/Upload-
recv.mv"

 METHOD="POST"

 ENCTYPE="multipart/form-data"

>

 <INPUT TYPE="FILE" NAME="FILEBOX">

 <P>
```

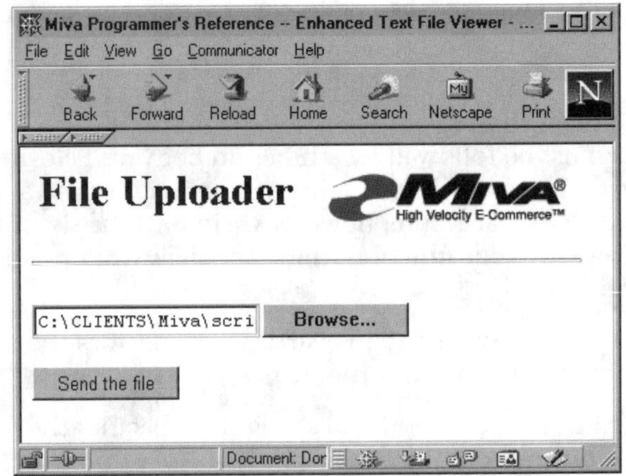

Figure 5-3: File Uploader display

```
 <INPUT TYPE="SUBMIT" VALUE="Send the file">
</FORM>
```

The File Uploader is very simple, since the actual file upload is done by the form. The only Miva Script here is the two macros in the form's `ACTION` attribute. By using the system variables `server_name` and `server_port`, the script is made portable: it can be moved to various servers without editing, and it will always send the upload to its own server. This script produces a display similar to Figure 5-3.

The Upload Viewer, shown in Listing 5-4, is a bit more complex. It contains definitions for the two functions needed to receive an uploaded file. The `Miva_ProcessFileUpload` function is very simple: it merely returns a value of 0 to accept the file. Then it uses macros to display several lines of information about the file. Finally, the script uses an `<MvIMPORT>` loop to display the text from the received file; this is equivalent to the text viewer shown in Listing 5-2.

Listing 5-4: Uploaded file viewer

```
<MvFUNCTION
 NAME="Miva_ValidateFileUpload"
 PARAMETERS="fieldvar,filename,mime_type"
>
 <MvFUNCRETURN VALUE="{0}">
</MvFUNCTION>
```

```
<MvFUNCTION
 NAME="Miva_ProcessFileUpload"
 PARAMETERS="fieldvar,filename,status,tempfile,mime_type,
size"
>
 Retrieved file: &[filename]; <BR>
 Stored in &[tempfile]; <BR>
 Data type: &[mime_type]; <HR>
 <MvIMPORT
  FILE="&[tempfile];"
  FIELDS="line"
  DELIMITER=""
 >
  &[line]; <BR>
 </MvIMPORT>
 <HR>
</MvFUNCTION>
```

The Upload Viewer is called by the File Uploader when you click the Send button. It produces a display similar to that shown in Figure 5-4.

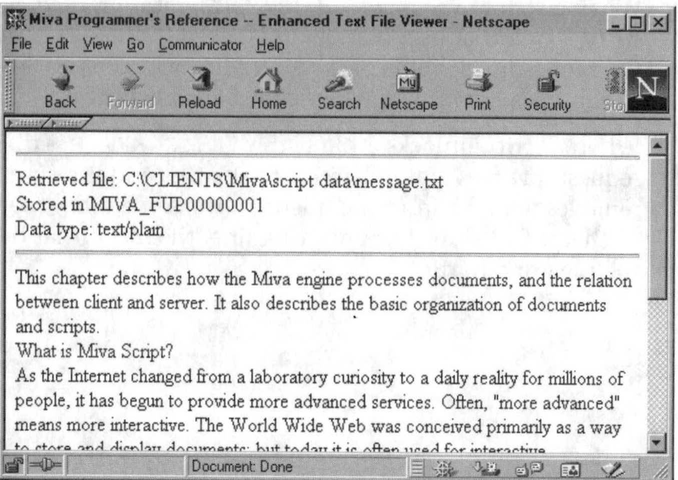

Figure 5-4: Viewing an uploaded file

File Locking

The World Wide Web is a multiuser environment, so it is quite likely that there will sometimes be multiple users accessing your Web site at the same time. It's possible that one user of your Web site might read a file while another user is modifying it; or several users might try to modify a file at the same time. These situations can cause loss of data and other problems. The `<MvLOCKFILE>` tag is used to prevent this from happening, by restricting a file so that only one script at a time can access it.

The tag has a single attribute, `FILE`, whose value is the pathname of the file to lock; for example,

```
<MvLOCKFILE FILE="employees.dbf">
```

locks a database file. This tag is always used with a corresponding `</MvLOCKFILE>` tag, which unlocks the file.

Files to be locked must be located in the standard Miva data directory, or a subdirectory of it. Locks can be applied to any type of file, including databases. Some Miva database operations use an internal locking mechanism: specifically, it is not necessary to use `<MvLOCKFILE>` with `<MvADD>`, `<MvUPDATE>`, `<MvDELETE>`, or `<MvUNDELETE>`. For other database operations, such as `<MvPACK>` or `<MvREINDEX>`, locking the database may be desirable. (For more information on databases, see Chapter 6).

Note that `<MvLOCKFILE>` is **not** an absolute guarantee of exclusive access to a file. It works "on the honor system;" that is, it only applies to scripts that also use `<MvLOCKFILE>`. Scripts that do not use `<MvLOCKFILE>`, or other users with non-Miva applications such as text editors, can still access the file at any time. If your application involves a number of scripts that modify a file, you should make sure that they all use locking (but be careful to avoid locking one file twice; see below).

When a script executes `<MvLOCKFILE>`, it is granted exclusive access to the file **only** if no other user has already locked it. If another user has locked the file, the requesting script is paused, and its lock request is placed in a holding area of the Miva engine's memory called a *request queue.*

When a script unlocks a file with `</MvLOCKFILE>`, the next script in the request queue is granted access to the file, and it resumes running. Miva removes requests from the queue in the same order that they were placed in it, so that it functions like a waiting line: the script that has waited the longest is the next one to run.

Precautions for File Locking

To prevent users from seeing noticeable delays, you should organize your scripts so that locks are used briefly. Only lock a file as long as necessary; keep other types of tags and text outside the `<MvLOCKFILE> ... </MvLOCKFILE>` block. Try to avoid having a script that needs to lock two or more files at the same time: this can result in "deadly embrace" situations where two users block each other, and neither can proceed. Also, never try to lock the same file twice, as the second attempt will stop the script permanently.

System Functions

Miva Script has a large number of system functions for manipulating files, as listed in the table below. The files must be located in one of the standard directories (for scripts or data). Except where noted, each of these functions returns 1 if it succeeds in its intended operation; if it fails, it returns 0.

Name	Action
`fchmod(f, n)`	Change permissions of a file in the data directory
`fcopy(f)`	Copy a file in the data directory
`fdelete(f)`	Delete a file in the data directory
`fexists(f)`	Return 1 if a file exists in the data directory
`fmkdir(d)`	Create a subdirectory in the data directory
`fmode(f)`	Return permission settings on a file in the data directory
`frename(f1, f2)`	Rename or move a file in the data directory
`fscopy(f1, f2)`	Copy a file from the data directory to the scripts directory
`fsize(f)`	Return the size of a file in the data directory
`fsrename(f1, f2)`	Rename or move a file from the data directory to the scripts directory
`fsymlink(f, s)`	Create a symbolic link or alias to a file in the data directory
`schmod(f, n)`	Change permissions of a file in the scripts directory
`scopy(f1, f2)`	Copy a file in the scripts directory

Name	Action
`sdelete(f)`	Delete a file in the scripts directory
`sexists(f)`	Return 1 if a file exists in the scripts directory
`sfcopy(f1, f2)`	Copy a file from the scripts directory to the data directory
`sfrename(f1, f2)`	Rename or move a file from the scripts directory to the data directory
`smkdir(d)`	Create a subdirectory in the scripts directory
`smode(f)`	Return permission settings on a file in the scripts directory
`srename(f1, f2)`	Rename or move a file in the scripts directory
`ssize(f)`	Return the size of a file in the scripts directory
`ssymlink(f, s)`	Create a symbolic link or alias to a file in the sripts directory

For More Information

For more detailed information on any of the tags and system functions discussed in this chapter, see the Reference section of this manual.

The scripts shown in the Listings are available online at this manual's companion Web site:

http://TopFloor.com/Miva/

6

Database Access

The ability to work with databases is one of Miva Script's most valuable features. A variety of tags are available for reading, writing, and managing databases. The tags are simple to use, and powerful enough to allow complete maintenance of databases without any software other than documents with scripts.

Miva Script can operate on two types of databases: Xbase3 and ODBC. Xbase3 is an industry-standard format that traces its roots all the way back to the dBase programs used on MS-DOS PCs. It is still widely supported and is compatible with many current applications. Miva Script supports a wide variety of operations on Xbase3 databases.

ODBC is a more advanced protocol. In ODBC terminology, the term *datasource* is often used instead of "database." This reflects the fact that data can be generated by a remote application or hardware device, rather than being simply read from a file on a hard drive. Currently, Miva Script support for ODBC is limited to performing SQL queries with the `<MvOPENVIEW>` and `<MvQUERY>` tags. Use of these tags requires an understanding of the SQL query language, which is beyond the scope of this manual.

Miva Script's repertoire of database operations includes:

- Creating a new database with `<MvCREATE>`.
- Opening an existing database with `<MvOPEN>`. If necessary, you can find out the database's record structure before opening it, by using `<MvREVEAL-STRUCTURE>`.

- Navigating to a specific record with `<MvFIND>`, `<MvGO>`, or `<MvSKIP>`. You can also make some records "invisible" to navigation by using `<MvFILTER>`.
- Adding new records with `<MvADD>`.
- Marking records for deletion with `<MvDELETE>`; unmarking them with `<MvUNDELETE>`; and deleting marked records with `<MvPACK>`.
- Modifying a record with `<MvUPDATE>`.
- Creating indexes for rapid searching by using `<MvMAKEINDEX>`. You can manage indexes with `<MvREINDEX>` and `<MvSETINDEX>`.
- Compressing a database with `<MvPACK>`.
- Performing SQL queries on ODBC databases with `<MvOPENVIEW>` and `<MvQUERY>`.

Database Fundamentals

A database is generally a file (except that in some cases, an ODBC datasource may be some other device) that is organized much like a table, with rows and columns. For instance, Figure 6-1 shows a table that could represent part of a company's employee database.

Figure 6-1:

Simple database table

ID number	Last name	First name	Gender	ZIP code
1001	Smith	John	M	12345
1002	Aardvark	Aaron	M	98765
1003	Bizzy	Bee	F	44444
1004	Bizzy	Dee	F	44444
1005	Zyvith	Yvonne	F	12346

Each row of the table represents one *record* of the database: it describes one employee. Each record is divided into sections called *fields;* these comprise the columns of the table. Each field contains one piece of information about the employee. (Of course, a real company's database would probably contain many other fields for the employee's complete address, age, etc.)

When you open a database in Miva Script, you define a set of variables that correspond to its fields. When you work with a database, you operate on one record at a time by using the field variables. For instance:

- To read a field, you navigate to the desired record, and then read the variable's value.

- To modify a field, you navigate to the desired record, modify the appropriate variable, and then store the new value back to the database with `<MvUPDATE>`.
- To create a new record, you write the values for all its fields to the appropriate variables, and then write the new record to the database with `<MvADD>`.

Aliases

When a script opens a database, it uses a nickname called an *alias* to refer to it. A script can open several databases simultaneously by using a different alias for each one.

The alias is specified by the `NAME` attribute for all Miva tags that perform database operations. However, in most cases this attribute is optional. When executing a tag without a `NAME` attribute, Miva uses the current *primary* alias for the script. The primary alias is normally the last one opened. If necessary, you can choose a different primary database at any time with the `<MvPRIMARY>` tag.

It is sometimes useful to open a single database several times, with several different aliases. For example, you can access different parts of a database by using `<MvFILTER>` to cause different records to appear to each alias. For this reason, it may be helpful to think of an alias as a "channel" or *connection* to a database, rather than an actual file.

Fields and Field Variables

Database field variables are named and used much like any other Miva Script variables. For example, to define the employee database shown in Figure 6-1, you could use five variables named `ID`, `lastname`, `firstname`, `gender`, and `zipcode`.

Database variables are in a different scope from other variables. So, for instance, if your script already has a variable named `zipcode`, you can still use `zipcode` as a field variable by referring to it as *dba*`.d.zipcode`, where *dba* is the alias for the database. To reference a field variable for the primary database, you could just write `d.zipcode`.

Caution: Since the `d.` scope has priority over `g.`, you must use the `g.` prefix with global variable names if they conflict with the names of database variables. See "Variable Scope" in Chapter 2 for details.

Unlike other Miva Script variables, field variables have a specific type that determines what kind of data they can hold. The available types are:

- `CHAR` fields hold character strings up to 254 characters long.
- `MEMO` fields hold character strings too long to fit in a `CHAR` field; their length is unlimited. `MEMO` fields are stored in a file separate from the rest of the database. The memo file will have the same name as the main database file, with a `.dbt` extension. Scripts that use `MEMO` fields may be slower than those without them, so these fields should be used sparingly.
- `NUMBER` fields hold numeric data. When you define a `NUMBER` field, you specify the number of digits and the location of the decimal point, if any.
- `BOOL` fields hold Boolean values: 1 for true, or 0 for false.
- `DATE` fields hold times and dates in the universal format used by all Miva Script tags and system functions. (See "Times and Dates" below for details about these.)

You determine the type for each field when you create a database. Once the database is created, the field types cannot be changed; so you should choose them carefully, with an eye to future expansion. For instance, even if your company only has a few hundred employees, if you use a six-digit field for the ID number, you will be able to expand up to a million employees without changing the database structure.

Times and Dates

As mentioned above, a `DATE` field contains a time and date in Miva universal format (see Chapter 2). To make working with these fields more convenient, when you create a `DATE` field, Miva creates four additional variables that reference the field. Specifically, when you create a `DATE` field variable named *ddd*, Miva creates the following variables:

- *ddd*`_day` returns the day of the month as a two-digit number.
- *ddd*`_month` returns the month as a two-digit number.
- *ddd*`_year` returns the year as a four-digit number
- *ddd*`_raw` returns the complete date as an eight-character string of the form *yyyymmdd*, where *yyyy* is the year, *mm* is the month, and *dd* is the day of the month.

For example, if your application reads a user's birth date from an HTML form, you can simply transfer the user's day, month, and year values into the appropriate variables. This is easier than using system functions to combine the separate values into a universal-format number.

Other Variables

Besides the field variables that are defined by the database creator, there are several other variables that Miva automatically creates for each database connection:

- `recno` is the *record pointer:* a number that identifies the current record (see "Navigation" below).
- `totrec` is the total number of records in the database, including any that have been marked for deletion, but not physically removed yet.
- `eof` is a Boolean variable. It is normally false (0), and becomes true (1) when the end of the database is reached, i.e., when an <MvSKIP> or <MvGO> attempts to navigate beyond the last record.
- `deleted` is true (1) if the current record has been marked for deletion by <MvDELETE>.

If you have other variables in your scripts with these names, you can reference the database variables by writing *dba*.d.*var*, where *dba* is an alias, and *var* is the variable; or by writing d.*var* for the primary database.

Caution: Since the `d.` scope has priority over `g.`, you must use the `g.` prefix with global variable names if they conflict with the names of database variables. See "Variable Scope" in Chapter 2 for details.

Creating a Database

To create a new database, you use the <MvCREATE> tag. Its attributes specify the alias to use, the pathname of the file, and the names and types of the field variables. For example, to create an employee database like that shown in Figure 6-1, you could write a tag such as:

```
<MvCREATE
 NAME="employees"
 DATABASE="employees.dbf"
 FIELDS=
 "ID NUMBER(6),
  lastname CHAR(32),
  firstname CHAR(32),
```

```
  gender CHAR(1),
  zipcode NUMBER(5)"
>
```

This tag creates a database file named `employees.dbf`. (`.dbf` is the usual filename extension for Xbase3 databases.) It assigns the alias `employees`, and creates the five field variables that correspond to the columns of the table.

Listing 6-1 shows a script that creates this database, and inserts some records using data from a text file. The text file should look like this:

```
1001; Smith; John; M; 12345
1002; Aardvark; Aaron; M; 98765
1003; Bizzy; Bee; F; 44444
1004; Bizzy; Dee; F; 44444
1005; Zyvith; Yvonne; F; 12346
...
```

The file contains one line of text for each employee. Each line contains values for the five fields, separated by a semicolon and a space.

Listing 6-1: Creating a database

```
<MvCREATE
 NAME="employees"
 DATABASE="employees.dbf"
 FIELDS=
 "ID NUMBER(6),
  lastname CHAR(32),
  firstname CHAR(32),
  gender CHAR(1),
  zipcode NUMBER(5)"
>

<MvIMPORT
 FILE="employees.txt"
 FIELDS="d.ID,d.lastname,d.firstname,d.gender,d.zipcode"
```

```
 DELIMITER="; "
>

Record &[g.recno]; ... <BR>

<MvADD>

</MvIMPORT>
```

The listing starts with the <MvCREATE> tag that creates the database as already described. This is followed by an <MvIMPORT> tag that creates a loop (see Chapter 5). The loop reads lines of text from the file employees.txt, which should have the format shown above. The FIELDS attribute specifies the names of the database's five field variables; this causes <MvIMPORT> to place values from the text file directly into the field variables. The DELIMITER attribute specifies that the values in the text file are separated by a semicolon and a space.

Inside the loop, the first thing that the script does is display a message on the browser; this is just to give you some indication of the script's progress. The &[g.recno] macro inserts the record number, based on the count of text lines read by <MvIMPORT>.

Next, the script executes <MvADD> to add a new record to the database. (<MvADD> is described in more detail later in this chapter.) The new record will contain the values that were read into the field variables by <MvIMPORT>. The loop will continue, creating one record for each line of text, until it reaches the end of the text file.

Opening and Closing Databases

To open a connection to an existing database, you use the <MvOPEN> tag. For example:

```
<MvOPEN
 NAME="employees"
 DATABASE="employees.dbf"
>
```

The tag's attributes specify the alias to use, and the pathname of the database file. Other attributes can optionally specify whether the database is Xbase3 or ODBC, and can also specify index files (described below) to use with the database. Note that there is no FIELDS attribute. Field variables are defined when a database is created; after that, their names are fixed, and they are available for use in scripts whenever the database is open.

To close a database connection, you use the <MvCLOSE> tag. After the connection is closed, the alias can be used to open a connection to a different database. Use of <MvCLOSE> is optional; if you don't use it, Miva automatically closes any open database connections when it finishes processing a document.

Navigation

As mentioned above, Miva Script accesses database records one at a time. To work with a record, you must first navigate to it. Several forms of navigation are available.

For each open database connection (alias), Miva maintains a record pointer in a variable named recno. (You can also reference it as *dba*.d.recno, where *dba* is an alias; or as d.recno for the primary database.) recno specifies the *current record* within the database, i.e., the specific record that can currently be read and modified using the field variables.

Records in a database file are stored in the order in which they are created. No facility is provided for sorting or rearranging the physical record order. The physical order may change when the database is packed (described below), so you generally should **not** use recno values as a key or index to find specific records.

You can use *indexes* (described below) to provide other ways to access the records, such as in alphabetical order by the contents of a CHAR field. However, the physical record order is often sufficient for simple tasks, such as reading all the records to compute some totals and averages. For such tasks, Miva Script supports simple navigation operations with <MvGO> and <MvSKIP>.

<MvGO> has a ROW attribute that specifies the physical record number to access. For instance, <MvGO NAME="employees" ROW="10"> will access the 10th record of the employees database. Instead of a number, you can use the keyword top or bottom to specify the first or last record. However, if any indexes are open for the database, top and bottom will navigate by using an index, which may give different results. To always navigate to the first or last physical record, use ROW="1" or ROW="{totrec}", respectively.

Whereas <MvGO> performs "absolute" positioning, <MvSKIP> performs "relative" movements through the database. The simplest case is probably the most common: <MvSKIP ROWS="1"> simply moves the record pointer forward to the next record. This is often used in loops, to step through the database one record at a time. In fact, if the ROWS attribute is omitted, Miva assumes a value of 1 as a default. ROWS can be a negative number, to move backwards (toward the first physical record). Note that if any indexes are open for the database, <MvSKIP>, like <MvGO>, will navigate by using an index.

Filtering

You can perform faster database searches by selecting records with <MvFILTER>. This tag has a FILTER attribute, whose value is a Miva Script expression that contains at least one field variable. As Miva navigates through a database, it uses the filter expression to perform a true/false check on every record. If the result of the expression is false (0), the record is considered "invisible;" in this case, <MvFIND>, <MvGO>, and <MvSKIP> will never navigate to the record. For example, using our employee database from Figure 6-1, suppose you want to do a report on all male employees. You can write:

```
<MvFILTER NAME="employees" FILTER="{gender EQ 'M'}">
```

After executing this tag, Miva will only navigate to records whose gender field contains M.

Indexes

In any database system, it may be necessary to rearrange the order of the records. For instance, when using an employee database to create an office phone list, you would want to read the records in alphabetical order. But when it's time to mail out paychecks, you want to print them in ZIP-code order, to get lower postage rates.

Rearranging the physical order of the records can be time-consuming, especially if the database is large. So modern databases solve this problem by using *indexes.* An index is a separate file that has the effect of specifying what order the records should be in, in order to be sorted in some specified way. Creating an index for a large database may be slow; but if you create the database and index at the same time, you can maintain the index as the database grows without a lot of overhead. You can create two (or more) indexes for the same database: this allows you to switch, say, from alphabetical to ZIP-code order at any time.

The order that an index defines is specified by a Miva Script expression, called the *key expression*, that references one or more of the database fields. The key expression is specified by the <MvMAKEINDEX> tag that creates the index. A simple example is shown below:

```
<MvMAKEINDEX
 NAME="employees"
 INDEXFILE="zip.mvx"
```

```
EXPR="{zipcode}"
>
```

This tag creates an index for the `employees` database. The index will be in a file named `zip.mvx` (`.mvx` is the standard extension for index files). The key expression is defined by the `EXPR` attribute. In this example, the "expression" simply the `zipcode` field variable. This has the effect of sorting the database b the value of `zipcode` in each record.

Sorting the records in alphabetical order by employee name may be a bit more complex, since the database has separate fields for the first and last names. In that case, we could use a tag such as:

```
<MvMAKEINDEX
NAME="employees"
INDEXFILE="alpha.mvx"
EXPR="{toupper(lastname) $ ',' $ toupper(firstname)}"
>
```

This time, the key expression consists of the `lastname` field variable concatenated to a comma and the `firstname` variable. The last name is placed first, since that is how we normally sort people's names. The `toupper()` system function is used to convert both names to uppercase, since all letters must be the same case for comparing and sorting. The comma is necessary to separate the first and last names; otherwise there could be some missorting. For instance, without the comma, the record for Ann Smithfield would be placed before Fielding Smith, since the concatenated string `smithfieldann` comes before `smithfielding` in alphabetical order.

`<MvMAKEINDEX>` also has a `FLAGS` attribute. It can be used to specify options such as alphabetic or numeric ordering, and ascending or descending sequenc

Managing Indexes

To create an index for a database, you use the `<MvMAKEINDEX>` tag as describ above. The database to be indexed must already be open. As mentioned earlie it is usually best to create the index at the same time as the database, so that they can grow together.

When you open an existing database that has indexes, you open the indexes specifying them in the `INDEXES` attribute of the `<MvOPEN>` tag. If you open the indexes, Miva will automatically update them as needed when changes ar made to the database.

If your database is large, and some indexes are not often used, you may prefer not to open all the indexes when running some scripts. In this case, the unopened indexes will become invalid if the database is modified. In order to resynchronize the indexes at a later time, you can use <MvREINDEX>. This tag reads the entire database, and rebuilds **all** indexes. Since this operation can be time-consuming, it may be best to do it offline, using Miva Mia and a copy of the database.

Navigation with Indexes

If more than one index is in use at one time, one of them is designated the *main index;* this is the one that is used for navigation. The main index is determined by the following rules:

- When you open a database with <MvOPEN>, the first index listed in the INDEXES attribute becomes the main index.
- When you use <MvMAKEINDEX> to create a new index, it becomes the main index.
- At any time, you can select a different main index with the <MvSETINDEX> tag.

When a database is opened with one or more indexes, a number of additional navigation features are provided:

- When using <MvGO>, ROW="top" and ROW="bottom" will navigate to the first or last record based on the order defined by the main index. (ROW with a numeric value will still navigate by physical record order.)
- When using <MvSKIP>, Miva moves from record to record according to the order defined in the main index.
- The <MvFIND> tag can be used to quickly find a specific record.

Listing 6-2 demonstrates the use of indexes by creating the ZIP-code and alphabetical indexes that we have been discussing. This script opens the employees database and creates the two indexes. It lists the contents of the database twice, to show the different sequences that the indexes provide.

Listing 6-2: Using database indexes

```
<MvFUNCTION  NAME="listrecords">
 <MvGO ROW="top">
 <MvWHILE EXPR="{not d.eof}">
  Employee #&[d.ID]; is &[d.firstname]; &[d.lastname];,
  &[d.gender];, ZIP code &[d.zipcode];. <BR>
  <MvSKIP ROWS="1">
 </MvWHILE>
```

```
</MvFUNCTION>
<MvOPEN  NAME="employees"  DATABASE="employees.dbf">

Making ZIP code index ... <BR>
<MvMAKEINDEX
 INDEXFILE="zip.mvx"
 EXPR="{zipcode}"
>
Result: <P>
<MvEVAL EXPR="{listrecords()}">

<P> Making alphabetical index ... <BR>
<MvMAKEINDEX
 INDEXFILE="alpha.mvx"
 EXPR="{toupper(lastname) $ ',' $ toupper(firstname)}"
>
Result: <P>
<MvEVAL EXPR="{listrecords()}">
```

At the beginning of this script is an `<MvFUNCTION>` tag that defines a function named `listrecords()`. This function simply displays all the records on the browser screen, in the order defined by the current main index. It uses `<MvGO ROW="top">` to navigate to the first record (see "Navigation" above). Then it uses an `<MvWHILE>` loop to display each record. The `<MvSKIP>` tag advances to the next record. The loop repeats until `d.eof` becomes true, indicating that the end of the database has been reached.

After defining the function, the script uses `<MvOPEN>` to open the `employees` database. Next, it uses `<MvMAKEINDEX>` with the key expression `{zipcode}` to create a ZIP-code index. Then the script uses `<MvEVAL>` to call the `listrecords()` function and display all the records in ZIP-code order.

Next, the script uses another `<MvMAKEINDEX>` to create the alphabetical index, using the key expression discussed earlier. Then it calls `listrecords()` again. This time, the just-created index has become the main index, so the records are displayed in alphabetical order.

Figure 6-2 shows the browser display produced by this script. In the first listing, the records are sorted by ZIP code. In the second listing, the records are sorted in alphabetical order; and Smithfield does indeed come after Smith.

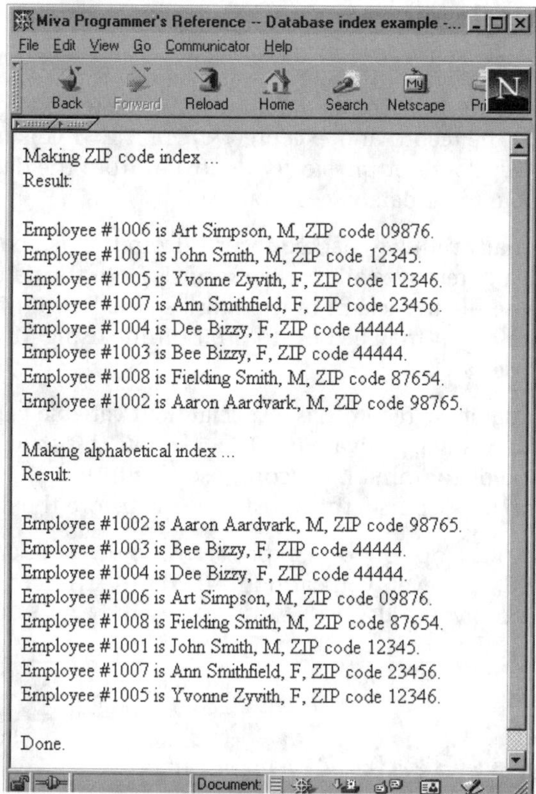

Figure 6-2: Database listings using indexes

Reading Records

Once you have navigated to a particular record, to read its values is trivial, because Miva automatically places the record's field values into the field variables. You simply use these variables in any Miva Script expression. There is no "MvREAD" tag.

Adding and Modifying Records

To add a record to a database, first assign the desired field values to the field variables. (Note that these variables may already contain values assigned by previous operations.) Then execute `<MvADD>` to write the new record. New records are always placed at the end of the database (in physical record order).

To modify a record, first navigate to it; then make the desired changes to any field variables. Then execute `<MvUPDATE>` to write the changes to the database.

Deleting Records

Deleting records from a database is a two-step process. The first step is to navigate to the record and execute <MvDELETE>. This marks the record for deletion, but does not physically remove it from the database. The record is still available to all database operations.

To actually remove marked records from the database, use <MvPACK>. This tag physically removes all marked records from the database, and compresses the database file to reclaim unused disk space. Since this operation can be time-consuming, it may be best to do it offline using Miva Mia and a copy of the database.

Every database record has a special field variable called `deleted` that is created automatically by Miva. <MvDELETE> sets this field to 1; this is how the record is marked. To unmark a record, use <MvUNDELETE> to set the `deleted` field back to 0; of course, this must be done before the database is packed.

You can use `deleted` in expressions, to determine whether or not a record is marked. However, you cannot use <MvASSIGN> to change the value of `deleted`; you must use <MvDELETE> and <MvUNDELETE> for that.

Reading a Database's Structure

If you receive an unknown database file from another user, you can determine its record format before opening it, by using <MvREVEALSTRUCTURE>. This tag examines a target database, and creates a new database that contains data describing the target. Specifically, the new database will contain one record for each field in the target database. Each record in the new database contains four fields:

`field_name`	Name of a field in the target database.
`field_type`	A single character that specifies the field type:

C	CHAR
N	NUMBER
D	DATE
L	logical (BOOL)
M	MEMO

`field_len`	Length of the field, depending on the field type:
	`CHAR` Number of characters.
	`NUMBER` Total number of digits, before and after the decimal point; plus 1 for the decimal point, if any.
	`DATE` Always 8.
	`BOOL` Always 1.
	`MEMO` Always 10.
`field_dec`	For NUMBER fields only, this field gives the number of digits after the decimal point.

Listing 6-3 shows how `<MvREVEALSTRUCTURE>` can be used. It examines the `employees` database, and displays the structure information in an HTML table.

Listing 6-3: Reading database structure

```
<MvOPEN NAME="employees" DATABASE="employees.dbf">

<MvREVEALSTRUCTURE
 NAME="employees"
 DATABASE="structure.dbf"
>

<MvOPEN NAME="structure" DATABASE="structure.dbf">

Database structure is: <P>

<TABLE BORDER>
 <TR>
  <TH> Name </TH>
  <TH> Type </TH>
  <TH> Length </TH>
  <TH> Digits after decimal point </TH>
 </TR>
```

```
<MvGO ROW="1">
<MvWHILE EXPR="{not d.eof}">
 <TR>
  <TD> &[field_name]; </TD>
  <TD> &[field_type]; </TD>
  <TD> &[field_len]; </TD>
  <TD> &[field_dec]; </TD>
 </TR>
 <MvSKIP ROWS="1">
</MvWHILE>
</TABLE>
```

This script starts by opening the `employees` database with `<MvOPEN>`. Next, it uses `<MvREVEALSTRUCTURE>` to read the structure of the `employees` database, and to store the structure data in a new database named `structure.dbf`. Then it opens the new database, and uses HTML tags to start a table and display a row of column headers.

Then the script uses an `<MvWHILE>` loop to read the structure records. Each record's fields are displayed as one row of the HTML table. The result is shown in Figure 6-3.

Figure 6-3: Database structure revealed

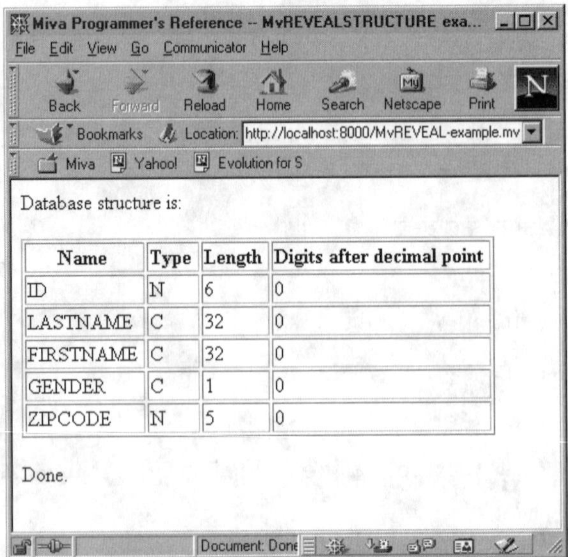

Name	Type	Length	Digits after decimal point
ID	N	6	0
LASTNAME	C	32	0
FIRSTNAME	C	32	0
GENDER	C	1	0
ZIPCODE	N	5	0

ODBC and SQL

At this time, Miva Script's support for ODBC datasources and SQL queries is rather basic; additional functionality will be provided in future versions. Currently, the following features are available:

- The `<MvOPEN>` tag can open an ODBC datasource by specifying the `TYPE="ODBC"` attribute. You can also use the `USER` and `PASSWORD` attributes to pass a user name and password to access the datasource.
- The `<MvQUERY>` tag can be used to execute an SQL query that does not return any results.
- The `<MvOPENVIEW>` tag can be used to execute an SQL query that returns results. The results are placed in a *view*, a table structure that functions much like a normal database. The tag's `VIEW` attribute specifies a name for the view. The view name is used like a database alias, to reference the view in other tags.
- The `<MvGO>` and `<MvSKIP>` tags can be used to navigate within a view by specifying the view name in the `VIEW` attribute.
- Miva provides the `eof` and `recno` variables for navigating in views (but not `totrec` or `deleted`). These can be referenced by expressions such as *`viewname`*`.d.eof`, where *`viewname`* is the name assigned when the view was opened.
- The `<MvCLOSEVIEW>` tag is used to close a view when a script no longer needs it.

For More Information

For more detailed information on any of the tags and system functions discussed in this chapter, see the Reference section of this manual.

The scripts shown in the Listings are available online at this manual's companion Web site:

http://TopFloor.com/Miva/

Sending and Receiving E-mail

Miva Script provides a number of tags for accessing e-mail servers. Scripts can send messages with the `<MvSMTP>` tag, and receive them with `<MvPOP>`. To use these tags, you must have the name of a mail server that Miva can access. In many cases, you can use `mail.`*`company.com`*, where *`company.com`* is the domain you use for your e-mail address (you might use a different suffix, such as `.net`, `.org`, etc. instead of `.com`).

Sending E-mail

Scripts can transmit e-mail by using the `<MvSMTP>` and `</MvSMTP>` tags. Miva redirects the portion of a script between these two tags: instead of displaying it on the user's browser, Miva places it in an e-mail message, and sends it to one or more destinations. A simple example is shown below:

```
<MvSMTP
 TO="<you@yourcompany.com>"
 CC="coworker@yourcompany.com"
 SUBJECT="Testing MvSMTP"
 MAILHOST="mail.myisp.com"
 FROM="me@mycompany.com"
```

```
>

Bcc: "Him" <otherguy@mycompany.com>


I am testing a new Miva Script program.  If you receive
this, please reply.


</MvSMTP>
```

This example illustrates several key points about using `<MvSMTP>`. The attributes provide the basic information needed to send the message. If you want to include additional mail headers, such as `Bcc:` or `Reply-to:`, put them immediately after the `<MvSMTP>` tag. After any additional headers, there **must** be at least one blank line to indicate the start of the message text. (This blank line is required even if there are no additional headers.)

A more sophisticated script is shown in Figures 7-1 and 7-2. This Mail Sender applet uses the two-pass structure discussed in Chapter 3. The applet starts (pass 1) by displaying a form in which the user enters the message text, addresses, and other necessary information.

When the user clicks the Send button, the script calls itself for pass 2, and passes the information from the form. It then uses `<MvSMTP>` to send the message.

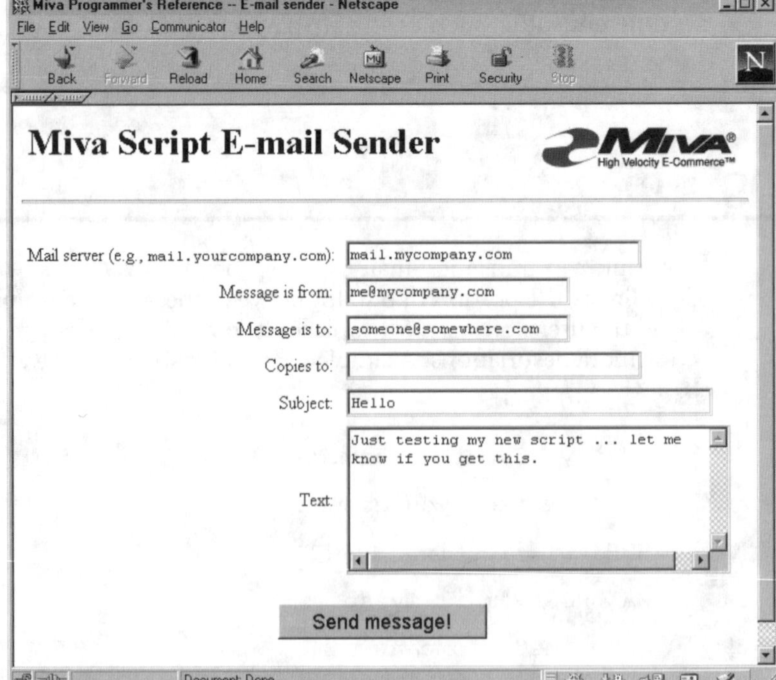

Figure 7-1: E-mail Sender applet, pass 1

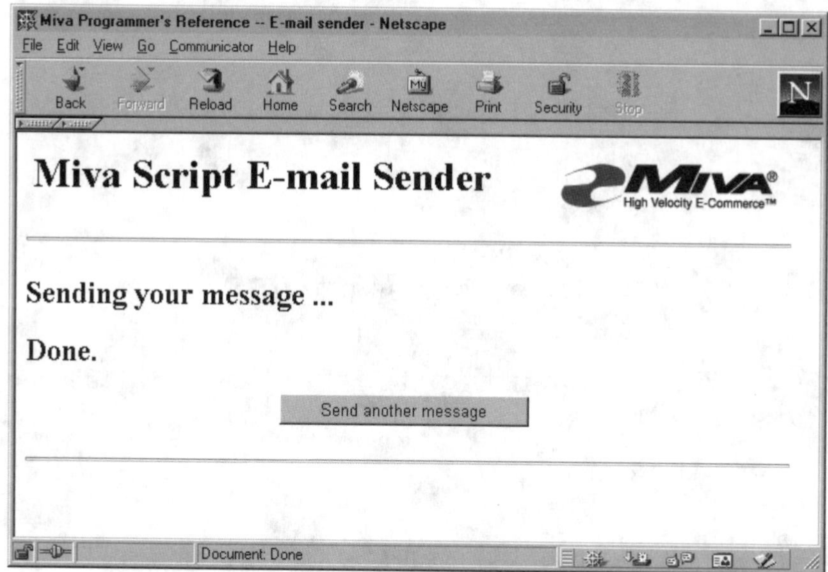

Figure 7-2: Mail Sender applet, pass 2

The complete applet is shown in Listing 7-1.

Listing 7-1: E-mail Sender applet

```
<HTML>

<HEAD>

<TITLE> Miva Programmer's Reference -- E-mail sender
</TITLE>

</HEAD>

<BODY>


<TABLE WIDTH="100%"> <TR>

 <TD> <H1> Miva Script E-mail Sender </H1>

 <TD ALIGN="RIGHT"> <IMG SRC="mivalogo.gif">

</TR> </TABLE>

<HR>


<MvIF EXPR="{pass NE 2}">
```

```
 <!-- Pass 1:  display form -->

 <FORM ACTION="&[s.documenturl];" METHOD="POST">
 <TABLE>
  <TR>
   <TD ALIGN="RIGHT"> Mail server (e.g.,
<TT>mail.yourcompany.com</TT>):
   </TD>
   <TD> <INPUT TYPE="TEXT" NAME="mailserver" SIZE="32">
</TD>
  </TR>
  <TR>
   <TD ALIGN="RIGHT"> Message is from: </TD>
   <TD> <INPUT TYPE="TEXT" NAME="returnaddress" SIZE="24">
</TD>
  </TR>
  <TR>
   <TD ALIGN="RIGHT"> Message is to: </TD>
   <TD> <INPUT TYPE="TEXT" NAME="recipient" SIZE="24">
</TD>
  </TR>
  <TR>
   <TD ALIGN="RIGHT"> Copies to: </TD>
   <TD> <INPUT TYPE="TEXT" NAME="copyrecip" SIZE="32">
</TD>
  </TR>
  <TR>
   <TD ALIGN="RIGHT"> Subject: </TD>
   <TD> <INPUT TYPE="TEXT" NAME="subjectline" SIZE="40">
</TD>
  </TR>
  <TR>
   <TD ALIGN="RIGHT"> Text: </TD>
```

```
    <TD> <TEXTAREA NAME="messagetext" ROWS="6"
COLS="40"></TEXTAREA>
    </TD>
   </TR>
  </TABLE>
  <CENTER> <H2> <INPUT TYPE="SUBMIT" VALUE="Send message!">
</H2> </CENTER>
  <INPUT TYPE="HIDDEN" NAME="pass" VALUE="2">
  </FORM>

<MvELSE>

  <!-- Pass 2:  send message -->

  <H2> Sending your message ... </H2>

  <MvSMTP
  TO="&[recipient];"
  CC="&[copyrecip];"
  SUBJECT="&[subjectline];"
  MAILHOST="&[mailserver];"
  FROM="&[returnaddress];">

&[messagetext];

  </MvSMTP>

  <H2> Done. </H2>

  <CENTER>
  <FORM ACTION="&[s.documenturl];" METHOD="POST">
  <INPUT TYPE="SUBMIT" VALUE="Send another message">
```

```
  </FORM>
  </CENTER>

</MvIF>

<HR>
</BODY> </HTML>
```

Receiving E-mail

To receive e-mail, scripts can use the <MvPOP> and </MvPOP> tags. A simple example is shown below:

```
<MvPOP
   MAILHOST="mail.mynet.net"
   LOGIN="joe_user"
   PASSWORD="secret007"
   DIRECTORY="inbox">

Retrieved message from &[messagesender]; stored in file
&[messagebody];.
<BR>

  </MvPOP>
```

The MAILHOST, LOGIN, and PASSWORD attributes specify the mail account to access. Miva retrieves some or all incoming messages in the account, and copies their contents to files in a directory specified by the DIRECTORY attribute. Miva ensures that each file has a unique name, such as MIVA_POP00000001, MIVA_POP00000002, etc. (The exact format of the names may vary depending on the platform on which Miva is running: Windows, Unix, etc.)

The <MvPOP> and </MvPOP> tags form a loop: everything between them is executed once for each retrieved message. Normally, the loop will run until all messages in the account have been retrieved. However, a script can use the <MvPOPSTOP> tag to interrupt the loop.

Inside the `<MvPOP> ... </MvPOP>` loop, the following variables are available, and provide information on each message as it is retrieved:

Name	Contents
`messagebody`	Name of the file in which the message is stored
`messagesubject`	Contents of the message's `Subject:` field
`messagereplyto`	Contents of the message's `Reply-To:` field
`messagesender`	Contents of the message's `From:` field
`messagedate`	Contents of the message's `Date:` field

Normally, `<MvPOP>` leaves retrieved messages on the server. However, if the script executes the `<MvPOPDELETE>` tag inside the loop, the corresponding message will be deleted from the server.

A more sophisticated example is shown in Figures 7-3 through 7-5. This E-mail Viewer applet starts (pass 1) by displaying a form in which users enter their mail server, username, and password.

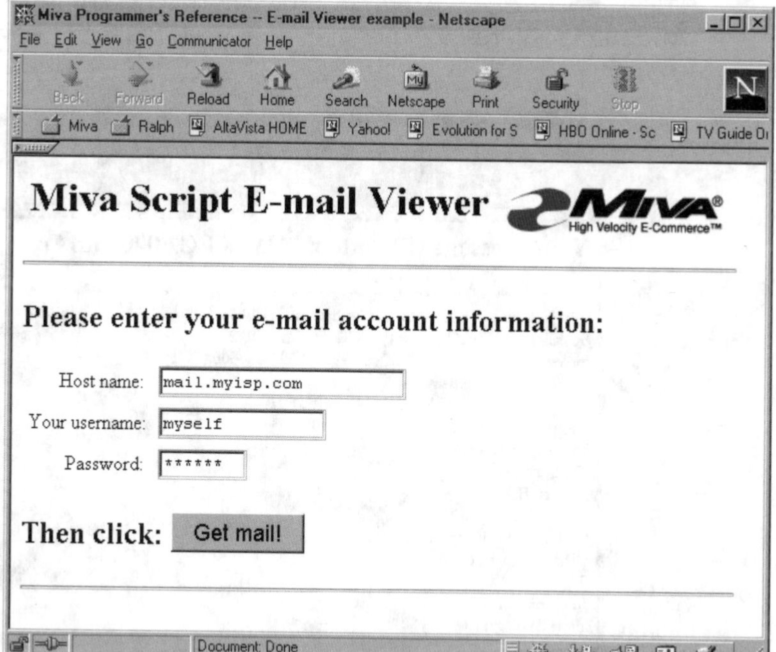

Figure 7-3: E-mail Viewer applet, pass 1

When the user clicks the Get Mail button, the script calls itself for pass 2, and passes the information from the form. It then uses `<MvPOP>` to read incoming messages from the server, and displays information about the messages in a table:

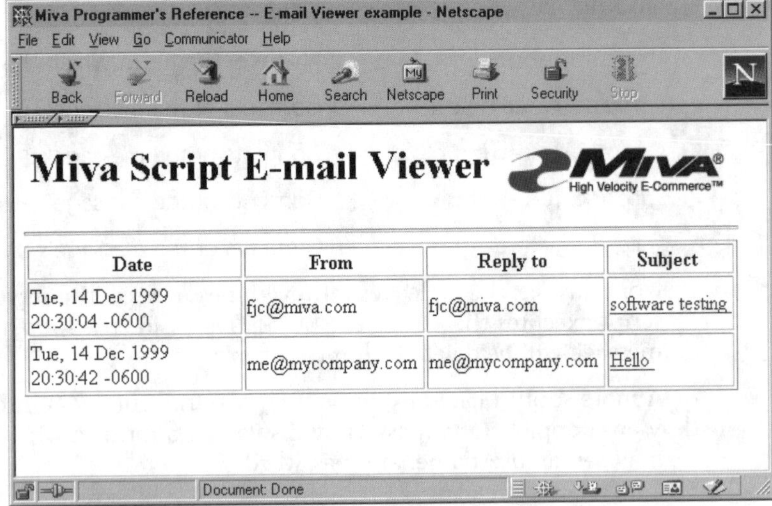

Figure 7-4:

E-mail Viewer applet, pass 2

The Subject field in each row of the table is a hyperlink. Clicking on one of these links will run another script that reads the mail message and displays its contents:

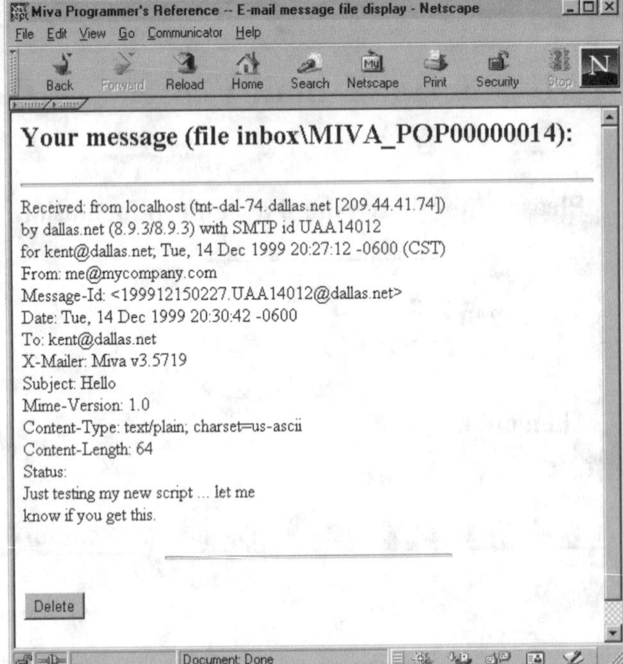

Figure 7-5:

Viewing a message

The message-display script includes a button that deletes the file in which the message is stored. (Note that this script does **not** delete the message from the mail server; you can use <MvPOPDELETE> to do that.)

The complete E-mail Viewer applet is shown in Listing 7-2. In the pass-2 part of this script, the <MvPOP>...</MvPOP> loop is interwoven with an HTML table. First, the <TABLE> tag starts the table, and a series of <TH> tags creates column headers. Next, the <MvPOP> starts the loop for retrieving messages. Inside the loop, the script uses <TR> and <TD> tags to add one row to the table, and fill in its columns with information about the retrieved message. The </MvPOP> terminates the message-reading loop, and the </TABLE> tag terminates the HTML table.

Note that each complete table row, from <TR> to </TR>, is created by code inside the <MvPOP>...</MvPOP> loop, so that each time Miva executes the loop, it builds one complete table row. The <TABLE> and </TABLE> tags, on the other hand, are outside the loop, so they are only executed once.

Note: This applet assumes that you will create a directory called inbox as a subdirectory of your Miva data directory. The applet places received messages in this directory. If you want the applet to store messages elsewhere, modify the DIRECTORY attribute of the <MvPOP> tag.

Listing 7-2: E-mail Viewer applet

```
<HTML> <HEAD>

<TITLE> Miva Programmer's Reference -- E-mail Viewer
example </TITLE>

</HEAD>

<BODY>


<TABLE WIDTH="100%"> <TR>

 <TD> <H1> Miva Script E-mail Viewer </H1>

 <TD ALIGN="RIGHT"> <IMG SRC="mivalogo.gif">

</TR> </TABLE>


<HR>
```

```
<MvIF EXPR="{username EQ ''}">

 <!-- Pass 1:  get user info -->

 <H2> Please enter your e-mail account information: </H2>

 <FORM ACTION="&[s.documenturl];" METHOD="POST">
  <TABLE>
   <TR>
    <TD ALIGN="RIGHT"> Host name: </TD>
    <TD> <INPUT TYPE="TEXT" NAME="hostname" SIZE="24">
</TD>
   </TR>
   <TR>
    <TD ALIGN="RIGHT"> Your username: </TD>
    <TD> <INPUT TYPE="TEXT" NAME="username" SIZE="16">
</TD>
   </TR>
   <TR>
    <TD ALIGN="RIGHT"> Password: </TD>
    <TD> <INPUT TYPE="PASSWORD" NAME="psw" SIZE="8"> </TD>
   </TR>
  </TABLE>
  <H2> Then click: <INPUT TYPE="SUBMIT" VALUE="Get mail!">
</H2>
 </FORM>
 <HR>

<MvELSE>

 <!-- Pass 2:  get mail and display info -->
```

```
<TABLE BORDER>
 <TR>
  <TH> Date </TH>
  <TH> From </TH>
  <TH> Reply to </TH>
  <TH> Subject </TH>
 </TR>

<MvPOP
 MAILHOST="&[hostname];"
 LOGIN="&[username];"
 PASSWORD="&[psw];"
 DIRECTORY="inbox">

 <TR>
  <TD> &[messagedate]; </TD>
  <TD> &[messagesender]; </TD>
  <TD> &[messagereplyto]; </TD>
  <TD>
  <MvASSIGN NAME="linkpath"
VALUE="{encodeattribute(messagebody)}">
  <A HREF="viewmail.mv?messagefile1=&[linkpath];">
  &[messagesubject]; </A>
  </TD>
 </TR>

</MvPOP>

</TABLE>
```

```
</MvIF>


</BODY> </HTML>
```

The script for displaying individual messages is shown in Listing 7-3. This is another two-pass script, but in this case, most of the action occurs in pass 1. The name of the file to display has been passed in the URL, and is available to the script in the variable `messagefile1`. The script copies this to the variable `messagefile`, after checking for any backslash characters that might be part of a pathname on a Windows system; slightly different handling may be needed on your system.

Next, the script passes the pathname to an `<MvIMPORT>` tag, which is used to read the file. The `DELIMITER` attribute is set to `asciichar(10)`, the Newline character; this causes `<MvIMPORT>` to read each line of the file into a single variable, `filetext`, which the script displays to the user.

After reading the message, the user may click the Delete button, which causes the script to call itself for pass 2. In this case, the script uses the `fdelete()` system function to delete the message file.

Listing 7-3: Single-message display

```
<HTML> <HEAD>
<TITLE> E-mail message file display </TITLE>
</HEAD>
<BODY>


<MvIF EXPR="{g.deletemessage NE 'yes'}">


 <!-- Pass 1:  view message -->


 <H2> Your message (file &[messagefile1];): </H2>
 <HR>
```

Note: The `<MvASSIGN>` statement below is for Windows systems. Different handling may be needed on other platforms.

```
 <MvASSIGN NAME="messagefile"
VALUE="{glosub(messagefile1,'\\','\\\\')}">


 <MvIMPORT
  FILE="&[messagefile];"
  FIELDS="filetext"
  DELIMITER="{asciichar(10)}"
  FILTER="{len(filetext) GT 1}">
 &[filetext]; <BR>
 </MvIMPORT>


 <P>
 <HR WIDTH="50%">


 <FORM ACTION="&[s.documenturl];" METHOD="POST">
  <MvHIDE FIELDS="messagefile">
  <INPUT TYPE="HIDDEN" NAME="deletemessage" VALUE="yes">
  <INPUT TYPE="SUBMIT" VALUE="Delete">
 </FORM>


<MvELSE>


 <!-- Pass 2:  delete message -->


 <MvIF EXPR="{fdelete('&[messagefile];')}">
  <H2> The file &[messagefile]; has been deleted. </H2>
 <MvELSE>
  <H2> Sorry, unable to delete the file &[messagefile];.
</H2>
 </MvIF>
```

```
</MvIF>


<HR>
</BODY> </HTML>
```

For More Information

For more detailed information on any of the tags and system functions discussed in this chapter, see the Reference section of this manual.

The scripts shown in the Listings are available online at this manual's companion Web site:

http://TopFloor.com/Miva/

8

E-commerce Access

The term *e-commerce* has come to be used for many types of commercial services that are being delivered via the World Wide Web. The most well known is retail shopping, but many other services are becoming available.

Miva Script can request transactions from commerce servers by using the <MvCOMMERCE> tag. A simple example of this tag is:

```
<MvCOMMERCE
 METAMETHOD="UPSCost"
 ACTION="http://www.ups.com/using/services/rave/
qcostcgi.cgi"
 FIELDS="accept_UPS_license_agreement, 10_action,
 13_product,
 15_origPostal, 19_destPostal, 22_destCountry, 23_weight">

 ... code ...

</MvCOMMERCE>
```

This tag could be used to access UPS's QuickCost server to determine the shipping cost for a package. (More on QuickCost will be found later in this chapter.)

The <MvCOMMERCE> tag must be used with a matching </MvCOMMERCE>. Between the two tags, some special-purpose variables may be available that allow your script to determine the results of the transaction.

The portion of the script between the two tags may be executed as a loop, if necessary for the transaction being performed. In that case, you may use `<MvCOMMERCESTOP>` to interrupt the loop, if necessary. It works like the other loop termination tags described in Chapter 3.

`<MvCOMMERCE>` takes three attributes.The `ACTION` attribute specifies the URL of the commerce server. The `FIELDS` attribute specifies the names of one or more variables to be included in the service request. The `METAMETHOD` attribute specifies the type of service to access. Currently, Miva Script supports protocols for three types of commercial services. The `METAMETHOD` values, and the protocols supported, are listed in the table below:

`METAMETHOD` attribute	Protocol/service
`UPSCost`	QuickCost service for finding the UPS shipping cost for a product.
`ICS2`	CyberSource ICS for online purchases and delivery.
`CyberCash`	CyberCash CashRegister API for credit card and check transactions.

The following sections of this chapter discuss the use of `<MvCOMMERCE>` with these three services.

Caution: Details of these commerce services are controlled by the companies that provide them and may change from time to time. When creating an application that uses a commerce server, be sure to check the service company's own documentation for any changes or updates. URLs for the three services' Web sites are given later in this chapter, as well as in Appendix D.

Note: E-commerce applications tend to be large and complex. When designing your application, please consider the "Programming Techniques and Considerations" described in Chapter 4, with particular attention to the sections on "Multiuser Applications" and "User-Friendliness."

Note: In this chapter, the term *field* will be used to mean variables used for exchanging data with commerce servers. This is a common practice in the commerce service's own documentation, so it is followed here for compatibility. However, these "fields" are ordinary Miva Script variables; they do not have the special behavior of database fields (see Chapter 6).

UPS QuickCost

QuickCost is a convenient service for retailers. It allows a script to determine the shipping cost for a parcel by specifying where it is, where it needs to go, how much it weighs, and some other related parameters. The QuickCost service is free, and no registration or log-in is required.

Field Variables

To send a QuickCost request, a script must create a number of variables with specific names and assign them values for the request. This can be done either with an HTML form, where the user can insert the values, or directly from a script using `<MvCALL>`. The QuickCost protocol supports several dozen variables, but most are optional. The required variables are listed in the table below.

Note: Most of the QuickCost variable names start with one or more digits. In Miva Script, variable names normally do not start with a digit, but you can write them by using the `g.` or `l.` prefix. For example, to use the variable named `13_product`, write `g.13_product`.

Name	Value
`accept_UPS_license_agreement`	Must have the value `'yes'` when the form is submitted.
`13_product`	UPS product code corresponding to the type of shipment service desired. For example, `'1DA'` for Next Day Air. See Listing ???-1, or obtain a list of codes from UPS's online documentation.
`10_action`	Set to `'3'` to obtain information only for the service specified with `13_product`, or `'4'` to obtain information on all applicable services.
`15_origPostal`	The ZIP code of the originating location (U.S. only).
`19_destPostal`	The ZIP or other postal code of the destination (all countries, as applicable).
`22_destCountry`	The 2-letter country code of the destination; for example, `'US'` for the United States, `'CA'` for Canada, `'MX'` for Mexico. A complete list of codes is available from UPS's online documentation.
`23_weight`	Weight in pounds (not required if the requested service is for letters only).

Besides the variables listed above, others can be used to specify options such as the shipment's value (for insurance purposes) and whether to allow Saturday pickup/delivery. A complete list of input variables is available in UPS's online documentation.

Returned Variables

Between `<MvCOMMERCE>` and `</MvCOMMERCE>`, a number of output variables are available for use by scripts. These variables specify the results of the transaction, such as the cost for the requested shipment, and other information as listed in the table below:

Name	Value
errmsg	Description of error, or empty if no error occurred.
errorcode	Numeric code of error, or empty if no error occurred.
message	Informational message.
product	UPS product code.
orig_postal	Shipment source ZIP code.
orig_country	Shipment source country code.
dest_postal	Shipment destination ZIP/postal code.
dest_country	Shipment destination country code.
zone	UPS shipping zone.
weight	Shipment weight (in pounds).
productchrg	Shipment charge, minus any accessory or surcharges.
accs_surcharg	Shipment accessory or surcharges.
totalchrg	Total cost of shipment.
time	Commit time, or -1 for end-of-day.

Using QuickCost

An example of a script that uses QuickCost is shown in Figures 8-1 and 8-2. This Shipping Cost Calculator uses the two-pass structure discussed in Chapter 3. The script starts (pass 1) by displaying a form in which the user enters the package weight, type of service, and other necessary information, as shown in Figure 8-1.

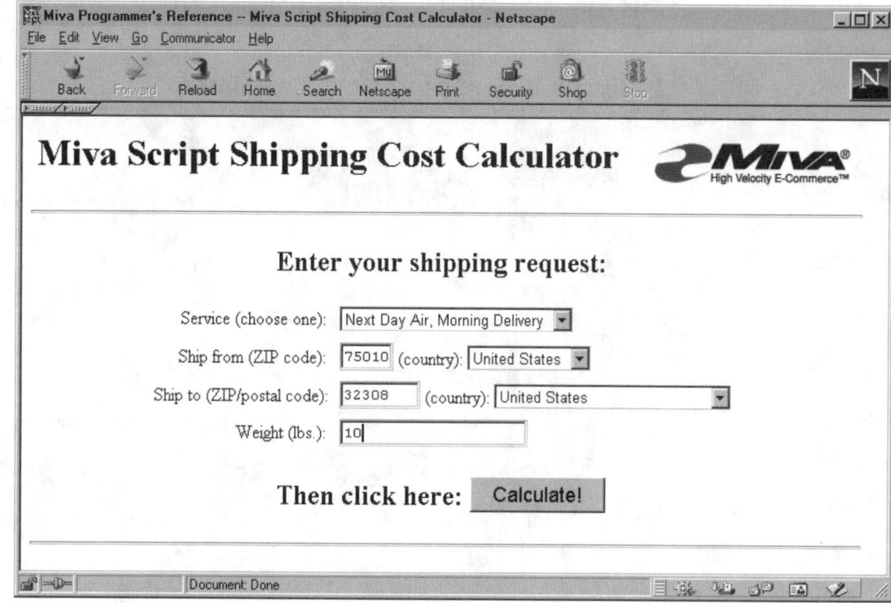

Figure 8-1: Shipping Cost Calculator, pass 1

When the user clicks the Calculate button, the script calls itself for pass 2 and passes the information from the form. It then uses <MvCOMMERCE> to send the request to the UPS server and displays the results, as shown in Figure 8-2.

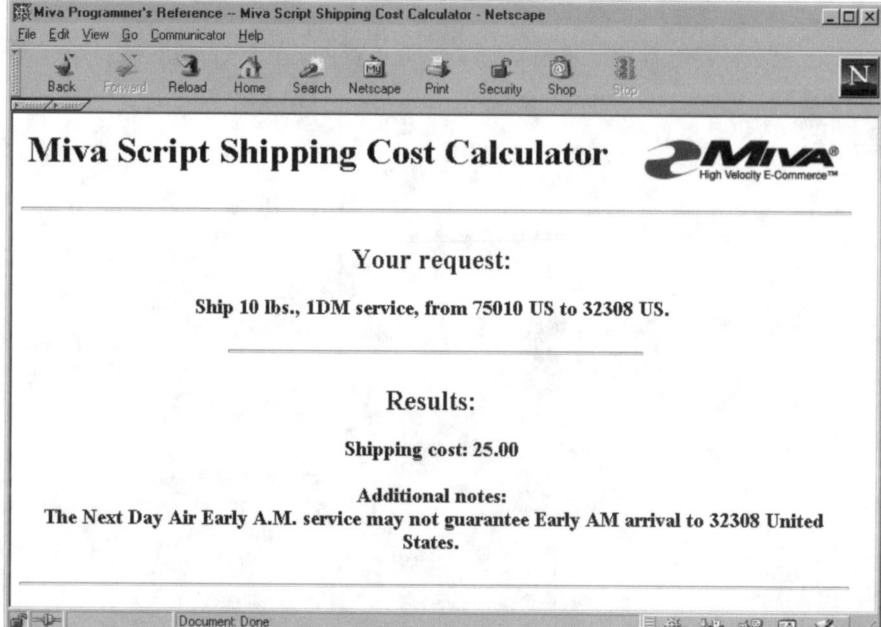

Figure 8-2: Shipping Cost Calculator, pass 2

The complete script is shown in Listing 8-1.

Listing 8-1: Shipping Cost Calculator

```
<HTML> <HEAD>

<TITLE> Miva Programmer's Reference -- Miva Script
Shipping Cost Calculator </TITLE>

</HEAD>

<BODY>

<TABLE WIDTH="100%"> <TR>

 <TD> <H1> Miva Script Shipping Cost Calculator </H1>

 <TD ALIGN="RIGHT"> <IMG SRC="mivalogo.gif">

</TR> </TABLE>

<HR>


<MvIF EXPR="{g.accept_UPS_license_agreement NE 'yes'}">


<!-- Pass 1:  Display the form -->


<CENTER>

<H2> Enter your shipping request: </H2>


 <FORM ACTION="&[s.documenturl];" METHOD="POST">

 <INPUT TYPE="HIDDEN" NAME="accept_UPS_license_agreement"
VALUE="yes">

 <TABLE>

  <TR>

   <TD ALIGN="RIGHT"> <INPUT TYPE="HIDDEN"
NAME="10_action" VALUE="3">

     Service (choose one): </TD>

    <TD> <SELECT NAME="13_product">

     <OPTION VALUE="1DM"> Next Day Air, Morning Delivery

     <OPTION VALUE="1DA"> Next Day Air, Regular Delivery
```

```
  <OPTION VALUE="1DP"> Next Day Air, Saver Rate
  <OPTION VALUE="2DM"> 2nd Day Air, Morning Delivery
  <OPTION VALUE="2DA"> 2nd Day Air, Regular Delivery
  <OPTION VALUE="3DS"> 3-day Select
  <OPTION VALUE="GND"> Regular Ground Service
  <OPTION VALUE="STD"> Canadian Standard Service
  <OPTION VALUE="XPR"> Worldwide Express
  <OPTION VALUE="XDM"> Worldwide Express Plus
  <OPTION VALUE="XPD"> Worldwide Expedited
 </SELECT> </TD>
</TR>
<TR>
 <TD ALIGN="RIGHT"> Ship from (ZIP code): </TD>
 <TD> <INPUT TYPE="TEXT" SIZE="5" NAME="15_origpostal">
  (country):
 <SELECT NAME="14_origCountry">
  <OPTION VALUE="US"> United States
  <OPTION VALUE="PR"> Puerto Rico
 </SELECT> </TD>
</TR>
<TR>
 <TD ALIGN="RIGHT"> Ship to (ZIP/postal code): </TD>
 <TD> <INPUT TYPE="TEXT" SIZE="8" NAME="19_destPostal">
  (country): <SELECT NAME="22_destCountry">
        <OPTION VALUE="AL">Albania
        <OPTION VALUE="BS">Bahamas
        <OPTION VALUE="CA">Canada
        <OPTION VALUE="MX">Mexico
        <OPTION VALUE="GB">United Kingdom
        <OPTION VALUE="US" SELECTED>United States
```

Note: A complete list of some 200 country codes is available from UPS. (See below for the location of UPS's online documentation.)

```
    <OPTION VALUE="ZW">Zimbabwe

   </SELECT> </TD>

  </TR>

  <TR>

   <TD ALIGN="RIGHT"> Weight (lbs.): </TD>

   <TD> <INPUT TYPE="TEXT" NAME="23_weight"> </TD>

  </TR>

 </TABLE>

 <H2> Then click here: <INPUT TYPE="SUBMIT"
VALUE="Calculate!"> </H2>

 </FORM>

<HR>

</CENTER>


<MvELSE>


<!-- Pass 2:  contact UPS server -->


<CENTER>

<H2> Your request: </H2>

<H3>

 Ship &[g.23_weight]; lbs., &[g.13_product]; service,

 from &[g.15_origPostal]; &[g.14_origCountry];

 to &[g.19_destPostal] &[g.22_destCountry];.

</H3>

<HR WIDTH="50%">

<H2> Results: </H2>
```

```
 <MvCOMMERCE
  METAMETHOD="UPSCost"
  ACTION="http://www.ups.com/using/services/rave/
qcostcgi.cgi"
  FIELDS="accept_UPS_license_agreement, 10_action,
13_product,
   15_origPostal, 19_destPostal, 22_destCountry,
23_weight">
  <H3>
   <MvIF EXPR="{s.errmsg}">
    Error: <MvEVAL EXPR="{s.errmsg}"><BR>
    <MvCOMMERCESTOP>
   <MvELSE>
Shipping cost: <MvEVAL EXPR="{s.totalchrg}">
    <P>
    <MvIF EXPR="{s.message}">
     Additional notes: <BR> &[s.message];
    </MvIF>
   </MvIF>
  </H3>
  <HR>
 </MvCOMMERCE>

</MvIF>
</BODY>
</HTML>
```

The pass-2 part of the script uses `<MvCOMMERCE>` to send a request to the UPS server, using the variables and values collected by the form in pass 1. Then the script uses an `<MvIF>` to check the `errmsg` output variable, to see if an error has occurred. If there is an error message, the script displays it and uses `<MvCOMMERCESTOP>` to terminate the transaction. Otherwise, the script uses the `totalchrg` and `message` output variables to display the shipping cost and any related information.

For More Information

For complete information on Quick Cost, UPS's documentation is available online at:

http://www.ups.com/tools/tools.html

The UPS OnLine Tools page at

http://www.ec.ups.com/ecommerce/ontools/index.html

has additional information about their e-commerce software and services.

The script shown in Listing 8-1 is available online at this manual's companion Web site:

http://TopFloor.com/Miva/

CyberSource ICS

Internet Commerce Services (ICS) from CyberSource Corporation provides a variety of functions for online retailing. ICS can process credit card transactions, assist with shipping and security checking, and can also perform licensing and delivery of downloadable products such as software, electronic books, and audio and video media.

In order to use CyberSource, you must first set up an account, which may involve some or all of the following:

- Obtain an account and merchant ID from CyberSource. You will also receive several files of security key data, which must be placed in specific locations on your hard drive.
- In order to process credit card transactions, you must have a merchant account with a bank or other service bureau, and this account must be set up for online access.
- If you plan to use certain services, such as third-party shippers or electronic distribution of products, additional registration or setup may be required. Consult your CyberSource representative for details.

To access the CyberSource services, use an `<MvCOMMERCE>` tag similar to:

```
<MvCOMMERCE
 ACTION="http://mycompany.ic3.com"
 METAMETHOD="ICS2"
 FIELDS="{'ics_applications,merchant_id,'
```

```
    $
'merchant_ref_number,bill_city,bill_state,bill_zip,bill_
country,'
    $ 'currency,offer0'}"
>
  ...
  ... (process returned variables) ...
  ...
</MvCOMMERCE>
```

The ACTION attribute value is a URL that contains the merchant ID that was issued to you by CyberSource (mycompany in the above example). This is the standard way to request a transaction: use your merchant ID as the "server" part of the URL. The METAMETHOD value of ICS2 is the required value for all CyberSource transactions. The FIELDS attribute is shown as a Miva Script expression, partly just because it is a long list and is easier to edit when it is broken into several lines of text. Also, the exact list of variables may need to be determined at run time, as described below for Listing 8-3. So it is common to use an expression here.

The following sections describe some details of the fields used in CyberSource transactions and give a sample script that uses <MvCOMMERCE> to compute sales tax. Complete information will be provided by CyberSource Corporation when you open your account.

Field Variables

The FIELDS attribute is a list of variables that specify detailed information about the transaction that you are requesting. In some cases, this list of variables may be quite long. The order of the variables is not significant, but all names must be spelled exactly as shown in this manual. (Upper- and lowercase letters are equivalent in ICS variables.)

There are four types of fields:

- Basic information about the transaction itself.
- Information about the end user (retail customer).
- Information about the credit card used for the transaction.
- Information about each product being purchased: these fields are called *offers*.

Four fields contain information about the transaction itself and are required for all transactions:

Name	Contents
`ics_applications`	One or more application names, separated by commas. These identify the specific services or actions that you are requesting from the CyberSource server (see "ICS Applications" below for details).
`merchant_ID`	The merchant ID issued to you by CyberSource.
`merchant_ref_number`	A reference number, generated by the merchant (i.e., your application), to be used for tracking the transaction.
`offer0, offer1, ... offerN`	One or more offer fields describing products to be purchased (see "Offers" below).

Other fields may or may not be used, depending on the particular services that you request. The specific fields used with each service are listed later in this chapter.

The following fields contain information about the retail customer:

Name	Contents
`customer_firstname`	Customer's first name. Spaces can be included; leading and trailing spaces are removed. For credit card transactions, this must be the cardholder's registered name.
`customer_lastname`	Customer's last name. Spaces can be included; leading and trailing spaces are removed. For credit card transactions, this must be the cardholder's registered name.
`customer_email`	Customer's e-mail address.
`customer_phone`	Customer's telephone number. ICS ignores nonnumeric characters.
`bill_address1`	Customer's mailing address for billing. If more space is needed, the optional `bill_address2` field may be used. If a separate shipping address is required, it is specified with other variables as listed below.
`bill_address2`	Additional text for billing address.

Name	Contents
`bill_city`	Customer's city (billing address).
`bill_state`	Customer's state (billing address).
`bill_zip`	Customer's ZIP code (billing address).
`bill_country`	Customer's country (billing address).
`currency`	Currency to use for the transaction.
`company_name`	Customer's business or organization name.
`ship_to_address1`	Customer's street address for shipping. If more space is needed, the optional `ship_to_address2` field may be used.
`ship_to_address2`	Additional text for shipping address.
`ship_to_city`	Customer's city (shipping address).
`ship_to_state`	Customer's state (shipping address).
`ship_to_zip`	Customer's ZIP code (shipping address).
`ship_to_country`	Customer's country (shipping address).

The following fields describe the credit card being used for the transaction:

Name	Contents
`customer_cc_number`	Credit card number. ICS ignores nonnumeric characters.
`customer_cc_expmo`	Expiration date month (2 digits).
`customer_cc_expyr`	Expiration date year (4 digits).

Offers

One other type of field that is used in CyberSource transactions is the description of the products being purchased. These fields are called *offers* in CyberSource terminology. The first offer in a transaction must be named `offer0`, and additional ones must be named `offer1`, `offer2`, etc. with no gaps in the sequence.

Note: In a typical online shopping session, a user may place items in a shopping cart and later remove them. Do not allow this to affect the naming of the offer variables; they must still form an unbroken series.

Caution: A security hazard may exist if the contents of the offer fields are exposed to the end user, e.g. if they are included in HTML source code that a skilled user could view. To prevent this, if necessary, store the user's order information in a database or other file on the server.

An offer is itself a fairly complex structure. It consists of a string divided into many segments, which are called *offer-level fields* or *subfields*, since each offer is itself a field. Each subfield consists of a name and value. A typical offer might be a string such as:

```
offerid:1^productsku:XYZ00123^quantity:10^amount:7.99
```

As you can see, the string consists of name/value pairs, with the name and value separated by a colon (`:`). Multiple pairs are separated by up-arrow or caret (^) characters. Some of the most commonly used subfields are listed below:

Name	Contents
`amount`	The price per item. ICS will multiply this by the `quantity` subfield to determine the total cost for this offer.
`product_name`	The name or description of the product, in a form clearly understandable by customers. Up to 30 characters.
`merchant_product_sku`	The retailer's catalog number or other unique identifier for the product. Up to 15 characters.
`product_code`	A keyword that identifies the type of product. This may affect whether sales tax is applied, how to distribute it, etc.
`quantity`	Number of units of the item to order.
`distributor`	Distributor from whom to request permission to generate a license for the product. If blank or not specified, CyberSource is assumed. For information on other distributors, contact your CyberSource representative.
`export`	A list of country codes, separated by commas, identifying countries to which the product may be exported. ICS compares this list to the customer's shipping address in order to determine whether or not to distribute the product. This subfield may be omitted, or blank. Regardless of its value, ICS will not export to countries on the U.S. government's Denials list.

Name	Contents
`nexus`	A list of state and/or province codes, specifying locations for which a tax should be paid. If this subfield is blank or omitted, ICS computes a tax based on the shipping address.
`score_threshold`	Score value used by `ics_score` service to identify possible fraud.
`serial_number`	If the `product_code` value is `electronic_software`, this is the serial number that the customer will receive for installing and using the product.
`tax_amount`	The cost of tax for the item. If this is omitted, the `ics_tax` service will compute a value. If this is included, even if the value is blank, `ics_tax` does not compute any additional tax.

Returned Variables

Inside the `<MvCOMMERCE> ... </MvCOMMERCE>` block, scripts can access variables that provide information about the success or failure of the transaction, as well as additional data depending on the specific services requested. Four variables are returned for all transactions, regardless of which services were requested:

Name	Meaning
`request_id`	Unique identifier for tracking the transaction; it remains constant for the life of the request.
`ics_rcode`	-1 if a software or network error occurs. 0 if at least one requested service was declined. 1 if all requested services were performed.
`ics_rmsg`	If `ics_rcode` is 0 or -1, this variable contains an error message explaining the error.
`ics_rflag`	An alphabetic code specifying the cause of the result, such as `DINVALIDADDRESS` or `ETIMEOUT`.

Three more variables, similar to the above, are returned for each service that was requested by the `ics_applications` field (see below). Specifically, if you requested the service named `ics_`*`xxx`*, the variables *`xxx`*`_rcode`, *`xxx`*`_rmsg`, and *`xxx`*`_rflag` will be returned. They are like the `ics_rcode`, `ics_rmsg`, and `ics_rflag` just described, but they pertain to individual services. If you requested several services in one transaction, your script will receive several sets of these variables.

Other variables are returned for most services and provide specific data needed for those transactions. These are described in the following section.

ICS Applications

The `ics_applications` field is a string that specifies the name of the specific service (or *application* in CyberSource terminology) that you are requesting. This field can contain several service names separated by commas, in order to combine several services into a single `<MvCOMMERCE>` transaction; this can allow your scripts to run faster, by eliminating network and server overhead. The available services and their names are listed below:

Name (string in `ics_applications`)	Service
`ics_auth`	Authorize a credit card purchase.
`ics_bill`	Bill a credit card for an order.
`ics_credit`	Issue a refund or credit to a credit card.
`ics_dav`	Checks for possible invalid delivery address, such as a ZIP code that does not match the city and state.
`ics_download`	Generate a URL for a customer to download purchased software or other electronically distributed product.
`ics_elc`	Issue a license or certificate for an electronically distributed product.
`ics_export`	Check whether products may be exported.
`ics_notify`	Notify a distributor or fulfillment company to ship a product.
`ics_score`	Check whether a transaction has a high probability of fraud.
`ics_tax`	Compute sales tax or VAT for an order.

The following sections describe the ICS services in detail.

`ics_auth`

This service performs several functions needed for a credit card purchase:

- Calculates the total price for the order.
- Requests authorization for the customer's credit card.
- Places a temporary hold for the purchase amount against the credit card account.

To use this service, a script provides fields describing the customer, shipping address, and credit card, as well as offer fields for each item being purchased. Each offer-level field specifies an item identifier, quantity being purchased, and unit price. Variables returned to the script include a request ID that can be used in a subsequent `<MvCOMMERCE>` to execute the purchase and bill the credit card.

`ics_bill`

This service immediately bills a credit card for an order. It confirms the temporary hold placed when the purchase was authorized by `ics_auth`. You can request this service simultaneously with `ics_auth`; in that case, no extra fields are required for `ics_bill`. Alternatively, you can request `ics_auth` first and use the returned `request_id` to identify the transaction later when you request `ics_bill`. In that case, a script must supply copies of some of the fields used in the original request. Variables returned to the script include the total amount billed to the credit card, and a time/date stamp.

`ics_credit`

This service issues a credit to a customer's credit card account. This service can be used to process product returns or cancelled orders.

Caution: Use this service with care, to prevent unauthorized credits. CyberSource recommends that you **not** provide this service directly to the public from a Web page. Instead, make it available through a customer service facility.

To use this service, a script provides fields describing the original transaction and credit card, as well as offer fields for each item being credited. Variables returned to the script include the total amount credited to the card, and a time/date stamp.

`ics_dav`

DAV stands for delivery address verification. This service checks whether the shipping address entered by a customer is invalid. To use this service, a script provides fields describing the address. The standard returned variable `dav_rcode` will be 1 if the address was valid, or 0 if it was invalid.

ics_download

This service generates a unique URL that a customer can use to download a product. Normally, you use `ics_elc` for this. `ics_download` is for use when credit authorization is not required from ICS. This might occur when you are providing a free product, such as demo software, or when you are handling credit approvals without going through ICS. To use this service, a script provides fields describing the customer and products being ordered. Variables returned to the script include URLs that the customer can use to download the products, but no serial or license numbers.

ics_elc

This service issues one or more electronic license certificates (ELCs) for electronically distributed products. To use this service, a script provides fields describing the customer, credit card, and products being ordered. Variables returned to the script include serial and license numbers for the products, as well as URLs that the customer can use to download them.

ics_export

This service checks whether a set of products can be exported to the destination specified by the customer's shipping address. To use this service, a script provides variables describing the customer's country and the products being ordered. The offers may include subfields that specify the exportability of the products. The standard returned variable `export_rcode` will be 1 if all products may be exported to the intended destination, or 0 if at least one product may not be exported.

ics_notify

This service notifies a distributor to ship one or more products. To use this service, you must already have made arrangements with CyberSource for third-party distribution. To use this service, a script provides variables describing the customer, credit card, and products being purchased, as well as additional information such as a purchase order number for use by the distributor.

ics_score

This service is used to evaluate the possibility that an order is invalid and/or fraudulent. ICS evaluates several factors about the order and computes a numeric score representing the likelihood of its being fraudulent. A lower returned value indicates a safer transaction.

To use this service, a script provides variables describing the customer, credit card, products being ordered, and a number of additional parameters that allow you to fine-tune the scoring process. The standard returned variable `score_rcode` will be 1 if the transaction appears to be valid, or 0 otherwise.

`ics_tax`

This service computes the U.S. or Canadian sales tax for an order; it can also compute Value Added Tax (VAT) for countries that require it. To use this service, a script provides fields describing the customer billing and shipping addresses, and offers with subfields identifying the taxability of individual products. Variables returned to the script include the tax amount for each offer, as well as the total tax.

Using CyberSource

As an example of how to use CyberSource services, we will enhance the Shopping Cart Simulator already presented in Chapter 3 (Listing 3-4). The new script calls CyberSource to determine the sales tax for the imaginary order. Since it does not perform any actual billing or credit transactions, this is a very safe demonstration. However, you will still need to have a CyberSource merchant account in order to run this script.

Figure 8-3 shows the form presented in pass 1, with some extra text boxes to allow you to enter a billing address: only the city, state, and ZIP code are needed for this demonstration.

The form has a Compute Tax button that calls a second script to perform the actual `<MvCOMMERCE>` transaction. This script displays the results of the transaction as shown in Figure 8-4.

Listing 8-2 shows the enhanced Simulator script. It now contains two forms. The first one is much like the original script: you type in information on items you want to order, and the script collects it in pseudoarray variables such as `qty0`, `name0`, ... `qty`*N*, `name`*N*, ... The second form rearranges this information for the CyberSource transaction. Instead of using many separate variables, it combines all the information for each item into a single offer variable named `offer0`, `offer1`, ... The second form also includes text boxes for the city, state, and ZIP code. Since the Simulator is only computing sales tax, it does not need information about the customer and credit card that would be required for a complete purchase.

Note: This demonstration script stores offer variables in HTML form fields. As noted earlier, this practice is not recommended for actual applications, since there could be a security hazard if the offers are exposed to customers. Your applications should either store the offers on a server or encrypt them to hide their meaning from customers.

Figure 8-3: Shopping Cart Simulator with CyberSource access

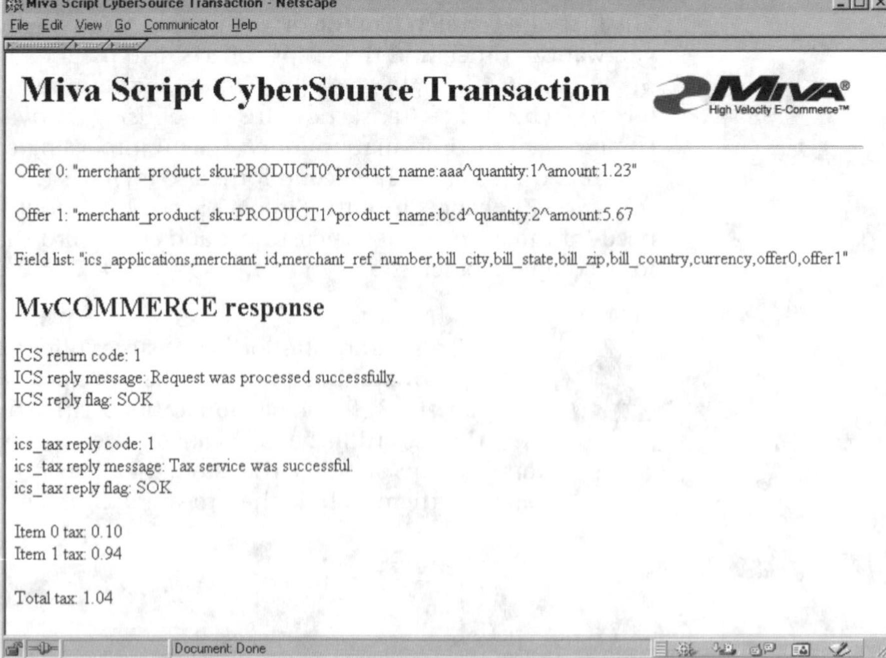

Figure 8-4: CyberSouce transaction results

Listing 8-2: Shopping Cart Simulator with CyberSource access

```
<FORM ACTION="&[s.documenturl];"
 METHOD="GET"
 ENCTYPE="multipart/form-data">

<TABLE BORDER="1">
 <TR>
  <TH> Item <TH> Qty. <TH> Name <TH> Price <TH> Weight
 <MvASSIGN NAME="n" VALUE="0">
 <MvWHILE EXPR="{n LT itemcount}">
  <TR>
   <TD> &[n];
   <TD> <MvEVAL EXPR="{qty&[n];}">
   <TD> <MvEVAL EXPR="{name&[n];}">
   <TD> <MvEVAL EXPR="{price&[n];}">
   <TD> <MvEVAL EXPR="{weight&[n];}">
  <MvHIDE
FIELDS="qty&[n];,name&[n];,price&[n];,weight&[n];">

  <MvASSIGN NAME="totalqty" VALUE="{totalqty + qty&[n];}">
  <MvASSIGN NAME="totalprice"
   VALUE="{totalprice + (qty&[n]; * price&[n];)}">
  <MvASSIGN NAME="totalweight"
   VALUE="{totalweight + (qty&[n]; * weight&[n];)}">
  <MvASSIGN NAME="n" VALUE="{n + 1}">
 </MvWHILE>
 <TR>
  <TD> &[n];
  <TD> <INPUT TYPE="TEXT" NAME="qty&[n];" SIZE="2">
  <TD> <INPUT TYPE="TEXT" NAME="name&[n];" SIZE="16">
```

```
  <TD> <INPUT TYPE="TEXT" NAME="price&[n];" SIZE="6">
  <TD> <INPUT TYPE="TEXT" NAME="weight&[n];" SIZE="4">
</TABLE>
<MvASSIGN NAME="itemcount" VALUE="{itemcount + 1}">
<MvHIDE FIELDS="itemcount">
<H3>
Total items: &[totalqty]; <BR>
Total price: &[totalprice]; <BR>
Total weight: &[totalweight]; <BR>
</H3>
<INPUT TYPE="SUBMIT" VALUE="Add item">
</FORM>
<HR>
<FORM
ACTION="http://&[server_name];:&[server_port];/compute-
tax.mv"
 METHOD="GET"
 ENCTYPE="multipart/form-data">
<MvASSIGN NAME="n" VALUE="0">
<MvWHILE EXPR="{n LT (itemcount - 1)}">
 <MvASSIGN NAME="offer&[n];" VALUE="{
   'merchant_product_sku:PRODUCT&[n];'
    $ '^product_name:' $ name&[n];
    $ '^quantity:' $ qty&[n];
    $ '^amount:' $ price&[n];
 }">
 <MvHIDE FIELDS="offer&[n];">
 <MvASSIGN NAME="n" VALUE="{n + 1}">
</MvWHILE>
City: <INPUT TYPE="TEXT" NAME="bill_city" SIZE="16">
State: <INPUT TYPE="TEXT" NAME="bill_state" SIZE="2">
```

```
ZIP Code: <INPUT TYPE="TEXT" NAME="bill_zip" SIZE="10">
<INPUT TYPE="SUBMIT" VALUE="Compute tax">
</FORM>
```

When you click the Compute Tax button, the Simulator calls a second script to contact CyberSource, and passes it all the offers as well as the billing address fields. The second script, shown in Listing 8-3, performs the actual <MvCOMMERCE> call and displays the result fields.

Listing 8-3: Using <MvCOMMERCE> to compute tax

```
<MvASSIGN NAME="fieldlist"
 VALUE="{'ics_applications,merchant_id,'
  $ 'merchant_ref_number,bill_city,bill_state,
bill_zip,bill_country,'
  $ 'currency,offer0'}">
Offer 0: "<MvEVAL EXPR="{offer0}">" <P>

<MvASSIGN NAME="n" VALUE="1">
<MvWHILE EXPR="{offer&[n];}">
 <MvASSIGN NAME="fieldlist" VALUE="{fieldlist $ ',offer' $
n}">
 Offer &[n];: "<MvEVAL EXPR="{offer&[n];}"> <P>
 <MvASSIGN NAME="n" VALUE="{n + 1}">
</MvWHILE>
Field list: "&[fieldlist];" <P>

<MvASSIGN NAME="ics_applications" VALUE="ics_tax">
<MvASSIGN NAME="merchant_id" VALUE="ICS2Test">
<MvASSIGN NAME="merchant_ref_number" VALUE="TEST00012345">
<MvASSIGN NAME="bill_country" VALUE="US">
<MvASSIGN NAME="currency" VALUE="USD">

<MvCOMMERCE
 ACTION="{'http://' $ merchant_id $ '.ic3.com'}"
```

```
 METAMETHOD="ICS2"
 FIELDS="{fieldlist}"
>
 <H2> MvCOMMERCE response </H2>
 ICS return code: &[ics_rcode]; <BR>
 ICS reply message: &[ics_rmsg]; <BR>
 ICS reply flag: &[ics_rflag]; <BR>
 <P>
 ics_tax reply code: &[tax_rcode]; <BR>
 ics_tax reply message: &[tax_rmsg]; <BR>
 ics_tax reply flag: &[tax_rflag]; <BR>
 <P>
 <MvASSIGN NAME="n2" VALUE="0">
 <MvWHILE EXPR="{n2 LT n}">
  Item &[n2] tax: <MvEVAL EXPR="{tax_tax_amount&[n2];}">
<BR>
  <MvASSIGN NAME="n2" VALUE="{n2 + 1}">
 </MvWHILE>
 <P>
 Total tax: &[tax_total_tax]; <BR>
</MvCOMMERCE>
```

This script starts by displaying the contents of the `fieldlist` variable and all the offers, for debugging and demonstration purposes. The `<MvWHILE>` loop that displays the offers is also used to add their names to the `fieldlist` variable. Then the script initializes a number of field variables and calls `<MvCOMMERCE>`. Note that the `ACTION` attribute is a Miva Script expression that includes the value of `merchant_ID` in the URL, as is required for CyberSource requests. The `FIELDS` attribute is an expression that uses the `fieldlist` variable's value. This technique of "building" the attribute at run time is necessary, since it is not known in advance how many items a user will purchase.

Inside the `<MvCOMMERCE>` block, the script displays a number of the returned variables. It displays the reply codes, and it uses another `<MvWHILE>` loop to display the individual tax amounts for each offer.

For More Information

For complete information on CyberSource services, see their Web site at:

http://www.cybersource.com/

Online documentation is available at:

http://www.cybersource.com/manuals/StartHere.html

Additional reference information is available on Miva's Web site at:

http://www.miva.com/commerce/cybersource/docs.html

A list of the ISO standard abbreviations for country names can be downloaded from:

ftp://ftp.ripe.net/iso3166-countrycodes

The scripts shown in Listings 8-2 and 8-3 are available online at this manual's companion Web site:

http://TopFloor.com/Miva/

CyberCash

Miva Script can access the CashRegister API from CyberCash, Inc. CashRegister provides the standard services for retail shopping, such as authorization, billing, and credits. It can process checking transactions as well as those using credit cards. It also has batch processing services that allow you to submit a group of transactions with a single `<MvCOMMERCE>` tag; and it provides a database of previous transactions that scripts can query.

In order to use CyberCash, you must first set up an account, which involves the following actions:

- You must have a merchant account with a bank or other service bureau, and this account must be set up for online access.
- Obtain an account and merchant ID from CyberCash. You will also receive a file of security key data, which must be placed in a subdirectory named `CyberCash` in your system's Miva data directory. The key data filename must be your merchant ID followed by `.key`.
- If you plan to use certain services, such as processing checks, additional registration or setup may be required. Consult your CyberCash representative for details.

To access the CyberCash services, use an <MvCOMMERCE> tag similar to:

```
<MvCOMMERCE
 ACTION="http://cr.cybercash.com/"
 METAMETHOD="CyberCash"
 FIELDS="cybercash\-id,operation,fld1,fld2,..."
>
  ... process returned variables ...
</MvCOMMERCE>
```

The ACTION and METAMETHOD attributes must have the standard values shown above. The FIELDS attribute must include two mandatory field variables, cybercash\-id and operation, followed by one or more additional variables needed for the specific transaction.

Caution: Some CyberCash field names include hyphen (-) characters. These are normally not used in Miva Script, and could be interpreted as subtractions. To prevent this, always use a backslash (\) in front of each hyphen, e.g. cybercash\-id.

Inside the <MvCOMMERCE> ... </MvCOMMERCE> block, a number of variables are available to the script that contain information returned by the CyberCash server. In some cases, the transaction returns a number of sets of variables, and the block is executed as a loop, once for each set.

Field Variables

The cybercash\-id field is required for all transactions. It must contain a string value that specifies your merchant ID as assigned by CyberCash.

The operation field, which is also required for all transactions, identifies the type of transaction you are requesting. It must contain a string specifying one of the operations (called *messages* in CyberCash documentation) listed in the following table:

String	Meaning
batch-commit	Commit (execute) a batch of transactions.
batch-prep	Prepare to execute a batch of transactions.
batch-query	Check or update the status of individual transactions in a batch.
batch-retry	Retry a batch of transactions that was interrupted by a system or network error.
batch-unroll	Check the status of a batch of transactions.
card-query	Query the database about a previous credit card transaction.
checkauth	Validate and authorize a payment from a checking account, using the ECP check-processing service.
checkreturn	Return (credit) funds to a customer's checking account.
mauthcapture	Authorize and capture (execute) a credit card transaction.
mauthonly	Authorize a credit card transaction, but do not capture it.
postauth	Capture a previously authorized credit card transaction, or mark it for batch processing.
query	Query the transaction database.
retry	Retry a pending transaction.
return	Return (credit) funds to a customer's credit card.
void	Void (cancel) a transaction.
merchant-check-payment	Validate and authorize a payment from a checking account, using the PayNow check-processing service.
check-query or check-query-order-status	Query the database of transactions processed by the PayNow service.
check-update-status	Update the database of transactions processed by the PayNow service.

Note that backslashes are **not** required before hyphens in these names as long as you use them as string values, not variable names.

After the `operation` field, a script must specify some additional field variables. The specific variables needed depend on the operation. The most commonly used ones are listed below:

Name	Meaning
`order\-id`	ID number for the transaction.
`passwd`	Password for database queries.
`amount`	Amount of money to be billed or credited.
`card\-number`	Number of credit card.
`card\-exp`	Expiration date of credit card.

`card\-name`
`card\-address`
`card\-city`
`card\-state`
`card\-zip`
`card\-country`
	Cardholder's name and address.

`txn\-type`
`txn\-status`
`origin`
`start\-time`
`end\-time`
`low\-amount`
`high\-amount`
	These fields are used in database queries, to select the transaction records to retrieve.

Additional variables may be required, depending on the specific type of transaction. For complete details, see your CyberCash documentation.

Returned Variables

There are four variables that are returned by all CyberCash transactions:

Name	Meaning
`MStatus`	A string specifying the success or failure status of the transaction.
`MErrLoc`	A string specifying the type of system or network error, if any.
`MErrMsg`	A string specifying an error message with additional details about the error that occurred, if any.
`MErrCode`	A numeric code identifying the specific error that occurred, if any.

Additionally, there are a number of standard variables that are returned by many transactions:

Name	Meaning
`merch\-txn`	Reference number for the transaction.
`order\-id`	Copy of the order ID used when the transaction was submitted.
`cust\-txn`	Reference number for a Microsoft Wallet transaction. For other types, this is the same as `merch\-txn`.
`aux\-msg`	Additional explanatory text.
`MSWErrMsg`	Additional error message for a Microsoft Wallet transaction.
`card\-type`	Type of credit card.
`card\-number`	Number of credit card.
`card\-exp`	Expiration date of credit card.
`auth\-code`	Authorization code returned by financial institution.
`action\-code`	Three-digit action code returned by financial institution.
`avs\-code`	Response code returned by Address Verification System (AVS), which checks for possible incorrect customer address (e.g., city name does not match ZIP code).
`ref\-code`	Reference number returned by financial institution.

Additional variables may be returned, depending on the specific type of transaction. For complete details, see your CyberCash documentation.

For More Information

For complete information on CyberCash services, see their Web site at:

http://www.cybercash.com/

A number of technical documents are available at:

http://www.cybercash.com/cybercash/merchants/support/doclib.html

Other Services

Miva Corporation is constantly expanding the range of e-commerce services available to Miva Script applications. At time of publication, several more services were becoming available. For the latest information, consult your Miva representative, or check the Miva Web site at:

http://www.miva.com

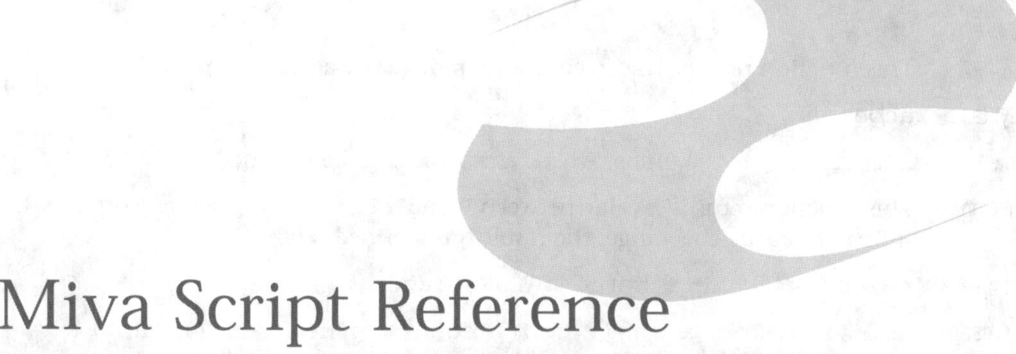

Miva Script Reference

This section contains descriptions of all Miva Script tags and system functions. They are listed in alphabetical order for easy reference. A more concise Quick Reference is contained in Appendix A.

abs()

Compute absolute value

This function returns the absolute value of a number (converts a negative value to positive).

Syntax `abs(num)`

Arguments *num* — Number whose absolute value is to be returned.

Example

```
<MvASSIGN NAME="aval" VALUE="{abs(x)}">
```

See Also `ceil()` `floor()` `int()` `rnd()`

acos()

Compute arccosine

This function returns the arccosine (in radians) of a number.

Syntax **acos(*num*)**

Arguments *num* Number whose arccosine is to be returned.

Discussion This function returns a value between 0 and π if *num* is in the range of –1 to 1. If *num* is outside this range, the result is undefined.

Example

```
<MvASSIGN NAME="theta" VALUE="{acos(x)}">
```

See Also `asin()` `atan()` `atan2()` `cos()` `cosh()` `sin()` `sinh()` `tan()` `tanh()`

asciichar()

Convert a number to a character

This function returns a string containing a single character that has a specified ASCII value.

Syntax **asciichar(*num*)**

Arguments *num* ASCII value.

Discussion This function allows you to create any character by specifying its numeric ASCII value. (A complete list of these values is contained in Appendix B) This can be helpful in dealing with control codes and other characters that cannot be simply typed into your script.

Example This example creates a string variable containing a long dash (emdash, "—") character:

```
<MvASSIGN NAME="emdash" VALUE="{asciichar(151)}">
```

See Also `asciivalue()`

asciivalue()

Convert a character to a number

This function returns a number representing the ASCII value of a character.

Syntax **`asciivalue(`*`str`*`)`**

Arguments *`str`* String expression or variable containing a single character.

Discussion This function allows you to determine the numeric ASCII value of any character. (A complete list of these values is contained in Appendix B.)

Example
```
<MvASSIGN NAME="charvalue" VALUE="{asciivalue(ch)}">
```

See Also `asciichar()`

asin()

Compute arcsine

This function returns the arcsine (in radians) of a number.

Syntax **`asin(`*`num`*`)`**

Arguments *`num`* Number whose arcsine is to be returned.

Discussion This function returns a value between $\pi/2$ and $-\pi/2$ if *num* is in the range of –1 to 1. If *num* is outside this range, the result is undefined.

Example
```
<MvASSIGN NAME="theta" VALUE="{asin(y)}">
```

See Also `acos() atan() atan2() cos() cosh() sin() sinh() tan() tanh()`

atan()

Compute arctangent

This function returns the arctangent (in radians) of a number.

Syntax **`atan(`*`num`*`)`**

Arguments *`num`* Number whose arctangent is to be returned.

Discussion This function returns a value between π/2 and –π/2.

Example
```
<MvASSIGN NAME="theta" VALUE="{atan(y / x)}">
```

See Also `acos()` `asin()` `atan2()` `cos()` `cosh()` `sin()` `sinh()` `tan()` `tanh()`

atan2()

Compute arctangent of quotient

This function returns the arctangent (in radians) of the quotient of two numbers.

Syntax **`atan2(`*`num1, num2`*`)`**

Arguments *num1, num2* Numbers whose arctangent is to be returned (see Discussion).

Discussion It is common to use arctangents to determine angles expressed as X and Y coordinates, by writing a statement such as:

```
<MvASSIGN NAME="angle" VALUE="{atan(y / x)}">
```

This has some problems: it may result in division by zero, and the quadrant of the result (0–360°) may be lost. `atan2()` solves these problems by allowing you to pass the X and Y values separately.

Example
```
<MvASSIGN NAME="theta" VALUE="{atan2(y, x)}">
```

See Also `acos()` `asin()` `atan()` `cos()` `cosh()` `sin()` `sinh()` `tan()` `tanh()`

ceil()

Compute "ceiling" of a number

This function returns the lowest integer value that is greater than the argument; in other words, it rounds up.

Syntax **`ceil(`*`num`*`)`**

Arguments *num* Number whose ceiling is to be returned.

Discussion — Note that "greater" means more positive. So, for instance, `ceil(4.5)` returns 5, but `ceil(-4.5)` returns -4, not -5.

Example

```
<MvASSIGN NAME="c" VALUE="{ceil(x)}">
```

See Also — `abs()` `floor()` `int()` `rnd()`

cos()

Compute cosine

This function returns the cosine of a number.

Syntax — **`cos(`*`num`*`)`**

Arguments — *num* — Number whose cosine is to be returned.

Discussion — This function returns a value between -1 and 1. Note that *num* represents an angle in radians, not degrees (see Example).

Example — To compute the cosine of an angle expressed in degrees, rather than radians, use a statement such as:

```
<MvASSIGN NAME="x" VALUE="{cos(theta / 57.2958)}">
```

See Also — `acos()` `asin()` `atan()` `atan2()` `cosh()` `sin()` `sinh()` `tan()` `tanh()`

cosh()

Compute hyperbolic cosine

This function returns the hyperbolic cosine of a number.

Syntax — **`cosh(`*`num`*`)`**

Arguments — *num* — Number whose hyperbolic cosine is to be returned.

Example

```
<MvASSIGN NAME="x" VALUE="{cosh(theta)}">
```

See Also — `acos()` `asin()` `atan()` `atan2()` `cos()` `sin()` `sinh()` `tan()` `tanh()`

decodeattribute()

Convert URL to normal text

This function returns a copy of a string in which URL-encoded characters are replaced with normal text.

Syntax **decodeattribute(*str*)**

Arguments *str* String to be decoded.

Discussion Since some characters are not allowed in URLs, it is sometimes necessary to encode strings before they can be used in HTTP requests. Characters are encoded by being converted to a per cent sign (%) and two hexadecimal digits.

This function returns a copy of a string in which any encoded character is replaced by the actual character. (To encode a string before passing it in a URL, use encodeattribute().)

Example

```
<MvASSIGN NAME="textaddress"
VALUE="{decodeattribute(URLaddress)}">
```

See Also decodeentities() encodeattribute() encodeentities()

decodeentities()

Convert entity-encoded characters to normal text

This function returns a copy of a string in which entity-encoded characters (such as <) are replaced with normal text.

Syntax **decodeentities(*str*)**

Arguments *str* String to be decoded.

Discussion Since some characters, such as < and >, have special meanings in HTML, it is sometimes necessary to represent them as *entities* that start with an ampersand (&) and end with a semicolon (;). This function returns a copy of a string in which any entities are replaced by the actual characters. (To encode a string before using it in HTML, use encodeentities().)

Example

```
<MvASSIGN NAME="rawtext"
VALUE="{decodeentities(HTMLtext)}">
```

See Also decodeattribute() encodeattribute() encodeentities()

encodeattribute()

Convert normal text to URL format

This function returns a copy of a string in which characters that are not allowed in URLs are replaced with encoded forms.

Syntax **`encodeattribute(str)`**

Arguments *`str`* String to be encoded.

Discussion Since some characters are not allowed in URLs, it is sometimes necessary to encode strings before they can be used in HTTP requests. Characters are encoded by being converted to a per cent sign (`%`) and two hexadecimal digits.

This function returns a copy of a string in which any character that is not allowed in URLs is replaced by the encoded form. (To decode a string passed to your script in a URL, use `decodeattribute()`.)

Example

```
<MvASSIGN NAME="URLaddress"
VALUE="{encodeattribute(textaddress)}">
```

See Also `decodeattribute()` `decodeentities()` `encodeentities()`

encodeentities()

Convert normal text to entity-encoded format

This function returns a copy of a string in which characters that are not allowed in HTML text are replaced with entity-encoded text.

Syntax **`encodeentities(str)`**

Arguments *`str`* String to be encoded.

Discussion Since some characters, such as < and >, have special meanings in HTML, it is sometimes necessary to represent them as *entities* that start with an ampersand (`&`) and end with a semicolon (`;`). This function returns a copy of a string in which any special character is replaced by an entity. (To replace entities with actual characters, use `decodeentities()`.)

Example

```
<MvASSIGN NAME="HTMLtext"
VALUE="{encodeentities(rawtext)}">
```

See Also `decodeattribute()` `decodeentitie()` `encodeattribute()`

exp()

Compute a power of *e*

This function returns *e* to the power of a number.

Syntax `exp(num)`

Arguments *num* — Exponent

Discussion This function computes *e* (Euler's constant, the base of natural logarithms, 2.71828 …) to the power of the specified number.

Example `<MvASSIGN NAME="y" VALUE="{exp(x)}">`

See Also `log()` `log10()` `power()`

fchmod()

Change permissions of a file in the data directory

This function changes the permission settings for a file. These settings control which users are allowed to read, modify, or execute the file.

Syntax `fchmod(path, num)`

Arguments

path — Pathname of the file whose permissions are to be changed. The path is specified relative to the Miva data directory.

num — Number specifying the new permissions to set.

Discussion On multiuser systems such as Unix, a file has permission data that determines how various classes of users may use the file. In Miva Script, a file's permission settings are represented by a nine-bit binary number, consisting of three fields of three bits each. The bit fields control access to the file by the file's owner, other users in the owner's group, and users in other groups. Within each bit field, the three bits determine whether the file can be read, written, or executed. A bit value of 1 allows the access, while a value of 0 prevents it. The positions of the specific bits are listed below.

Binary	Decimal	Meaning
100000000	256	Owner may read the file.
010000000	128	Owner may write the file.
001000000	64	Owner may execute the file.
000100000	32	Other users in owner's group may read the file.

Binary	Decimal	Meaning
000010000	16	Other users in owner's group may write the file.
000001000	8	Other users in owner's group may execute the file.
000000100	4	Users in other groups may read the file.
000000010	2	Users in other groups may write the file.
000000001	1	Users in other groups may execute the file.

Example This example sets a file's permissions so that the owner may read or write it, while all other users may only read it. To determine the correct value, add up the values from the above table: 256 + 128 + 32 + 4 equals 420.

```
<MvIF EXPR="{fchmod('myfile.dbf', 420) EQ 0}">
 <B> ERROR: couldn't change file permission. </B>
</MvIF>
```

The call to `fchmod()` is placed inside an `<MvIF>` in order to check for success or failure. (Like all file-system functions, `fchmod()` returns 1 if it succeeds or 0 if it fails.)

See Also `fmode()` `schmod()` `smode()`

fcopy()

Copy a file in the data directory

This function makes a copy of the specified file.

Syntax **`fcopy(`*`from`*`, `*`to`*`)`**

Arguments

from	Pathname of the file to copy. The path is specified relative to the Miva data directory.
to	Pathname of the file to create. The path is specified relative to the Miva data directory.

Discussion This function makes a copy of the file specified by *from*, and places it at the location specified by *to*. It returns 1 if the copy is successful, or 0 if it fails.

Example

```
<MvIF EXPR="{NOT fcopy('work/catalog.dbf',
'backup/catalog.dbf')}">
 ERROR: Unable to make backup copy!!!
</MvIF>
```

In this example, the call to `fcopy()` is placed in an `<MvIF>`. If the returned value is 0, indicating that the copy did not succeed, the script displays an error message.

See Also `fscopy()` `scopy()` `sfcopy()`

fdelete()

Delete a file in the data directory

This function deletes the specified file.

Syntax **fdelete(*path*)**

Arguments *path* Pathname of the file to delete. The path is specified relative to the Miva data directory.

Discussion This function deletes the specified file. It returns 1 if it succeeds, or 0 if it fails. It cannot be used to delete directories.

Example

```
<MvASSIGN NAME="dummy" VALUE="{fdelete('tempfile.dat')}">
```

In this example, the result returned by `fdelete()` is assigned to a dummy variable, in order to prevent it from appearing on the user's screen.

See Also `sdelete()`

fexists()

Check whether a file exists in the data directory

This function returns 1 if the specified file exists, or 0 otherwise.

Syntax **fexists(*path*)**

Arguments *path* Pathname to check, specified relative to the Miva data directory.

Example This example checks if a database file exists. If it does, the script opens it; otherwise, the script creates it.

```
<MvIF EXPR="{fexists('shopping.dbf')}">
 <MvOPEN NAME="shoppingcart" DATABASE="shopping.dbf">
<MvELSE>
```

```
<MvCREATE NAME = "shoppingcart" DATABASE="shopping.dbf"
  FIELDS="customer NUMBER(8), itemnum NUMBER(8),
qty NUMBER(4)">
</MvIF>
```

See Also `sexists()`

floor()

Compute "floor" of a number

This function returns the greatest integer value that is less than the argument; in other words, it rounds down.

Syntax **`floor(`*`num`*`)`**

Arguments *`num`* Number whose floor is to be returned.

Discussion Note that "less" means more negative. So, for instance, `floor(4.5)` returns 4, but `floor(-4.5)` returns -5, not -4.

Example

```
<MvASSIGN NAME="f" VALUE="{floor(x)}">
```

See Also `abs()` `ceil()` `int()` `rnd()`

fmkdir()

Create a subdirectory in the data directory

This function creates the specified directory.

Syntax **`fmkdir(`*`path`*`)`**

Arguments *`path`* Pathname of the directory to create. The path is specified relative to the Miva data directory.

Discussion This function creates the specified directory. It returns 1 if it succeeds, or 0 if it fails.

Example

```
<MvIF EXPR="{NOT fmkdir('tempdir')}">
 ERROR: Unable to make temporary directory!!!
</MvIF>
```

In this example, the call to `fmkdir()` is placed in an `<MvIF>`. If the returned value is 0, indicating that Miva was not able to create the directory, the script displays an error message.

See Also `smkdir()`

fmod()

Compute floating-point remainder

This function returns the remainder (modulus) produced by dividing two numbers. All arithmetic is done in floating-point.

Syntax **`fmod(`*`num1, num2`*`)`**

Arguments *num1* Dividend.

num2 Divisor.

Discussion This function returns the floating-point remainder of *num1* divided by *num2*.

For conventional (integer) remainders, use the `MOD` operator (see Chapter 2).

fmode()

Check permissions of a file in the data directory

This function returns a number representing the permission settings for a file. These settings control which users are allowed to read, modify, or execute the file.

Syntax **`fmode(`*`path`*`)`**

Arguments *path* Pathname of the file to check. The path is specified relative to the Miva data directory.

Discussion On multiuser systems such as Unix, a file has permission data that determines how various classes of users may use the file. In Miva Script, a file's permission settings are represented by a nine-bit binary number, consisting of three fields of three bits each. The bit fields control access to the file by the file's owner, other users in the owner's group, and users in other groups. Within each bit field, the three bits determine whether the file can be read, written, or executed. A bit value of 1 allows the access, while a value of 0 prevents it. The positions of the specific bits are listed below.

Binary	Decimal	Meaning
100000000	256	Owner may read the file.
010000000	128	Owner may write the file.
001000000	64	Owner may execute the file.
000100000	32	Other users in owner's group may read the file.
000010000	16	Other users in owner's group may write the file.
000001000	8	Other users in owner's group may execute the file.
000000100	4	Users in other groups may read the file.
000000010	2	Users in other groups may write the file.
000000001	1	Users in other groups may execute the file.

Example

To test individual permission settings, use bitwise operators with bit masks taken from the above table. For instance, to check whether users in other groups may read the file, use a mask value of 4 in an expression such as:

```
<MvIF EXPR="{fmode('myfile.dbf') BITAND 4"}>
 Reading is permitted.
<ELSE>
 <B> ERROR: cannot read the file. </B>
</MvIF>
```

If reading the file is permitted, the `BITAND` expression will return 4; otherwise, it will return 0.

See Also

`fchmod()` `schmod()` `smode()`

frename()

Rename or move a file in the data directory

This function changes the name of the specified file, and/or moves it to a different directory.

Syntax

`frename(`*`from,`* *`to`*`)`

Arguments

`from`	Pathname of the file to rename or move. The path is specified relative to the Miva data directory.
`to`	New name and/or location of the file. The path is specified relative to the Miva data directory.

Discussion This function removes the file from the name and directory specified by *from*, and assigns it the name and directory location specified by *to*. It returns 1 if it is successful, or 0 if it fails.

Example

```
<MvIF EXPR="{NOT frename('temp/catalog.dbf',
'work/catalog.dbf')}">

 ERROR: Unable to move file to working directory!!!

</MvIF>
```

In this example, the call to `frename()` is placed in an `<MvIF>`. If the returned value is 0, indicating that `frename()` did not succeed, the script displays an error message.

See Also `fsrename()` `sfrename()` `srename()`

fscopy()

Copy a file from the data directory to the scripts directory

This function makes a copy of the specified file.

Syntax **`fscopy(`*`from, to`*`)`**

Arguments

from	Pathname of the file to copy. The path is specified relative to the Miva data directory.
to	Pathname of the file to create. The path is specified relative to the Miva scripts directory.

Discussion This function makes a copy of the file specified by *from*, and places it at the location specified by *to*. It returns 1 if the copy is successful, or 0 if it fails.

Example

```
<MvIF EXPR="{NOT fscopy('script.txt', 'newscript.mv')}">

 ERROR: Unable to make backup copy!!!

</MvIF>
```

In this example, the call to `fscopy()` is placed in an `<MvIF>`. If the returned value is 0, indicating that the copy did not succeed, the script displays an error message.

See Also `fcopy()` `scopy()` `sfcopy()`

fsize()

Check size of a file in the data directory

This function returns a number that specifies the number of bytes of data in a file.

Syntax **fsize(*path*)**

Arguments *path* — Pathname of the file to check. The path is specified relative to the Miva data directory.

Discussion If this function is unable to determine the file size, it returns –1.

Example

```
The file named <MvEVAL EXPR="{myfile}">
contains <MvEVAL EXPR="{fsize(myfile)}"> bytes.
```

See Also `ssize()`

fsrename()

Rename or move a file from the data directory to the scripts directory

This function can change the name of the specified file, and also moves it to a new location relative to the scripts directory.

Syntax **fsrename(*from, to*)**

Arguments

from — Pathname of the file to rename or move. The path is specified relative to the Miva data directory.

to — New name and/or location of the file. The path is specified relative to the Miva scripts directory.

Discussion This function removes the file from the name and directory specified by *from*, and assigns it the name and directory location specified by *to*. It returns 1 if it is successful, or 0 if it fails.

Example

```
<MvIF EXPR="{NOT fsrename('script.txt', 'newscript.mv')}">
 ERROR: Unable to move file to scripts directory!!!
</MvIF>
```

In this example, the call to `fsrename()` is placed in an `<MvIF>`. If the returned value is 0, indicating that `fsrename()` did not succeed, the script displays an error message.

See Also `frename()` `sfrename()` `srename()`

fsymlink()

Create a symbolic link to a file in the data directory

This function creates a symbolic link to a file (also called an alias or shortcut on some platforms).

Syntax **fsymlink(*file, lnk*)**

Arguments

file	Pathname of the file to which to link. The path is specified relative to the Miva data directory.
lnk	Pathname of the link. The path is specified relative to the Miva data directory.

Discussion This function creates a symbolic link, which allows one physical file to appear in several directories. It returns 1 if it is successful, or 0 if it fails.

Example

```
<MvIF EXPR="{NOT fsymlink('archive/data.dbf',
'olddata.dbf')}"> ERROR: unable to create link to old
database.

</MvIF>
```

See Also `ssymlink()`

gettoken()

Find a token in a string

This function examines a string as a series of tokens, and returns a copy of one token.

Syntax **gettoken(*str, separators, n*)**

Arguments

str	String to search for the token.
separators	String containing characters to be considered as separators between tokens.
n	Number specifying which token to return.

Discussion This function looks for a "token" or substring within the string *str*. It considers *str* to be a series of tokens, separated by occurrences of any of the characters in the *separators* argument. It then returns a copy of the *n*th token. If the string contains fewer than *n* tokens, this function returns the null string ('').

Example If a variable named `txt` contains the string `'The quick brown fox'`, then the expression

```
gettoken(txt, ' ', 3)
```

will return the value `'brown'`.

See Also `substring()`

glosub()

Perform global substitution on a string

This function returns a copy of a string in which all occurrences of a specified substring have been replaced by a new value.

Syntax **`glosub(`*`str, old, new`*`)`**

Arguments

str	String to search.
old	Substring for which to search.
new	Substring to replace occurrences of *old*.

Example

```
<MvASSIGN NAME="nationality" VALUE="{glosub(str, 'USA', 'America')}">
```

See Also `tolower()` `toupper()`

int()

Return integer part of a number

This function returns the integer part of a number; this is equivalent to rounding towards zero.

Syntax **`int(`*`num`*`)`**

Arguments

num	Number whose integer part is to be returned.

Discussion This function returns the number computed by removing all digits of *num* to the right of the decimal point.

Example

```
<MvASSIGN NAME="ival" VALUE="{int(x)}">
```

See Also `abs()` `ceil()` `floor()` `rnd()`

isalnum() isalpha() isascii() iscntrl() isdigit() isgraph() islower() isprint() ispunct() isspace() isupper() isxdigit()

Test characters in a string

These functions are used to test whether the characters in a string are of a certain type. Each function returns 1 if all the characters in the string meet the condition, and 0 otherwise.

Syntax	**isalnum(*str*)**	Returns 1 if all characters in the string are alphanumeric (letters or digits).
	isalpha(*str*)	Returns 1 if all characters in the string are letters.
	isascii(*str*)	Returns 1 if all characters in the string are valid ASCII characters (values 0–127).
	iscntrl(*str*)	Returns 1 if all characters in the string are control characters (values 0–31 or 127).
	isdigit(*str*)	Returns 1 if all characters in the string are decimal digits.
	isgraph(*str*)	Returns 1 if all characters in the string are graphic characters (values 33–127).
	islower(*str*)	Returns 1 if all characters in the string are lowercase letters.
	isprint(*str*)	Returns 1 if all characters in the string are printable characters (values 32–127).
	ispunct(*str*)	Returns 1 if all characters in the string are punctuation symbols (graphic characters that are not letters or digits).
	isspace(*str*)	Returns 1 if all characters in the string are white space: space (32), tab (9), vertical tab (11), Newline (10), or form feed (12).
	isupper(*str*)	Returns 1 if all characters in the string are uppercase letters.
	isxdigit(*str*)	Returns 1 if all characters in the string are hexadecimal digits: decimal digits, or letters A–F (upper- or lowercase).
Arguments	*str*	String to be tested.

Example

```
<MvIF EXPR="{NOT isalnum(username)}">
 Sorry, your username must consist only of letters and
digits.<P>
</MvIF>
```

See Also `tolower()` `toupper()`

len()

Return the length of a string

This function returns the number of characters in a string.

Syntax **`len(`*`str`*`)`**

Arguments *`str`* String to measure.

Example

```
<MvIF EXPR="{len(passwd) LT 4}">
 ERROR: password must be at least 4 characters long.
<MvELSE>
 <MvIF EXPR="{len(passwd) GT 8}">
  ERROR: password may not be more than 8 characters long.
 <MvELSE>
  New password accepted.
 </MvIF>
</MvIF>
```

This example uses two calls to `len()` to check the length of a password entered by the user. If it is too short or too long, the script displays an appropriate error message.

log()

Compute natural logarithm

This function returns the natural logarithm of a number.

Syntax **`log(`*`num`*`)`**

Arguments *`num`* Number whose natural logarithm is to be returned.

Discussion This function computes the logarithm of the specified number to the base *e* (Euler's constant, 2.71828 …).

Example

```
<MvASSIGN NAME="y" VALUE="{log(x)}">
```

See Also `exp()` `log10()` `power()`

log10()

Compute base-10 logarithm

This function returns the logarithm of a number to the base 10.

Syntax `log10(num)`

Arguments *num* — Number whose base-10 logarithm is to be returned.

Example

```
<MvASSIGN NAME="y" VALUE="{log10(x)}">
```

See Also `exp()` `log()` `power()`

ltrim()

Remove spaces from the left (front) of a string

This function returns a copy of a string in which any leading spaces are removed.

Syntax `ltrim(str)`

Arguments *str* — String to be "trimmed."

Discussion In databases and some other types of files, record fields are required to be a certain length. If the actual data does not use all the available space, the remainder is commonly *padded* with space characters. This function removes padding from a string by returning a copy in which any spaces at the left side (beginning) have been removed.

To remove spaces from the right side, use `rtrim()`. To add padding, use `padl()` or `padr()`.

Example This example reads a database field, and places a "trimmed" copy in the variable `item`:

```
<MvASSIGN NAME="item" VALUE="{ltrim(catalog.d.itemname)}">
```

See Also `padl()` `padr()` `rtrim()`

makesessionid()

Return the session identifier

This function returns a 128-bit number that is guaranteed to be unique among all scripts running on a server at any given time.

Syntax **`makesessionid()`**

Arguments None.

Discussion The value returned by this function can be used to uniquely identify information from multiple Web site users, such as "shopping cart" data for online retail customers.

<MIVA>

Configure Miva processing

This tag controls settings that affect how Miva processes tags and sends information to the user.

Syntax (**`bold face text`** is required, `plain text` is optional)

```
<MIVA
  INTERPRET="str"
  STANDARDOUTPUTLEVEL="str"
  ERROROUTPUTLEVEL="str"
  ERRORMESSAGE="txt"
  tagname_ERROR="str"
>
```

Attributes

`INTERPRET="str"` Controls how Miva processes scripts. *`str`* is one of the following keywords, or both keywords separated by a comma:

`macros`	Enable processing of Miva macros.
`tags`	Enable processing of Miva tags.

`str` may also be null (`''`), or any other value, to suppress all processing.

The default value is `macros,tags`, so that both tags and macros will be processed.

`STANDARDOUTPUT-LEVEL="`*`str`*`"`	Controls what Miva sends to the browser after processing. *`str`* is one of the following keywords, or both keywords separated by a comma: `html` — Enable sending of HTML tags. `text` — Enable sending of text. *`str`* may also be null (`''`), or any other value, to suppress all output. The default value is `html,text`, so that both HTML tags and text will be sent to the browser.
`ERROROUTPUT-LEVEL="`*`str`*`"`	Controls what types of errors Miva will report. *`str`* is one of the following keywords, or two or more keywords separated by a comma: `expression` — Enable reporting of improper expressions. `runtime` — Enable reporting of runtime errors. `syntax` — Enable reporting of improper tags or attributes. `str` may also be null (`''`) to suppress all output. The default value is `expression,runtime, syntax`, so that all types of errors will be reported.
`ERRORMESSAGE="`*`text`*`"`	Specifies a "custom" error message for your application. If this attribute is specified, Miva will send *`text`* to the browser as the first part of any error message. Note that Miva will send this text even if the `ERROROUTPUTLEVEL` attribute has been used to turn off other types of error messages.
`tagname_ERROR ="`*`str`*`"`	Controls how Miva will report errors related to a specific tag. *`str`* is one of the following keywords, or two keywords separated by a comma: `fatal` or `nonfatal` — `fatal` causes Miva to stop processing if an error occurs ; `nonfatal` allows Miva to continue processing. `display` or `nodisplay` — `display` causes Miva to display error messages for this tag; `nodisplay` causes Miva to suppress error mes sages for this tag.

Note: If the `ERROROUTPUTLEVEL` attribute is specified, the presence or absence of the `runtime` keyword overrides the settings for specific tags made with the *tagname*_ERROR attributes.

Discussion

This tag has two attributes that allow you to control Miva processing. As seen by Miva, the contents of a file include several kinds of data:

- Miva tags
- Miva macros
- HTML tags and entities
- Document text

The `INTERPRET` attribute allows you to enable and disable the processing of Miva tags and/or macros. This has the effect of filtering the input to the Miva engine.

Similarly, the `STANDARDOUTPUTLEVEL` attribute has the effect of filtering the output of the Miva engine. It allows you to enable and disable the passing of HTML tags and/or document text to the browser.

This tag has a number of attributes that control Miva error handling. Miva recognizes threee kinds of errors:

- *Syntax errors* are caused by incorrect Miva tag or attribute names in a script.
- *Expression errors* are caused by incorrectly formed expressions in a script.
- *Runtime errors* are caused by conditions that occur when Miva processes a script, such as attempting to read from a file that does not exist.

The `ERROROUTPUTLEVEL` tag allows you to enable or disable the reporting of each of these types of errors. The `ERRORMESSAGE` tag allows you to add some additional text to Miva's standard error messages. For more detailed customizing of error reporting, you can use the *tagname*_ERROR attributes to control the handling of errors for specific Miva tags.

Example

This example causes Miva to regard errors caused by `<MvIMPORT>` tags as nonfatal, and to suppress error messages for them—effectively causing Miva to ignore these errors.

```
<MIVA

 MvIMPORT_ERROR="nonfatal,nodisplay"

>
```

miva_getvarlist()

Return a list of script variable names

This function returns a list of currently assigned variable names in the specified scope: local, global, or system.

Syntax **miva_getvarlist('*scope*')**

Arguments

scope	String that specifies the scope:	
	`local` or `l`	Local variables.
	`global` or `g`	Global variables.
	`system` or `s`	System variables.

Discussion This function can be used to obtain lists of all active variables in the Miva session. It returns a string consisting of all the variable names in the specified scope, separated by commas. You can use `gettoken()` to extract individual variable names from the list.

Example This example will display a complete list of the names and values of the Miva system variables:

```
<MvASSIGN NAME="list" VALUE="{miva_getvarlist('system')}">
<MvASSIGN NAME="token" VALUE="dummy">
<MvASSIGN NAME="count" VALUE="1">
<MvWHILE EXPR="{gettoken(list, ',', count)}">
 <MvASSIGN NAME="token" VALUE="{gettoken(list, ',',
count)}">
 <MvASSIGN NAME="vval" VALUE="{&[token];}">
 &[count];. &[token]; = &[vval]; <BR>
 <MvASSIGN NAME="count" VALUE="{count + 1}">
</MvWHILE>
```

This example uses an `<MvWHILE>` loop to extract single tokens from the list returned by `miva_getvarlist()`, and place them one at a time in the variable `token`. It then uses `token` in a macro, in order to obtain its value.

mktime_t()

Create a universal time/date value

This function returns a specified time and date in universal format.

Syntax **mktime_t(*yr, mo, dy, hr, min, sec, zone*)**

Arguments

yr	Year.
mo	Month.
dy	Day of the month.
hr	Hour.
min	Minute.
sec	Second.
zone	Time zone.

Discussion Miva supports storing times and dates in a universal format consisting of a single large number representing the number of seconds since midnight, January 1, 1970, universal time (also called Greenwich Mean Time or GMT). This function accepts individual arguments, and combines them into a single value. Note that you must specify the time zone, so that Miva can adjust from the local time zone to universal time.

Caution: Miva time functions cannot be used with dates earlier than January 1, 1970, or later than January 19, 2038.

Example This example will determine the day of the week for a particular date, such as someone's birthday:

```
<MvASSIGN NAME="wkday1" VALUE="Sunday">
<MvASSIGN NAME="wkday2" VALUE="Monday">
<MvASSIGN NAME="wkday3" VALUE="Tuesday">
<MvASSIGN NAME="wkday4" VALUE="Wednesday">
<MvASSIGN NAME="wkday5" VALUE="Thursday">
<MvASSIGN NAME="wkday6" VALUE="Friday">
<MvASSIGN NAME="wkday7" VALUE="Saturday">

<P> Your birthday was a
<MvASSIGN NAME="bday"
```

```
VALUE="{mktime_t(byear, bmonth, bdate, 0, 0, 0, bzone)}">
<MvASSIGN NAME="day" VALUE="{time_t_dayofweek(bday, -5)}">
<MvEVAL EXPR="{wkday&[day];}">.
```

This example first sets up the variables wkday1, wkday2, etc. as a pseudoarray (see Chapter 3). Then it uses mktime_t() to create a universal time value for the desired date, which is assumed to be available in the variables byear, bmonth, and bdate, along with the user's time zone in bzone. Then the script obtains the day of the week for this date by calling time_t_dayofweek(), and uses the result in a macro to select the proper name for the day.

See Also time_t_dayofmonth() time_t_dayofweek() time_t_dayofyear() time_t_hour() time_t_min() time_t_month() time_t_sec() time_t_year() timezone()

<MvADD>

Add a record to a database

This tag adds a record to a database. Miva creates the new record using data from the database's field variables. The new record is placed at the end of the database.

Syntax (**bold face text** is required, plain text is optional)

<MvADD

NAME="*alias*"

>

Attributes NAME="*alias*" Specifies a database to use. If this attribute is not present, the record is added to the current primary database.

Discussion When adding a record to a database, Miva sets the record fields equal to the current values of the database field variables. These variables are used for both reading and writing records; so unless your script modifies them, they will contain the values of the last record that was accessed by a navigation tag such as <MvGO>. Before executing <MvADD>, you may need to set some of these fields to the empty string '', in order to prevent the current record's values from being copied to the new record.

When adding a record with a date field, recall that Miva creates additional variables that allow you to read or write portions of the date:

*df*_year Specifies the year as a 4 digit number.

*df*_month Specifies the month as a 2 digit number.

*df*_day — Specifies the day of the month as a 2 digit number.

*df*_raw — Specifies the entire date as an 8 character string: 'YYYYMMDD' for year, month, and day.

(where *df* is the name of the date field variable.) You can set the field's value by assigning appropriate numbers or strings to any of these variables, or by assigning a time/date value in universal format directly to *df*. For more details on storing times and dates in databases, see Chapter 6.

Example This example creates a very simple database and adds one record to it:

```
<MvCREATE
 NAME="utensils"
 DATABASE="utenfile"
 FIELDS="itemname CHAR(20), price NUMBER(6.2)"
>
<MvASSIGN NAME="itemname" VALUE="knife">
<MvASSIGN NAME="price" VALUE="2.79">
<MvADD>
```

See Also <MvDELETE> <MvPACK> <MvUNDELETE> <MvUPDATE>

<MvASSIGN>

Assign a value to a Miva variable

This tag evaluates a Miva expression, and assigns the resulting value to a variable.

Syntax

```
<MvASSIGN
 NAME="var"
 VALUE="expr"
>
```

Attributes

NAME="*var*" — Name of the variable to which the value will be assigned.

VALUE="*expr*" — Miva expression to be evaluated.

Examples This example computes a total price by adding sales tax to a subtotal. (The salestax variable is assumed to be a numeric form of a percentage, e.g. 0.06 for a 6% tax.)

```
<MvASSIGN NAME="totalPrice" VALUE="{subtotal * (1 +
salestax)}">
```

The following example simulates an array reference by using a Miva macro in the NAME attribute. It assigns the value "75010" to a variable named zipcode0, zipcode1, zipcode2, etc., depending on the value of the variable named entry.

```
<MvASSIGN NAME="zipcode&[entry];" VALUE="75010">
```

(For more on arrays, see Chapter 3.)

See Also <MvEVAL>

<MvCALL>

Send an HTML request

This tag causes Miva to read an HTML document, and break it into a series of objects. <MvCALL> and </MvCALL> form a loop that receives the objects and processes them one at a time.

Syntax (**bold face text** is required, plain text is optional)

```
<MvCALL
 ACTION="URL"
 METHOD="str"
 FIELDS="var1,var2,var3..."
 FILES="file1,file2,file3..."
>
...
</MvCALL>
```

Attributes

Attribute	Description
ACTION="*URL*"	Specifies the URL to which to send the request.
METHOD="*str*"	Specifies how to send the request. *str* may be either GET or POST.
FIELDS="*var1, var2,var3...*"	Specifies the names of any Miva variables to include in the request.
FILES="*file1, file2,file3...*"	Specifies the names of any files to upload with the request.

Variables Inside the `<MvCALL> ... </MvCALL>` loop, a number of variables are available to provide information about each object from the document:

`callobjecttype`	Contains `'text'` or `'tag'` to specify the type of the object.
`callvalue`	Contains the actual text of the entire object. If the object is text, `callvalue` includes all white space. If the object is a tag, `callvalue` includes all attributes, values, and punctuation, including the opening and closing angle brackets.

If the object is a tag, a number of additional variables are available that describe it:

`callobjectelement`	The tag name, without angle brackets, e.g. `'IMG'` or `'/TABLE'`
`callobjectnumattributes`	The number of attributes for the tag.
`callobjectattribute`*N*	(where *N* is 1, 2, …) The name of tag attribute number *N*
`callobjectvalue`*N*	(where *N* is 1, 2, …) The value assigned to tag attribute number *N*

In addition, a number of variables provide information about the HTTP headers that Miva received with the document:

`callnumberofheaders`	The number of headers received.
`callreturnheader`*N*	(where *N* is 1, 2, …) The text of header number *N*

Discussion This tag's main function is to read an HTML document. However, HTTP requests can also be used to submit data or upload files to a server. When `<MvCALL>` is used that way, the "document" that it reads is actually the response from the server that received the submitted or uploaded data. (For more details, see Chapter 5.)

Example Assuming that a file named `calltest.htm` contains the following text:

```
<HTML><BODY>

<H1>Miva Demo</H1>

Here is a sample <B>processed</B> document.

</BODY></HTML>
```

Then the following script:

```
<MvCALL
 ACTION="http://localhost:8000/calltest.htm"
 METHOD="GET">
 <MvEVAL EXPR="{callobjecttype}">:
 <MvIF EXPR="{callobjecttype EQ 'text'}">
  "<MvEVAL EXPR="{callvalue}">"
 <MvELSE>
  <MvEVAL EXPR="{callobjectelement}">
 </MvIF>
 <BR>
</MvCALL>
```

will produce the following display:

tag: HTML
tag: BODY
text: " "
tag: H1
text: "Miva Demo"
tag: /H1
text: " Here is a sample "
tag: B
text: "processed"
tag: /B
text: " document. "
tag: /BODY
tag: /HTML
text: " "

Inside the loop, the first <MvEVAL> inserts the tag type into the output stream. The <MvIF> is used to follow this with either the text itself, or the tag name, depending on the type.

See Also <MvCALLSTOP> <MvDO>

<MvCALLSTOP>

Interrupt an HTML request

This tag interrupts an <MvCALL> ... </MvCALL> loop, and stops the processing of the received document.

Syntax

```
<MvCALL attrs>
 ...
 <MvCALLSTOP>
 ...
</MvCALL>
```

Attributes None.

Discussion This tag may only be used inside an <MvCALL> ... </MvCALL> loop. It causes Miva to discard the rest of the received document, and continue processing the current script at the point after the </MvCALL> tag.

Example This example reads the first five objects from a document:

```
<MvASSIGN NAME="count" VALUE="1">
<MvCALL
 ACTION="http://localhost:8000/test.htm"
 METHOD="GET">
 <MvIF EXPR="{count GT 5}">
  <MvCALLSTOP>
 </MvIF>
 &[count]; :
 <MvEVAL EXPR="{callobjecttype}">
 <MvASSIGN NAME="count" VALUE="{count + 1}">
 <BR>
</MvCALL>
```

The script counts the received objects with the variable `count`. It executes <MvCALLSTOP> when count reaches 6, so only the first 5 objects are reported to the output stream.

See Also <MvCALL>

<MvCLOSE>

Close a database

This tag closes a connection to a database.

Syntax (**bold face text** is required, plain text is optional)

```
<MvCLOSE
 NAME="alias"
>
```

Attributes

NAME="*alias*" — The alias that specifies the database connection to close. If NAME is not specified, Miva will close the current primary database.

Discussion Note that this tag closes a single connection to a database. If multiple aliases are in use, there may be other connections to the same file; these connections will remain open.

Example

```
<MvCLOSE NAME="employees">
```

See Also <MvCREATE> <MvOPEN> <MvPRIMARY> <MvREVEALSTRUCTURE>

<MvCLOSEVIEW>

Close a database view

This tag closes a database view that was created by <MvOPENVIEW>.

Syntax (**bold face text** is required, plain text is optional)

```
<MvCLOSEVIEW
 NAME="alias"
 VIEW="viewname"
>
```

Attributes

NAME="*alias*" — The alias that specifies the database. If NAME is not specified, Miva will close a view of the current primary database.

VIEW="*viewname*" — The name of the view to close. This must match the NAME specified when the view was opened.

Discussion This tag may only be used on ODBC databases.

Example `<MvCLOSEVIEW NAME="employees" VIEW="managers">`

See Also `<MvOPENVIEW> <MvQUERY>`

<MvCOMMENT>

Provide descriptive text

This tag marks the beginning of a Miva comment. All text between `<MvCOMMENT>` and `</MvCOMMENT>` is ignored: it will not be placed in the output stream or processed in any way.

Syntax

```
<MvCOMMENT>
  ... any type of text ...
</MvCOMMENT>
```

Attributes None.

Discussion You can also enclose comments with the standard HTML markers, `<!--` and `-->`. These comments will be placed in the output stream and passed to the browser, so they cause more overhead. However, their use may be required in some cases, for compatibility with other systems.

Example

```
<MvCOMMENT>
  Script written 5/24/99 by I. M. Busy, XYZZY Corp.
</MvCOMMENT>
```

<MvCOMMERCE>

Request commercial service

This tag generates a request to a commerce server.

Syntax (**bold face text** is required, plain text is optional)

```
<MvCOMMERCE
  ACTION="URL"
  METAMETHOD="str"
  FIELDS="var1,var2,..."
>
```

```
   ...
</MvCOMMERCE>
```

Attributes

ACTION="URL"	Specifies the URL from which to request the service.	
METAMETHOD="*str*"	Specifies the type of service. *str* may be one of:	
	ICS2	Simple Commerce Messaging Protocol
	CyberCash	CyberCash CashRegister API
	UPSCost	UPS Quick Cost shipping-cost server
FIELDS="*var1, var2,...*"	Specifies one or more variables that contain information to be included in the request.	

Discussion

This tag provides access to a number of commercial services. Currently Miva supports the following services:

Simple Commerce Messaging Protocol (SCMP) for access to ICS services provided by CyberSource Corporation. ICS can perform actions such as ordering products and billing credit cards.

UPS Quick Cost service for customers of United Parcel Service (UPS). It allows your script to find out the cost to ship a parcel after specifying its size, sending and receiving locations, etc.

CyberCash CashRegister API for access to services of CyberCash, Inc., which provides functions such as purchases, refunds, and queries.

For details on using <MvCOMMERCE>, see Chapter 8.

See Also <MvCOMMERCESTOP>

<MvCOMMERCESTOP>

Interrupt a commercial service transaction

This tag interrupts an <MvCOMMERCE> ... </MvCOMMERCE> block or loop. It causes Miva to skip forward in the script, and continue execution at the point after </MvCOMMERCE>.

Syntax

```
<MVCOMMERCE attrs>
   ...
 <MVCOMMERCESTOP>
```

```
...
</MvCOMMERCE>
```

Attributes None.

Discussion Some types of commercial transactions cause Miva to loop between the <MvCOMMERCE> and </MvCOMMERCE> tags. In that case, you can place <MvCOMMERCESTOP> inside the loop to interrupt it. This tag is also useful in case your script detects an error condition, to provide a quick exit from the <MvCOMMERCE> ... </MvCOMMERCE> block.

Example See Chapter 8.

See Also <MvCOMMERCE>

<MvCREATE>

Create a database

This tag creates a new database file. It defines its structure, assigns an alias, and opens it for processing.

Syntax (**bold face text** is required, plain text is optional)

```
<MvCREATE
 NAME="alias"
 DATABASE="pathname"
 TYPE="str"
 FIELDS="name1 type1, name2 type2, ..."
>
```

Attributes

NAME="*alias*"	Specifies an alias to use for referencing the database in scripts.
DATABASE= "*pathname*"	Specifies a file location and name for the database file.
TYPE="*str*"	Specifies the type of database. Currently, the only supported value is xbase3 (since this tag is not supported for ODBC databases), so this attribute is optional.
FIELDS="*name1 type1, name2 type2, ...*"	Specifies names of record fields, and the type of data stored in each field. (See Discussion below.)

Discussion

This tag creates a new database file, with its name and location specified by the DATABASE attribute. By default, the file is located in the Miva data directory. However, the DATABASE attribute may specify a subdirectory, e.g. `DATABASE="store/orders/active.dbf"`. (If necessary, you can create subdirectories using the Miva `fmkdir` function.) It is recommended that you make all database filenames end with the `.dbf` extension.

If a file with the same pathname already exists, <MvCREATE> deletes it and creates a new, empty file. After creating the database, <MvCREATE> opens a connection to it and assigns the specified alias for referencing it.

The structure of the database is determined by the FIELDS attribute, which consists of a series of names and type specifiers separated by spaces and commas as shown. Each name must be a valid Miva variable name. Each type specifier must be one of those in the table below:

Specifier	Meaning
CHAR(*n*)	The field may contain a string of up to *n* characters. The maximum value for *n* is 254.
NUMBER	The field may contain a number up to 19 digits long. The value may not include a decimal point, i.e., integer value only.
NUMBER(*n*)	The field may contain a number up to *n* digits long. The value may not include a decimal point, i.e., integer value only.
NUMBER(*m.n*)	The field may contain a number with up to *m* digits before the decimal point, and up to *n* digits after it.
BOOL	The field may contain a logical or Boolean value: 0 representing False, and 1 representing True.
DATE	The field may contain a date and time in universal format. When you create a DATE field with name *df*, Miva also creates the following variables to provide a convenient way to read and change the value: *df*_year — Specifies the year as a 4-digit number. *df*_month — Specifies the month as a 2-digit number. *df*_day — Specifies the day of the month as a 2-digit number. *df*_raw — Specifies the entire date as an 8-character string: 'YYYYMMDD' for year, month, and day. For more details on storing times and dates in databases, see Chapter 2.

Specifier	Meaning
MEMO	This field may contain a string of any size; unlike CHAR, there is no limit on MEMO fields. This flexibility comes at the cost of some additional overhead, since the fields are stored in a separate file from the rest of the database. This file will have the same name as the main database file, but with an extension of .dbt. For efficiency, you should use CHAR fields when possible.

Example This example creates a simple database that could be used to store items for an online catalog.

```
<MvCREATE
 NAME="items"
 DATABASE="items.dbf"
 FIELDS="catalog_num NUMBER(8),
  description CHAR(64),
  weight NUMBER(3.1),
  price NUMBER(6.2)">
```

This file provides an 8-digit field for the item's catalog number and a 64-character description. It specifies an item's shipping weight with one digit to the right of the decimal point, allowing accuracy to the nearest tenth of a pound. It specifies the item's price with 6 digits before the decimal point and 2 digits after, allowing prices up to $999999.99.

See Also <MvCLOSE> <MvOPEN> <MvPRIMARY> <MvREVEALSTRUCTURE>

<MvDELETE>

Mark a database record for deletion

This tag marks the current record in a database as having been deleted. (The record is not actually removed until the database is packed.)

Syntax (**bold face text** is required, plain text is optional)

```
<MvDELETE
 NAME="alias"
>
```

Attributes

`NAME="alias"`	Specifies the alias assigned to the database connection. If this is not specified, Miva deletes a record from the current primary database.

Discussion Every database record has a special `deleted` field that can be referenced in scripts. `<MvDELETE>` sets this field to 1 (true). The record is not actually removed from the database until you execute an `<MvPACK>`. In the meantime, the record is still visible for searching and navigation. Until the database is packed, you can use `<MvUNDELETE>` to set `deleted` back to 0 (false).

Example

```
<MvDELETE NAME="shoppingcart">
```

See Also `<MvADD>` `<MvPACK>` `<MvUNDELETE>` `<MvUPDATE>`

<MvDO>

Run a script in an external file

This tag reads Miva tags or text from an external file. Depending on the attributes, it may read the entire file, or just run a single Miva function.

Syntax (**bold face text** is required, plain text is optional)

```
<MvDO
  FILE="pathname"
  NAME="var"
  VALUE="{func(args)}"
>
```

Attributes

`FILE="pathname"`	Specifies the location of the file to read. If the path starts with a directory name, the path is relative to the current file (in case of a nested `<MvDO>`). If it starts with a slash (/), the path is relative to the Miva standard document directory.
`NAME="var"`	Name of a variable to receive the result returned by the function.
`VALUE="{func(arg1, arg2,...)}"`	A Miva expression consisting of a function name *func* and one or more arguments *arg1, arg2, ...*

Discussion This tag operates in two different ways. If only the `FILE` attribute is specified, Miva reads the entire contents of the file, as if it were part of the current file; this is largely equivalent to a "server-side include" (see Example). However, note that any Miva functions defined in the included file are not preserved: the definitions are not available to scripts after the `<MvDO>` is processed.

If the NAME and VALUE attributes are specified, <MvDO> allows you to use a file as a runtime library, by calling a single function in the file and returning a result. The function name is specified in the VALUE attribute, as are any arguments that the function requires.

<MvDO> tags can be nested: a script read by <MvDO> can itself contain <MvDO> tags. The maximum number of nesting levels is fixed at 23 for Miva Mia. For Miva Empresa, the limit is set to 23 by default, but it can be changed by changing the maxfunctiondepth setting in the global configuration file. A relative pathname can be used in the FILE attribute of a nested <MvDO>, so that the included script can access files in its own directories.

Example A standard HTML server-side include such as

```
<!-- #include file="otherfile.html" -->
```

is equivalent to a Miva tag:

```
<MvDO FILE="otherfile.html">
```

To call a single function in a file, use a tag such as

```
<MvDO FILE="orders/access.mv" NAME="ordersToday"
VALUE="{howMany(today)}">
```

This tag reads a file named access.mv in the orders subdirectory. It finds a function named howMany, and calls it using the variable today as an argument. The result of the function call will be placed in the variable ordersToday.

See Also <MvCALL>

<MvELSE>

Specify alternate part of a conditional block

This tag specifies the part of an <MvIF> ... </MvIF> block that is executed if its expression is false.

Syntax

```
<MvIF EXPR="{expr}">
  ... "true" part ...
<MvELSE>
  ... "false" part ...
</MvIF>
```

For more details, see <MvIF> or Chapter 3.

<MvEVAL>

Evaluate an expression and place it in the output stream

This tag evaluates a Miva expression, and places the result in the output stream so that it will be displayed on the user's browser.

Syntax

```
<MvEVAL
 EXPR="{expr}"
>
```

Attributes

`EXPR="{expr}"` Specifies the Miva expression to be evaluated.

Discussion

This tag is used to place the values of Miva expressions into the output stream, so that they will be included as part of the HTML document sent to the user's browser. The expression may return any type of numeric or string result.

Note that to insert the value of a single variable in the output stream, it may be simpler to use a macro. For details, see Chapter 1.

Example

To compute a percentage result after administering an online quiz, you could use a script such as:

```
Your final score is
<MvEVAL EXPR="{(correctAnswers / totalAnswers) * 100}">
% correct.
```

See Also

`<MvASSIGN>`

<MvEXIT>

Terminate script processing

This tag causes Miva to end its current session.

Syntax

```
<MvEXIT>
```

Attributes

None.

Discussion

This tag causes Miva to stop reading the current script. If the script was called by `<MvDO>`, the calling script is also terminated, as are any additional nested calls. (To return from a function called by `<MvDO>` and resume execution of the calling script, use `<MvFUNCRETURN>`.) Any HTML tags or text that had already been generated by the script will be "flushed" out to the browser.

Note that scripts may also be terminated by timeouts, as described in Chapter 3.

See Also <MvFUNCRETURN>

<MvEXPORT>

Write data to an external file

This tag writes a record to an external file. The record consists of one or more values converted to strings, separated by a specified delimiter.

Syntax

```
<MvEXPORT
 FILE="pathname"
 FIELDS="var1,var2,..."
 DELIMITER="str"
>
```

Attributes

FILE="*pathname*"	Specifies the file to write. The path is relative to the Miva data directory.
FIELDS="*var1, var2,...*"	Specifies one or more variables to write.
DELIMITER="*str*"	Specifies a string that will be written between variable values.

Discussion This tag writes the variable values as text; that is, it converts the values to strings. The complete record consists of the variable values, separated by the delimiter string, and followed by a Newline (asciichar(10)) character.

Miva always adds new data at the end of an existing file. If the file does not exist, Miva creates it.

Note that, unlike <MvIMPORT>, <MvEXPORT> does *not* form a loop. To write a series of records, you must construct a loop in your script using <MvWHILE>.

Example This example writes values to a file, separated by a semicolon:

```
<MvEXPORT FILE="catalog.txt" FIELDS="itemname,price"
DELIMITER=";">
```

See Also <MvIMPORT>

<MvFILTER>

Apply a filter to a database

This tag defines a filter expression for a database. The filter makes some database records invisible to navigation functions.

Syntax (**bold face text** is required, plain text is optional)

```
<MvFILTER
 NAME="alias"
 FILTER="{expr}"
>
```

Attributes

NAME="*alias*"	Specifies the alias assigned to the database connection. If this attribute is omitted, Miva uses the current primary database.
FILTER="{*expr*}"	A Miva expression. If this attribute is omitted, Miva removes any filter that may currently be in effect for this database connection.

Discussion This tag is helpful in searching databases. When a filter is in effect, the <MvFIND>, <MvGO>, and <MvSKIP> tags will only move the record pointer to records for which the filter expression is true.

Note that a filter is associated with a database connection (alias), not a file. If you have several aliases assigned to one file, each alias can have a separate filter.

Example This example applies a filter to a personnel database, allowing Miva to find only records for men of a minimum age:

```
<MvFILTER
 NAME="employees"
 FILTER="{(sex EQ 'M') AND (birthdate_year LE 1969)}"
>
```

See Also <MvFIND> <MvGO> <MvSKIP>

<MvFIND>

Find a database record

This tag searches a database, and finds the first record with a specified key value.

Syntax (**bold face text** is required, plain text is optional)

```
<MvFIND
  NAME="alias"
  VALUE="str"
  EXACT="EXACT"
>
```

Attributes

NAME="*alias*"	Alias assigned to the database connection. If this attribute is omitted, Miva uses the current primary database.
VALUE="*str*"	Value to search for.
EXACT="*EXACT*"	If this attribute is present, Miva searches for a record whose field is an exact match. If this attribute is omitted, Miva searches for a record whose field *starts* with the search value.

Discussion

This tag is used to perform quick searches on a database. In order to use <MvFIND>, you must have created an index for the database. If several indexes are open, the main index is used for the search.

<MvFIND> searches the database, and positions the record pointer to the first record whose key value matches the VALUE attribute. Normally, a record is considered to match if the search value occurs at the beginning of the key value; this is helpful if the field values are padded with trailing spaces. If you want to only match records where the entire key value is equal to the search value, use the EXACT="EXACT" attribute.

<MvFIND> always finds the first matching record in the database. To find all matching records, you can use <MvFIND> to get the first one, and then use <MvSKIP> to find the others. Since the database is indexed, all the matching records will be found immediately after the first one. (You can also search for multiple records by using <MvFILTER>.)

Example

This example searches a product database for records where the key value contains the string Acme. Since this is not an exact search, it will find a record with a key value of Acme Inc., Acme Tools, Acme Toys, etc.

```
<MVFIND NAME="products.dbf" VALUE="Acme">
```

See Also

<MvFILTER> <MvGO> <MvSKIP>

<MvFUNCRETURN>

Return from a function

This tag terminates a Miva function, and passes control back to the script that called it. It can also return a value to the caller.

Syntax (**bold face text** is required, plain text is optional)

```
<MvFUNCTION attrs>
  ...
  <MvFUNCRETURN
   VALUE="{expr}"
  >
  ...
</MvFUNCTION>
```

Attributes VALUE="{*expr*}" A Miva expression specifying a value to return to the caller.

Discussion This tag is used inside a Miva function definition (<MvFUNCTION> ... </MvFUNCTION>). It causes Miva to stop executing the function and return to the script that called it. If the VALUE attribute is present, Miva evaluates the specified expression and returns that value to the caller.

For more details on functions, see Chapter 3, as well as the <MvFUNCTION> tag described below.

<MvFUNCTION>

Define a function

This tag defines a function that can be called by scripts.

Syntax (**bold face text** is required, plain text is optional)

```
<MvFUNCTION
 NAME="funcname"
 PARAMETERS="var1,var2,..."
 STANDARDOUTPUTLEVEL="str"
 ERROROUTPUTLEVEL="str"
```

```
>
  ...
</MvFUNCTION>
```

Attributes

NAME="*funcname*"	Specifies a name for the function.
PARAMETERS= "*var1,var2,...*"	Specifies one or more local variables to receive parameters from the caller.
STANDARDOUTPUT-LEVEL="*str*"	Controls what Miva sends to the browser while processing the function. *str* is one of the following keywords, or both keywords separated by a comma: `html` Enable sending of HTML tags. `text` Enable sending of text. *str* may also be null (''), or any other value, to suppress all output. The default value is `html,text`, so that both HTML tags and text will be sent to the browser.
ERROROUTPUTLEVEL ="*str*"	Controls what types of errors Miva will report while processing the function. *str* is one of the following keywords, or two or more keywords separated by a comma: `expression` Enable reporting of improper expressions. `runtime` Enable reporting of runtime errors. `syntax` Enable reporting of improper tags or attributes. str may also be null ('') to suppress all output. The default value is `expression,runtime, syntax`, so that all types of errors will be reported.

Discussion For more details on Miva functions, see Chapter 3.

Example This example defines a function that computes the square root of a number, except that if the number is negative, it returns the string `Invalid`:

```
<MvFUNCTION NAME="sq_root" PARAMETERS="num">
 <MvIF EXPR="{num LT 0}">
  <MvFUNCRETURN VALUE="{'Invalid'}">
 <MvELSE>
  <MvFUNCRETURN VALUE="{sqrt(num)}">
```

```
 </MvIF>
</MvFUNCTION>
```

See Also <MvDO> <MvFUNCRETURN>

<MvGO>

Access a specific record in a database

This tag moves a database record pointer to a specific position.

Syntax (**bold face text** is required, plain text is optional)

```
<MvGO
 NAME="alias"
 ROW="position"
 VIEW="viewname"
>
```

Attributes

NAME="*alias*"	Specifies the alias assigned to the database connection. If this attribute is omitted, Miva uses the current primary database.
ROW="*position*"	Specifies the record number to go to. *position* may be a number, Miva expression, or the keyword top or bottom.
VIEW="*viewname*"	Specifies a database view to use (for ODBC databases only).

Discussion This tag moves a database record pointer to a specified position. Normally, the ROW attribute specifies a numeric value, which specifies the record's physical position in the database, i.e., the order in which the records were created.

Instead of a number, the ROW attribute value may be top or bottom to position the pointer at the first or last record. Note, however, that if the database has an open index, <MvGO> using one of these literals will position the pointer to the first or last record as specified by the index. For convenient access to the first physical record, regardless of whether the database is indexed, use ROW="1". To access the last physical record, use ROW="{totrec}".

Example

```
<MvGO NAME="my_db" ROW="{previousOrder}">
```

See Also <MvFILTER> <MvFIND> <MvSKIP>

<MvHIDE>

Add hidden data to a form

This tag creates hidden input elements in a form, providing a convenient way to pass data to a server.

Syntax

```
<MvHIDE
 FIELDS="var1,var2,..."
>
```

Attributes

`FIELDS="`*`var1, var2,...`*`"`	Specifies one or more Miva variables to include in the form.

Discussion This tag may only be used inside an HTML form (between `<FORM>` and `</FORM>`). It creates one or more hidden form elements and assigns them values. These values will then be passed to a server when the form is submitted. `<MvHIDE>` is equivalent to one or more `<INPUT TYPE="HIDDEN">` tags, as shown in the example below.

Example The Miva tag:

```
<MvHIDE FIELDS="firstname,lastname">
```

is equivalent to the HTML tags:

```
<INPUT TYPE="HIDDEN" NAME="firstname" VALUE="val1">
<INPUT TYPE="HIDDEN" NAME="lastname" VALUE="val2">
```

where *`val1`* and *`val2`* represent the actual values of the Miva variables `firstname` and `lastname`.

<MvIF>

Conditionally execute parts of a script

This tag allows parts of a script to be executed or skipped, depending on the value of a Miva expression.

Syntax (**`bold face text`** is required, `plain text` is optional)

```
<MvIF EXPR="{expr}">
 ... "true" part ...
<MvELSE>
```

```
 ... "false" part ...
</MvIF>
```

Attributes

EXPR="{*expr*}" A Miva expression to be evaluated as true or false.

Discussion

This tag is used to control execution of a script, depending on whether some condition is true or false. Miva evaluates the expression in the EXPR attribute. If the result is 0 or the null string '', it is considered false; any other value is considered true.

If there is no <MvELSE> inside the <MvIF> ... </MvIF> block, Miva will execute the text and tags inside the block only if the expression is true. If the expression is false, Miva skips to the point after the </MvIF>.

If the block includes an <MvELSE>, then Miva executes the text and tags between <MvIF> and <MvELSE> if the expression is true. If the expression is false, Miva skips to the point after the <MvELSE>, and executes the text and tags between <MvELSE> and </MvIF>.

Example

This use of <MvIF> is useful for certain types of online businesses:

```
<MvIF EXPR="userAge GE 18">
 <A HREF="http://www.somewhere.com/adult/"> Click here to
enter </A>
<MvELSE>
 <B>Sorry, this site is not available to you.</B>
</MvIF>
```

This example assumes that the variable userAge has been set by some previous Miva tag, or entered into an HTML form by the user. If the age is greater than or equal to 18, the display will include a link to read a new Web page. If the age is less than 18, the user will see a message; the link is not even presented to the browser.

See Also

<MvEXIT> <MvWHILE>

<MvIMPORT>

Read data from an external file

This tag creates a loop that reads a series of records from an external data file.

Syntax

(**bold face text** is required, plain text is optional)

```
<MvIMPORT
 FILE="pathname"
```

```
  FIELDS="var1,var2,..."
  DELIMITER="str"
  FILTER="{expr}"
>
  ...
</MvIMPORT>
```

Attributes

FILE="*pathname*"	Specifies the file from which to read. The path is relative to the Miva data directory.
FIELDS="*var1, var2,...*"	Specifies one or more variables to receive the data read from the file.
DELIMITER="*str*"	Specifies one or more characters that will occur between fields of each record.
FILTER="{*expr*}"	Specifies an expression that is used to filter incoming records. If this attribute is present, Miva will skip over any records for which the expression is false.

Variables

recno	Within the <MvIMPORT> ... </MvIMPORT> block, Miva updates the global variable recno as a count of the records read, starting with 1. Note that in scripts that use both <MvIMPORT> and databases, you should write g.recno and *alias*.d.recno (or d.recno for the primary database), in order to distinguish the two variables.

Discussion

This tag is used to read one or more records from an external text file. <MvIMPORT> and </MvIMPORT> form a loop that is executed once for each record read. The loop will read all records in the file, unless it is terminated by an <MvIMPORTSTOP> tag.

To quickly search for a particular record, you can define a filter expression. Note, however, that a text file is not as efficient as a database for searching and managing a large amount of data. If your file has more than a few hundred records, a database will probably be a better choice. <MvIMPORT> is ideally suited for creating a script that reads a text file and converts it to a database (see Example).

Example

Assume the file utensils.txt contains data such as:

```
100001; knife; 2.79; 0.2
100002; dinner fork; 2.39; 0.1
100003; salad fork; 2.29; 0.1
100004; dessert spoon; 2.49; 0.1
100005; soup spoon; 2.59; 0.1
```

To read records from the file, and use the data to create new records in a database, use a script such as:

```
<MvIMPORT
 FILE="utensils.txt"
 FIELDS="catalog_num,name,price,weight"
 DELIMITER="; ">
Record &[g.recno]; is &[name]; <BR>
<MvASSIGN NAME="d.itemnum" VALUE="{catalog_num}">
<MvASSIGN NAME="d.itemname" VALUE="{name}">
<MvASSIGN NAME="d.price" VALUE="{price}">
<MvASSIGN NAME="d.weight" VALUE="{weight}">
<MvADD>
</MvIMPORT>
```

The <MvIMPORT> reads the data from the file into variables named catalog_num, name, price, and weight. Then the script assigns those variables to the database field variables d.itemnum, d.itemname, d.price, and d.weight, and uses <MvADD> to create the new database record. (The database in this example was created with the <MvCREATE> example seen earlier in this manual.)

If the <MvIMPORT> tag included the FILTER="{'spoon' CIN name}" attribute, then the script would ignore records from the file that did not have the string 'spoon' in their name field. In this case, the script would create only two database records.

See Also <MvEXPORT> <MvIMPORTSTOP>

<MvIMPORTSTOP>

Interrupt reading of an external file

This tag is used inside an <MvIMPORT> ... </MvIMPORT> loop. It causes Miva to stop reading from the file, and continue executing the script at a point after the </MvIMPORT>.

Syntax

```
<MvIMPORT attrs>
 ...
 <MvIMPORTSTOP>
```

```
...
</MvIMPORT>
```

Attributes None.

Variables

recno — Within the <MvIMPORT> ... </MvIMPORT> block, Miva updates the global variable recno as a count of the records read, starting with 1. Note that in scripts that use both <MvIMPORT> and databases, you should write g.recno and *alias*.d.recno (or d.recno for the primary database), in order to distinguish the two variables.

Discussion Normally, an <MvIMPORT> loop reads all the records in a file. This tag is used to stop reading a file when some condition is reached.

Example This example reads only the first three records in a file:

```
<MvIMPORT
 FILE="utensils.txt"
 FIELDS="catalog_num,name,price,weight"
 DELIMITER="; "
>
 Record &[g.recno]; is &[name]; <BR>
 <MvIF EXPR="{recno GE 3}">
  <MvIMPORTSTOP>
 </MvIF>
</MvIMPORT>
```

When recno reaches 3, the script executes <MvIMPORTSTOP>.

See Also <MvIMPORT>

<MvLET>

(Replaced by <MvASSIGN>)

This tag was used instead of <MvASSIGN> in early versions of Miva Script. It is still supported for compatibility with older scripts. However, it is recommended that you use <MvASSIGN>.

<MvLOCKFILE>

Request exclusive use of a file

This tag requests Miva to lock a file to prevent other users from accessing it. If another user has already locked the file, the requesting script will be paused until the file becomes available.

Syntax

```
<MvLOCKFILE
  FILE="filename"
>
  ...
</MvLOCKFILE>
```

Attributes

FILE="*filename*"	Specifies the file to lock.

Discussion

If two or more users of your Web site run the same script at the same time, one user might read a file while another user is modifying it; or both users might try to modify a file at the same time. <MvLOCKFILE> is used to prevent more than one user from accessing a file simultaneously.

When a script executes <MvLOCKFILE>, it is granted exclusive access to the file *only* if no other user has already locked it. If another user has locked the file, the requesting script is paused, and its lock request is placed in a queue.

The </MvLOCKFILE> tag unlocks a file. When a user unlocks a file, the next script in the request queue is granted access to the file, and it resumes running. To prevent users from being delayed, you should organize your scripts so that locks are used briefly. Only lock a file as long as necessary; keep other types of tags and text outside the <MvLOCKFILE> ... </MvLOCKFILE> block.

Note that <MvLOCKFILE> is *not* an absolute guarantee of exclusive access to a file. It only applies to scripts that use <MvLOCKFILE>. Scripts that do not use <MvLOCKFILE>, or other users with non-Miva applications such as text editors, can still access the file at any time. You may need to design your application carefully, to ensure that file access is both reliable and fast.

Locks can be applied to any type of file, including a database.

For more details, see the section on "File Locking" in Chapter 5.

Example

To lock a database while compressing it and updating indexes, use a script such as:

```
<MvOPEN NAME="catalog"
 DATABASE="catalog.dbf"
 INDEXES="alpha.mvx,numeric.mvx">
<MvLOCKFILE FILE="catalog.dbf">
```

```
 <MvPACK NAME="catalog">
</MvLOCKFILE>
```

Note that packing a database can be time-consuming. If the database is large, it is best to do this offline, using Miva Mia on a separate copy of the database files.

<MvMAKEINDEX>

Create a database index

This tag creates a new index file for a database, and makes it the main index for the database.

Syntax (**bold face** text is required, plain text is optional)

```
<MvMAKEINDEX
 NAME="alias"
 INDEXFILE="pathname"
 EXPR="{expr}"
 FLAGS="str"
>
```

Attributes

NAME="*alias*"	Alias assigned to the database connection. If this attribute is omitted, Miva uses the current primary database.
INDEXFILE= "*pathname*"	Pathname for the new index file. It is recommended that the filename end with `.mvx`. The path is relative to the Miva data directory.
EXPR="{*expr*}"	Miva key expression to use for sorting database records.
FLAGS="*str*"	String of one or more keywords separated by commas:

ascending	Sort records in ascending order (default).
descending	Sort records in descending order.
unique	Key values must be unique; duplicates are not allowed.
nounique	Multiple records with same key value are allowed (default).
string	Use string comparisons, not numeric, when comparing key values.

Discussion

This tag creates a new index file for a database. An index file makes it possible for the <MvSKIP> and <MvFIND> functions to work more quickly, especially for large databases.

To index a database, you define a *key expression*. Miva evaluates this expression for each record in the database. The expression can be as simple as the name of a single field, or it can be a complex combination of several fields. The results of this expression, called *key values*, determine the order of records defined in the index file.

If a file with the same name exists, <MvMAKEINDEX> deletes it. The newly created index becomes the main index for the database (this can be changed with <MvSETINDEX>).

<MvMAKEINDEX> can use a lot of processor time and/or memory, so it may be preferable to do it offline using Miva Mia. It is generally a "management" function that does not need to be readily available to Web users.

Example

This example indexes a product database by a single field:

```
<MvMAKEINDEX
 NAME="catalog"
 INDEXFILE="inum.mvx"
 EXPR="{catalog.d.itemnum}"
>
```

The catalog database contains a field, `itemnum`, that is a unique number for each item. Since it is common to search for records by item number, indexing the database this way will make the application more efficient. The variable name is written `catalog.d.itemnum` to make sure that it does not conflict with any other variables named `itemnum` that might be in use.

A printed price list, on the other hand, may be more useful if it lists items in alphabetical order, and includes the item's color. An index for that can be created with a tag such as:

```
<MvMAKEINDEX
 NAME="shoelist"
 INDEXFILE="prices.mvx"
 EXPR="{shoelist.d.itemname $ shoelist.d.color}"
>
```

Here, the key expression concatenates the name and color into a single string. So, for example, a red shirt would be listed after a blue shirt (since `shirtred` comes after `shirtblue` in alphabetical sequence).

See Also

<MvREINDEX> <MvSETINDEX>

<MvOPEN>

Open a database

This tag makes a database available for use in a script, and also creates an alias for the connection.

Syntax

(**bold face text** is required, plain text is optional)

```
<MvOPEN
 NAME="alias"
 DATABASE="pathname"
 TYPE="str"
 USER="str"
 PASSWORD="str"
 INDEXES="file1,file2,..."
>
```

Attributes

Attribute	Description
`NAME="alias"`	Specifies the alias that Miva will assign to the database connection.
`DATABASE="pathname"`	Pathname for the database file.
`TYPE="str"`	Specifies the type of database. `str` may contain `xbase3` or `odbc` . If this attribute is omitted, `xbase3` is assumed.
`INDEXES="file1, file2,..."`	One or more index files to open with the database.
`USER="str"`	Specifies the username for accessing an ODBC datasource.
`PASSWORD="str"`	Specifies the password for accessing an ODBC datasource.

Discussion

This tag opens a database connection, and assigns it an alias that can be used to reference it in other Miva tags. The connection remains open until the script either terminates, or closes with `<MvCLOSE>`. Note that you can open several connections simultaneously to one database file; this may be useful if each connection uses different indexes, filters, etc.

The file specified by the `DATABASE` parameter must already exist. To create a new database, use `<MvCREATE>`.

The newly opened database becomes the *primary database* for the script: it will be used for any subsequent Miva tags that operate on a database but do not include the NAME attribute. To change the primary database without opening a new connection, use <MvPRIMARY>.

Any index files specified in the INDEXES attribute will be opened, and Miva will update them as needed when records are added or changed. The first file specified becomes the *main index* for the connection: the one used for navigation with <MvFIND> and <MvSKIP>. To select a different main index, use <MvSETINDEX>. To update indexes when a database connection is not open, use <MvREINDEX>.

When opening an ODBC database, the DATABASE attribute contains an ODBC connection string instead of a pathname.

Example: This example opens a catalog database with two index files:

```
<MvOPEN NAME="catalog"
 DATABASE="catalog.dbf"
 INDEXES="alpha.mvx,numeric.mvx">
```

See Also: <MvCLOSE> <MvCREATE> <MvPRIMARY> <MvREVEALSTRUCTURE>

<MvOPENVIEW>

Create a view of a database and run an SQL query

This tag opens a view of an ODBC database and retrieves the results of an SQL query into the view.

Syntax: (**bold face text** is required, plain text is optional)

```
<MvOPENVIEW
 NAME="alias"
 VIEW="viewname"
 QUERY="str"
>
```

Attributes:

NAME="*alias*"	Specifies the alias assigned to the database connection. If this attribute is omitted, Miva uses the current primary database.
VIEW="*viewname*"	Specifies a name for the view.
QUERY="*str*"	An SQL query that is used to request data.

Discussion

This tag is used to retrieve results of SQL queries. The view will contain all fields of all records returned by the query. Once the view is opened, you can navigate through it using the `VIEW` attribute on the `<MvSKIP>` and `<MvGO>` tags.

Note that views can only be used with ODBC databases. Currently, these databases are only supported for offline use with Miva Mia.

When you are finished using a view, close and delete it with `<MvCLOSEVIEW>`.

Example

This example creates a view of an employee database that only contains the names, employee ID numbers, and salaries:

```
<MvOPENVIEW
 NAME="staff"
 VIEW="salary"
 QUERY="select lastname,firstname,empID,salary from
employees>
```

See Also

`<MvCLOSEVIEW>` `<MvQUERY>`

<MvPACK>

Compress a database

This tag permanently removes from the database all records that have been marked for deletion. It also updates all open index files.

Syntax

(**bold face text** is required, plain text is optional)

```
<MvPACK
 NAME="alias"
>
```

Attributes

`NAME="`*`alias`*`"`	Specifies the alias assigned to the database connection. If this attribute is omitted, Miva uses the current primary database.

Discussion

This tag physically removes from the database all records that have been marked for deletion by `<MvDELETE>`. After the database is packed, `<MvUNDELETE>` can no longer retrieve deleted records.

Note that if the database is large, compressing it may take a lot of processing time. It may be best to do this offline, using Miva Mia and a separate copy of the database. If it is necessary to do it while the database is online, you can use `<MvLOCKFILE>` to prevent other users from accessing the database while the `<MvPACK>` is in progress.

<MvPACK> also updates any index files that are open, so that their contents reflect the current state of the database. If any index is not open during <MvPACK>, you can update it later with <MvREINDEX>.

Example To lock a database while compressing it, use a script such as:

```
<MvOPEN NAME="catalog"
 DATABASE="catalog.dbf"
 INDEXES="alpha.mvx,numeric.mvx">
<MvLOCKFILE FILE="catalog.dbf">
<MvPACK NAME="catalog">
</MvLOCKFILE>
```

See Also <MvADD> <MvDELETE> <MvLOCKFILE> <MvUNDELETE> <MvUPDATE>

<MvPOP>

Read e-mail

This tag reads one or more e-mail messages from a server and stores them in files on the Miva host.

Syntax

```
<MvPOP
 MAILHOST="host"
 LOGIN="username"
 PASSWORD="pwd"
 DIRECTORY="path"
>
 ...
</MvPOP>
```

Attributes

MAILHOST="*host*"	Specifies a POP3 mail server, such as mail.mycompany.com.
LOGIN="*username*"	Username to use for logging in to the mail host.
PASSWORD="*pwd*"	Password to use for logging in to the mail host.
DIRECTORY="*path*"	Directory in which to store retrieved messages. The path is relative to the Miva data directory.

Variables Inside the <MvPOP> ... </MvPOP> loop, the following variables are available, and apply to each message as it is retrieved:

`messagebody`	Name of the file in which the message is stored.
`messagesubject`	Contents of the message's `Subject:` field.
`messagereplyto`	Contents of the message's `Reply-To:` field.
`messagesender`	Contents of the message's `From:` field.
`messagedate`	Contents of the message's `Date:` field.

Discussion This tag logs in to a specified mail server account. The <MvPOP> ... </MvPOP> loop is executed once for each message on the specified mail server. Miva retrieves each message, and places it in a file in the specified directory. Miva creates a unique name for each file, and returns filename in the `messagebody` variable.

Miva normally leaves messages on the mail server. To delete a message from the server after it is read, use <MvPOPDELETE>.

<MvPOP> normally executes once for each message in the mail server account. To exit from the loop before the last message is read, use <MvPOPSTOP>.

Example This example retrieves e-mail and displays information about the retrieved messages in an HTML table:

```
<TABLE BORDER>
  <MvPOP
   MAILHOST="mail.myisp.net"
   LOGIN="myname"
   PASSWORD="mypassword"
   DIRECTORY="inbox"
  >
    <TR>
      <TD> &[messagebody];     </TD>
      <TD> &[messagesender];   </TD>
      <TD> &[messagereplyto]; </TD>
      <TD> &[messagedate];     </TD>
    </TR>
    <TR>
      <TD COLSPAN="4"> <B>Subject:</B> &[messagesubject];
</TD>
```

```
        </TR>
    </MvPOP>
</TABLE>
```

In this script, the `<MvPOP> ... </MvPOP>` loop is enclosed by HTML `<TABLE>` and `</TABLE>` tags. Each pass through the loop generates one row for the table, using `<TR>` and `<TD>` tags. Miva macros are used to insert variable values into the table cells. A typical display generated by this script looks like:

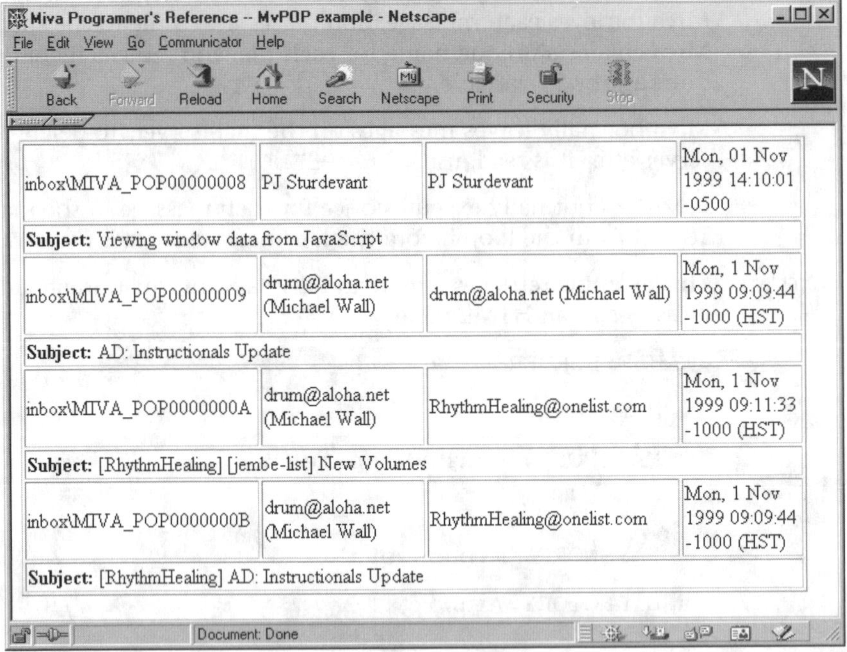

Caution: Inserting an actual password into a script could be a security risk. It is shown here only to keep the example simple. In actual practice, it would be better to use an HTML form to get the host, username, and password from the user at run time, and pass them to a script that does the actual retrieval.

See Also `<MvPOPDELETE>` `<MvPOPSTOP>` `<MvSMTP>`

<MvPOPDELETE>

Delete an e-mail message from a server

This tag is used inside an <MvPOP> ... </MvPOP> loop. It deletes the current e-mail message from the mail server.

Syntax

```
<MvPOP attrs>
  ...
  <MvPOPDELETE>
  ...
</MvPOP>
```

Attributes None.

Variables See <MvPOP>

Discussion Normally, <MvPOP> leaves retrieved e-mail messages on the server from which it retrieves them. If you want to delete a message, execute this tag inside the <MvPOP> ... </MvPOP> loop.

Note that <MvPOPDELETE> deletes a message after it has been retrieved onto the Miva host, so variables such as `messagebody` will still contain correct values, and the file containing the retrieved message text will remain in the directory specified by <MvPOP>. To delete the text file, use the `fdelete()` system function.

Example This example retrieves messages, deletes them from the mail server, and also deletes the retrieved message body text file:

```
<MvPOP
  MAILHOST="mail.my_isp.com"
  LOGIN="me"
  PASSWORD="xyzzy"
  DIRECTORY="inbox">
  ... process message ...
  <MvEVAL EXPR="{fdelete('inbox/' $ messagebody)}">
  <MvPOPDELETE>
</MvPOP>
```

<MvPOP> retrieves messages and places the text files in a directory named `inbox`. <MvPOPDELETE> deletes the messages from the mail server, and the `fdelete()` call deletes the text files from the `inbox` directory.

See Also <MvPOP> <MvPOPSTOP>

<MvPOPSTOP>

Stop reading e-mail

This tag interrupts an <MvPOP> ... </MvPOP> loop.

Syntax

```
<MvPOP attrs>
 ...
 <MvPOPSTOP>
 ...
</MvPOP>
```

Attributes None.

Variables See <MvPOP>

Discussion Normally, <MvPOP> retrieves all the messages in the specified account. <MvPOPSTOP> can interrupt the loop before all messages are read. Miva will continue executing the script at the point after the </MvPOP>.

Example This example retrieves just the first ten messages in an account:

```
<MvASSIGN NAME="messagecount" VALUE="0">
<MvPOP
 MAILHOST="mail.my_isp.com"
 LOGIN="me"
 PASSWORD="xyzzy"
 DIRECTORY="inbox">
 ... process message ...
 <MvASSIGN NAME="messagecount" VALUE="{messagecount + 1}">
 <MvIF EXPR="{messagecount GE 10}">
  <MvPOPSTOP>
 </MvIF>
</MvPOP>
```

This script uses a variable `messagecount` to count the retrieved messages. It starts at 0, and is incremented after each message is read and processed. An <MvIF> tag is used to execute <MvPOPSTOP> when the count reaches 10. If there are less than 10 messages on the server, the script will of course terminate after reading the last one; in that case, `messagecount` will contain the actual number of messages retrieved.

See Also <MvPOP> <MvPOPDELETE>

<MvPRIMARY>

Select a primary database

This tag specifies a database connection that becomes the primary connection for this script. It will then be used as the default by all database tags that do not include the NAME attribute.

Syntax

```
<MvPRIMARY
 NAME="alias"
>
```

Attributes

NAME="*alias*" Specifies the alias assigned to the database connection.

Discussion

A script may have two or more database connections open at one time. One connection is always designated the primary connection, and is used as the default by any database tag that does not include a NAME="*alias*" attribute. The <MvCREATE> and <MvOPEN> tags automatically make a connection primary when they open it.

Scripts can use <MvPRIMARY> to change the primary database at any time. The new primary database must already have been opened by <MvOPEN> or <MvCREATE>.

Example

```
<MvPRIMARY NAME="data1998">
```

See Also

<MvCLOSE> <MvCREATE> <MvOPEN> <MvREVEALSTRUCTURE>

<MvQUERY>

Submit an SQL query

This tag submits an SQL query to an ODBC database. No results are returned.

Syntax (**bold face** text is required, plain text is optional)

```
<MvQUERY 1
 NAME="alias"
 QUERY="str"
>
```

Attributes

NAME="*alias*" Specifies the alias assigned to the database connection. If this attribute is omitted, Miva uses the current primary database.

QUERY="*str*" A valid SQL query string.

Discussion

This tag is used only with ODBC databases. It submits a query, but does not accept any returned results; to return a result, you must use <MvOPENVIEW>.

For more details, see Chapter 6.

Example

```
<MvQUERY
 NAME="my_db"
 QUERY="create table newtable
      (numfield integer,
       textfield char(64))"
>
```

See Also

<MvCLOSEVIEW> <MvOPENVIEW>

<MvREINDEX>

Rebuild database index files

This tag rebuilds all open index files for a database.

Syntax

(**bold face text** is required, plain text is optional)

```
<MvREINDEX
 NAME="alias"
>
```

Attributes

NAME="*alias*" Specifies the alias assigned to the database connection. If this attribute is omitted, Miva uses the current primary database.

Discussion

Miva updates all open database index files whenever the database is modified. However, there may be times when a database is modified while some indexes are not open. In that case, <MvREINDEX> is used to rebuild the indexes at a later time. The database, and the index files to rebuild, must be opened in order to use this tag.

Caution: <MvREINDEX> can consume a lot of processing time and resources, so it may be better to do it offline, using Miva Mia and a copy of the database. If you must do it online, use <MvLOCKFILE> to lock the database and index files while the rebuild is in progress. Remember that in order for <MvLOCKFILE> to be effective, it must be used by all scripts that use the database.

Example `<MvREINDEX NAME="catalog">`

See Also `<MvMAKEINDEX>` `<MvSETINDEX>`

<MvREVEALSTRUCTURE>

Read database record format

This tag examines a database to determine the format of its records, and creates a new database with information about the type and size of each field.

Syntax (**bold face text** is required, plain text is optional)

<MvREVEALSTRUCTURE

NAME="*alias*"

DATABASE="*pathname*"

>

Attributes

NAME="*alias*"	Specifies the alias assigned to the database connection. If this attribute is omitted, Miva uses the current primary database.
DATABASE="*pathname*"	Filename for the new database to be created. If a path is specified, it is relative to the Miva data directory.

Variables Each record of the newly created database contains fields that give information about one field of the database being examined:

field_name	Name of the field.	
field_type	A single character that specifies the field type:	
	C	CHAR
	N	NUMBER
	D	DATE
	L	logical (BOOL)
	M	MEMO
field_len	Length of the field:	
	CHAR	Number of characters.
	NUMBER	Total number of digits, before and after the decimal point; plus 1 for the decimal point, if any.
	DATE	Always 8.

	BOOL	Always 1.
	MEMO	Always 10.
field_dec	For NUMBER fields only, this field gives the number of digits after the decimal point.	

Discussion This tag can be used for scripts that must access a database when its record structure is not known in advance. It creates a new database, in which each record gives descriptive information about one field of the database being examined. After creating this database, you must use <MvOPEN> to access it. This information it contains can then be used to access records in the original database.

Example

```
<MvREVEALSTRUCTURE NAME="unknownDB"
DATABASE="structure.dbf">
```

See Also <MvCLOSE> <MvCREATE> <MvOPEN> <MvPRIMARY>

<MvSETINDEX>

Select indexes for database navigation

This tag opens one or more index files for use with a database. It also selects one index file to be the main index for a database connection.

Syntax (**bold face text** is required, plain text is optional)

<MvSETINDEX

NAME="*alias*"

INDEXES="*file1,file2,...*"

>

Attributes

NAME="*alias*"	Specifies the alias assigned to the database connection. If this attribute is omitted, Miva uses the current primary database.
INDEXES="*file1, file2,...*"	Specifies one or more index files to open.

Discussion This tag first closes any index files that are open to the specified database connection. It then opens all index files specified by the INDEXES attribute. The first file specified becomes the main index, which will be used by the <MvFIND> and <MvSKIP> tags for database navigation. <MvSETINDEX> also positions the record pointer to the first record, based on the order specified by the main index.

Example

```
<MvSETINDEX NAME="customers"
INDEXES="calpha.mvx,czipcode.mvx">
```

See Also <MvMAKEINDEX> <MvREINDEX>

<MvSKIP>

Move sequentially through a database

This tag moves a database record pointer forward or back a specified number of records.

Syntax (**bold face text** is required, plain text is optional)

```
<MvSKIP
 NAME="alias"
 ROWS="num"
 VIEW="viewname"
>
```

Attributes

NAME="*alias*"	Specifies the alias assigned to the database connection. If this attribute is omitted, Miva uses the current primary database.
ROWS="*num*"	Number of records to advance. Positive values move forward; negative values move back. If this attribute is omitted, a default value of 1 is used.
VIEW="*viewname*"	Specifies a database view to which this tag applies (for ODBC databases only).

Discussion

This tag is most often used to step through a database, accessing one record at a time. However, it can also move forward or backward by larger amounts. If the database has any open indexes, <MvSKIP> moves through the records in the order defined by the main index. If the database has no open indexes, <MvSKIP> moves through the records in physical order .

Movement with <MvSKIP> is always relative to the current record. To reference a specific record, regardless of the current record pointer, use <MvFIND> or <MvGO>.

Example

To create a simple database report, use a script such as:

```
<MvWHILE EXPR="{d.eof EQ 0}">
 Record &[recno]; :
 <MvEVAL EXPR="{d.itemnum}">
```

```
<MvEVAL EXPR="{d.itemname}">
<MvEVAL EXPR="{d.price}">
<MvEVAL EXPR="{d.weight}">.
<BR>
<MvSKIP>
</MvWHILE>
```

This example uses `<MvWHILE>` to loop on the variable `d.eof`, which will become 1 when the end of the database is reached. It displays each record's number and field values on one line of the browser screen. Then it uses `<MvSKIP>` to advance to the next record. The `ROWS` attribute is not used, since 1 is the default value.

See Also `<MvFILTER>` `<MvFIND>` `<MvGO>`

<MvSMTP>

Send e-mail

This tag sends an e-mail message using a specified server account.

Syntax (**bold face text** is required, plain text is optional)

```
<MvSMTP
 TO="dest1,dest2,..."
 SUBJECT="text"
 CC="dest1,dest2,..."
 MAILHOST="host"
 FROM="addr">
 ... headers ...
(blank line)
 ... message body ...
</MvSMTP>
```

Attributes `TO="dest1,dest2,..."` One or more e-mail addresses to whom the message will be sent.

`SUBJECT="text"`	A line of text that will be used as the message's `Subject:` line.
`CC="dest1,dest2,..."`	One or more e-mail addresses to whom the message will be sent as a copy (`Cc:`).
`MAILHOST="host"`	A valid mail host, such as `mail.yourcompany.com`.
`FROM="addr"`	E-mail address of the sender.

Discussion

This tag connects to a mail host and sends an e-mail message. Attributes specify basic information: mail host, addresses of sender and recipients, and a subject line. If you wish to include additional mail header information, such as `Bcc:` or `Reply-To:`, you may place these immediately after the `<MvSMTP>` tag, and follow them with a blank line. The blank line must be present even if there are no headers.

Everything in your script after the header's blank line until the `</MvSMTP>` tag becomes the body of the e-mail message. You may include additional Miva tags in the body. For instance, you can use `<MvCALL>` or `<MvDO>` to read another file, and include it in the message.

Note: The specific formats of e-mail addresses, and the range of allowed headers, may vary depending on the particular mail host being used. You may need to test your application to ensure that your messages will be accepted by your host.

Example

This example sends a simple message:

```
<MvSMTP
 TO="<someone@company.com>"
 SUBJECT="Hey there"
 MAILHOST="mail.myisp.net"
 FROM="myname@myisp.net"
>

Hi, just testing my new Miva script ...
</MvSMTP>
```

Note the blank line just before the message body; this is required.

See Also

`<MvPOP>`

<MvUNDELETE>

Restore deleted records to a database

This tag clears the `deleted` variable for a database record, allowing it to be accessed by database navigation tags. This can only be done for records that have not been physically removed from the database with `<MvPACK>`.

Syntax (**`bold face text`** is required, `plain text` is optional)

<MvUNDELETE

NAME="*alias*"

>

Attributes

NAME="*alias*" Specifies the alias assigned to the database connection. If this attribute is omitted, Miva uses the current primary database.

Discussion Every database record has a special `deleted` field that can be referenced in scripts. `<MvDELETE>` sets this field to 1 (true). The record is not actually removed from the database until you execute an `<MvPACK>`. In the meantime, the record is still visible for searching and navigation. Until the database is packed, you can use `<MvUNDELETE>` to set `deleted` back to 0 (False).

Example

```
<MvUNDELETE NAME="shoppingcart">
```

See Also `<MvADD>` `<MvDELETE>` `<MvPACK>` `<MvUPDATE>`

<MvUPDATE>

Modify a database record

This tag modifies a database record by setting its fields equal to the field variables defined for the database connection (alias).

Syntax (**`bold face text`** is required, `plain text` is optional)

<MvUPDATE

NAME="*alias*"

>

Attributes

NAME="*alias*" Specifies the alias assigned to the database connection. If this attribute is omitted, Miva uses the current primary database.

Discussion

This tag copies the values from a set of database field variables, and stores them in the actual fields of the current database record. If any index files are open, they will be updated if necessary, based on the new values of the record's fields.

Example

To change the price of an item in a catalog, use a script such as:

```
<MvFIND VALUE="salad fork">

<MvASSIGN NAME="price" VALUE="1.99">

<MvUPDATE>
```

See Also

<MvADD> <MvDELETE> <MvPACK> <MvUNDELETE>

<MvWHILE>

Create a program loop

This tag marks the beginning of a loop. Text and tags between <MvWHILE> and </MvWHILE> will be executed repeatedly.

Syntax

```
<MvWHILE
  EXPR="{expr}"
>
  ...
</MvWHILE>
```

Attributes

EXPR="{*expr*}"	Miva expression that is evaluated to determine whether to continue looping.

Discussion

This tag creates loops that cause the portion of a script to be executed repeatedly. Everything between <MvWHILE> and the corresponding </MvWHILE> will be executed as long as the expression specified by the EXPR attribute returns a true value (anything other than 0 or the null string ''). An <MvWHILE> loop can also be terminated by <MvWHILESTOP>.

Note that if the expression returns a false value the first time <MvWHILE> is executed, the loop will not be executed at all.

Example

This example reads 25 records from a database, and displays them to the user. This could be used to display results of a search in one-page-size segments:

```
<MvASSIGN NAME="count" VALUE="1">

<MvWHILE EXPR="{count LE 25}">
```

```
  ... process one record ...

 <MvASSIGN NAME="count" VALUE="{count + 1}">
 <MvSKIP ROWS="1">
</MvWHILE>
```

The script uses a variable named `count` to keep track of the loop's progress. It is set to 1 before the <MvWHILE>, and is incremented by 1 each time Miva executes the loop. When it reaches 26, the <MvWHILE> expression will no longer be true, so the loop will stop after 25 iterations.

Another form of loop is useful when you want to process all the records in a database:

```
<MvWHILE EXPR="{d.eof EQ 0}">
  ... process one record ...
 <MvSKIP ROWS="1">
</MvWHILE>
```

This loop uses an expression based on the database variable `eof`, which becomes true (1) when the end of the database has been reached. This <MvWHILE> loops as long as `eof` is false, i.e., as long as it has not reached the end of the database.

See Also <MvWHILESTOP>

<MvWHILESTOP>

Interrupt a loop

This tag is used to stop an <MvWHILE> ... </MvWHILE> loop at any time, even if the condition for loop termination has not occurred.

Syntax

```
<MvWHILE EXPR="{expr}">
 ...
 <MvWHILESTOP>
 ...
</MvWHILE>
```

Attributes None.

Discussion

Normally, an <MvWHILE> loop executes repeatedly until the condition specified by the EXPR attribute becomes false. This tag can be used to break out of a loop before that.

Example

<MvWHILESTOP> is generally enclosed by <MvIF> and </MvIF>, so that it will not execute until some termination condition occurs, as in:

```
<MvWHILE EXPR="{something}">
 ...
 <MvIF EXPR="{scripterror}">
  <MvWHILESTOP>
 </MvIF>
 ...
</MvWHILE>
```

In this script, the variable scripterror is assumed to be normally 0, and to be set to 1 if some kind of error is detected. In that case, the <MvIF> will cause the <MvWHILESTOP> to be executed, terminating the loop.

See Also

<MvWHILE>

padl()

Pad a string with characters at the left (beginning)

This function returns a copy of a string with leading characters added to make the length equal a specified value.

Syntax

padl(*str, len, char*)

Arguments

str	String to be padded.
len	Number specifying the desired length of the string.
char	Character to use for padding.

Discussion

In databases and some other types of files, record fields are required to be a certain length. If the actual data does not use all the available space, the remainder is commonly *padded* with space characters. This function adds padding to a string by returning a copy in which one or more of the specified padding character, *char*, have been added at the left side (beginning) to make the string equal the length specified by *len*. If the string's length is already equal to or greater than *len*, no characters are added.

To add padding to the right side of a string, use padr(). To remove padding, use ltrim() or rtrim().)

Example This example places a padded copy of the variable `item` into a database field:

```
<MvASSIGN NAME="catalog.d.itemname" VALUE="{padl(item, 32,
' ')}">
```

The call to `padl()` pads the variable `item` with leading spaces to reach a length of 32 characters.

See Also `ltrim()` `padr()` `rtrim()`

padr()

Pad a string with characters at the right (end)

This function returns a copy of a string with trailing characters added to make the length equal a specified value.

Syntax **`padr(str, len, char)`**

Arguments

str	String to be padded.
len	Number specifying the desired length of the string.
char	Character to use for padding.

Discussion In databases and some other types of files, record fields are required to be a certain length. If the actual data does not use all the available space, the remainder is commonly *padded* with space characters. This function adds padding to a string by returning a copy in which one or more of the specified padding character, *char*, have been added at the right side (end) to make the string equal the length specified by *len*. If the string's length is already equal to or greater than *len*, no characters are added.

To add padding to the left side of a string, use `padl()`. To remove padding, use `ltrim()` or `rtrim()`.)

Example This example places a padded copy of the variable `item` into a database field:

```
<MvASSIGN NAME="catalog.d.itemname" VALUE="{padr(item, 32,
' ')}">
```

The call to `padr()` pads the variable `item` with leading spaces to reach a length of 32 characters.

See Also `ltrim()` `padl()` `rtrim()`

power()

Raise a number to a power

This function returns a number raised to a specified power ($base^{exponent}$).

Syntax **`power(base, exp)`**

Arguments *base* Number to be raised.

exp Power value (exponent).

Example This example sets the variable `p` to 256 (2 to the 8th power):

```
<MvASSIGN NAME="p" VALUE="{power(2, 8)}">
```

See Also `exp()` `log()` `log10()`

random()

Generate a random number

This function returns a random integer with a value between zero and the specified maximum.

Syntax **`random(max)`**

Arguments *max* Maximum value for the returned number.

Example For a simple "yes/no" decision, the expression:

```
<MvEVAL EXPR="{random(1)}">
```

will return either 0 or 1, randomly chosen.

rnd()

Round a number to a specified number of decimal places

This function returns a number that has been rounded off to have a specified number of digits to the right of the decimal point.

Syntax **`rnd(val, precision)`**

Arguments
: *val* — Number to round.
: *precision* — Number specifying how many digits to leave after the decimal point.

Discussion
: This function rounds up or down in order to return the most accurate result (see Examples).

Examples
: Assuming that the variable `x` contains the value 2.3456, the expression

```
rnd(x, 3)
```

returns 2.346 (rounding up), while the expression

```
rnd(x, 1)
```

returns 2.3 (rounding down).

See Also
: `abs()` `ceil()` `floor()` `int()`

rtrim()

Remove spaces from the right side (end) of a string

This function returns a copy of a string in which any trailing spaces are removed.

Syntax
: **`rtrim(`*`str`*`)`**

Arguments
: *str* — String to be "trimmed."

Discussion
: In databases and some other types of files, record fields are required to be a certain length. If the actual data does not use all the available space, the remainder is commonly *padded* with space characters. This function removes padding from a string by returning a copy in which any spaces at the right side (end) have been removed.

To remove spaces from the left side, use `ltrim()`. To add padding, use `padl()` or `padr()`.

Example
: This example reads a database field, and places a "trimmed" copy in the variable `item`:

```
<MvASSIGN NAME="item" VALUE="{rtrim(catalog.d.itemname)}">
```

See Also
: `ltrim()` `padl()` `padr()`

schmod()

Change permissions of a file in the scripts directory

This function changes the permission settings for a file. These settings control which users are allowed to read, modify, or execute the file.

Syntax **`schmod(`*`path`*`, `*`num`*`)`**

Arguments

path	Pathname of the file whose permissions are to be changed. The path is specified relative to the Miva scripts directory.
num	Number specifying the new permissions to set.

Discussion On multi-user systems such as Unix, a file has permission data that determines how various classes of users may use the file. In Miva Script, a file's permission settings are represented by a nine-bit binary number, consisting of three fields of three bits each. The bit fields control access to the file by the file's owner, other users in the owner's group, and users in other groups. Within each bit field, the three bits determine whether the file can be read, written, or executed. A bit value of 1 allows the access, while a value of 0 prevents it. The positions of the specific bits are listed below.

Binary	Decimal	Meaning
100000000	256	Owner may read the file.
010000000	128	Owner may write the file.
001000000	64	Owner may execute the file.
000100000	32	Other users in owner's group may read the file.
000010000	16	Other users in owner's group may write the file.
000001000	8	Other users in owner's group may execute the file.
000000100	4	Users in other groups may read the file.
000000010	2	Users in other groups may write the file.
000000001	1	Users in other groups may execute the file.

Example This example sets a file's permissions so that the owner may read or write it, while all other users may only read it. To determine the correct value, add up the values from the above table: 256 + 128 + 32 + 4 equals 420.

```
<MvIF EXPR="{schmod('myscript.mv', 420) EQ 0}">
 <B> ERROR: couldn't change file permission. </B>
</MvIF>
```

The call to schmod() is placed inside an <MvIF> in order to check for success or failure. (Like all file-system functions, schmod() returns 1 if it succeeds or 0 if it fails.)

See Also fchmod() fmode() smode()

scopy()

Copy a file in the scripts directory

This function makes a copy of the specified file.

Syntax **scopy(*from*, *to*)**

Arguments

from	Pathname of the file to copy. The path is specified relative to the Miva scripts directory.
to	Pathname of the file to create. The path is specified relative to the Miva scripts directory.

Discussion This function makes a copy of the file specified by *from*, and places it at the location specified by *to*. It returns 1 if the copy is successful, or 0 if it fails.

Example

```
<MvIF EXPR="{NOT scopy('work/shopping.mv',
'backup/shopping.mv')}">

 ERROR: Unable to make backup copy!!!

</MvIF>
```

In this example, the call to scopy() is placed in an <MvIF>. If the returned value is 0, indicating that the copy did not succeed, the script displays an error message.

See Also fcopy() fscopy() sfcopy()

sdelete()

Delete a file in the scripts directory

This function deletes the specified file.

Syntax **sdelete(*path*)**

Arguments

path	Pathname of the file to delete. The path is specified relative to the Miva scripts directory.

Discussion

This function deletes the specified file. It returns 1 if it succeeds, or 0 if it fails. It cannot be used to delete directories.

Example

```
<MvASSIGN NAME="dummy" VALUE="{sdelete('tempfile.dat')}">
```

In this example, the result returned by `sdelete()` is assigned to a dummy variable, in order to prevent it from appearing on the user's screen.

See Also

`fdelete()`

sexists()

Check whether a file exists in the scripts directory

This function returns 1 if the specified file exists, or 0 otherwise.

Syntax

`sexists(`*`path`*`)`

Arguments

path	Pathname to check, specified relative to the Miva scripts directory.

Example

This example checks if a script file exists. If it does, the script reads it; otherwise, the script displays an error message.

```
<MvIF EXPR="{sexists('somefile.htm')}">
 <MvDO FILE="somefile.htm">
<MvELSE>
 ERROR: Couldn't find file.
</MvIF>
```

See Also

`fexists()`

sfcopy()

Copy a file from the scripts directory to the data directory

This function makes a copy of the specified file.

Syntax

`sfcopy(`*`from, to`*`)`

Arguments

from	Pathname of the file to copy. The path is specified relative to the Miva scripts directory.
to	Pathname of the file to create. The path is specified relative to the Miva data directory.

Discussion — This function makes a copy of the file specified by *from*, and places it at the location specified by *to*. It returns 1 if the copy is successful, or 0 if it fails.

Example

```
<MvIF EXPR="{NOT sfcopy('work/shopping.mv',
'shopmiva.txt')}">
 ERROR: Unable to make copy!!!
</MvIF>
```

In this example, the call to `sfcopy()` is placed in an <MvIF>. If the returned value is 0, indicating that the copy did not succeed, the script displays an error message.

See Also — `fcopy()` `fscopy()` `scopy()`

sfrename()

Rename or move a file from the scripts directory to the data directory

This function can change the name of the specified file, and also moves it to a new location relative to the data directory.

Syntax — **`sfrename(`*`from, to`*`)`**

Arguments

from	Pathname of the file to rename or move. The path is specified relative to the Miva scripts directory.
to	New name and/or location of the file. The path is specified relative to the Miva data directory.

Discussion — This function removes the file from the name and directory specified by *from*, and assigns it the name and directory location specified by *to*. It returns 1 if it is successful, or 0 if it fails.

Example

```
<MvIF EXPR="{NOT sfrename('shopping.mv',
'scriptdata.txt')}">
 ERROR: Unable to move file to data directory!!!
</MvIF>
```

In this example, the call to `sfrename()` is placed in an <MvIF>. If the returned value is 0, indicating that the `sfrename()` did not succeed, the script displays an error message.

See Also — `frename()` `fsrename()` `srename()`

sin()

Compute sine

This function returns the sine of a number.

Syntax **`sin(`*`num`*`)`**

Arguments *num* — Number whose sine is to be returned.

Discussion This function returns a value between –1 and 1. Note that *num* represents an angle in radians, not degrees (see Example).

Example To compute the sine of an angle expressed in degrees, rather than radians, use a statement such as:

```
<MvASSIGN NAME="y" VALUE="{sin(theta / 57.2958)}">
```

See Also `acos()` `asin()` `atan()` `atan2()` `cos()` `cosh()` `sinh()` `tan()` `tanh()`

sinh()

Compute hyperbolic sine

This function returns the hyperbolic sine of a number.

Syntax **`sinh(`*`num`*`)`**

Arguments *num* — Number whose hyperbolic sine is to be returned.

Example

```
<MvASSIGN NAME="y" VALUE="{sinh(theta)}">
```

See Also `acos()` `asin()` `atan()` `atan2()` `cos()` `cosh()` `sin()` `tan()` `tanh()`

smkdir()

Create a subdirectory in the scripts directory

This function creates the specified directory.

Syntax **`smkdir(`*`path`*`)`**

Arguments *path* — Pathname of the directory to create. The path is specified relative to the Miva scripts directory.

Discussion This function creates the specified directory. It returns 1 if it succeeds, or 0 if it fails.

Example

```
<MvIF EXPR="{NOT smkdir('tempdocs')}">
 ERROR: Unable to create directory!!!
</MvIF>
```

In this example, the call to smkdir() is placed in an <MvIF>. If the returned value is 0, indicating that Miva was not able to create the directory, the script displays an error message.

See Also fmkdir()

smode()

Check permissions of a file in the scripts directory

This function returns a number representing the permission settings for a file. These settings control which users are allowed to read, modify, or execute the file.

Syntax **smode(*path*)**

Arguments *path* Pathname of the file to check. The path is specified relative to the Miva scripts directory.

Discussion On multi-user systems such as Unix, a file has permission data that determines how various classes of users may use the file. In Miva Script, a file's permission settings are presented by a nine-bit binary number, consisting of three fields of three bits each. The bit fields control access to the file by the file's owner, other users in the owner's group, and users in other groups. Within each bit field, the three bits determine whether the file can be read, written, or executed. A bit value of 1 allows the access, while a value of 0 prevents it. The positions of the specific bits are listed below.

Binary	Decimal	Meaning
100000000	256	Owner may read the file.
010000000	128	Owner may write the file.
001000000	64	Owner may execute the file.
000100000	32	Other users in owner's group may read the file.
000010000	16	Other users in owner's group may write the file.
000001000	8	Other users in owner's group may execute the file.

Binary	Decimal	Meaning
000000100	4	Users in other groups may read the file.
000000010	2	Users in other groups may write the file.
000000001	1	Users in other groups may execute the file.

Example

To test individual permission settings, use bitwise operators with bit masks taken from the above table. For instance, to check whether users in other groups may read the file, use a mask value of 4 in an expression such as:

```
<MvIF EXPR="{smode('somescript.mv') BITAND 4"}>
 Reading is permitted.
<ELSE>
 <B> ERROR: cannot read the file. </B>
</MvIF>
```

If reading the file is permitted, the `BITAND` expression will return 4; otherwise, it will return 0.

See Also

`fchmod()` `fmode()` `schmod()`

sqrt()

Compute square root

This function returns the square root of a number.

Syntax

`sqrt(`*`num`*`)`

Arguments

num	Number whose square root is to be returned.

Example

```
<MvASSIGN NAME="y" VALUE="{sqrt(x)}">
```

srename()

Rename or move a file in the scripts directory

This function changes the name of the specified file, and/or moves it to a different directory.

Syntax **`srename(`*`from, to`*`)`**

Arguments

`from` — Pathname of the file to rename or move. The path is specified relative to the Miva scripts directory.

`to` — New name and/or location of the file. The path is specified relative to the Miva scripts directory.

Discussion This function removes the file from the name and directory specified by *`from`*, and assigns it the name and directory location specified by *`to`*. It returns 1 if it is successful, or 0 if it fails.

Example

```
<MvIF EXPR="{NOT srename('temp/shopping.mv',
'work/shopping.mv')}">

 ERROR: Unable to move file to work directory!!!

</MvIF>
```

In this example, the call to `srename()` is placed in an `<MvIF>`. If the returned value is 0, indicating that the `srename()` did not succeed, the script displays an error message.

See Also `frename()` `fsrename()` `sfrename()`

ssize()

Check size of a file in the scripts directory

This function returns a number that specifies the number of bytes of data in a file.

Syntax **`ssize(`*`path`*`)`**

Arguments

`path` — Pathname of the file to check. The path is specified relative to the Miva scripts directory.

Discussion If this function is unable to determine the file size, it returns –1.

Example

```
The file named <MvEVAL EXPR="{myfile}">

contains <MvEVAL EXPR="{ssize(myfile)}"> bytes.
```

See Also `fsize()`

ssymlink()

Create a symbolic link to a file in the scripts directory.

This function creates a symbolic link to a file (also called an alias or shortcut on some platforms).

Syntax **`ssymlink(`*`file, lnk`*`)`**

Arguments

`file`	Pathname of the file to which to link. The path is specified relative to the Miva scripts directory.
`lnk`	Pathname of the link. The path is specified relative to the Miva scripts directory.

Discussion This function creates a symbolic link, which allows one physical file to appear in several directories. It returns 1 if it is successful, or 0 if it fails.

Example

```
<MvIF EXPR="{NOT ssymlink('archive/dec99.mv',
'lastmonth.mv')}"> ERROR: unable to create link to old
script.

</MvIF>
```

See Also `fsymlink()`

substring()

Return part of a string

This function returns a string containing a specified part of a longer string.

Syntax **`substring(`*`str, pos, len`*`)`**

Arguments

`str`	String from which to copy the substring.
`pos`	Number specifying the position of the substring to copy.
`len`	Number of characters to copy.

Discussion This function returns a copy of a portion of the source string *`str`* with the specified position and length. If the length would extend beyond the end of *`str`*, only characters up to the end of *`str`* are returned.

Example To obtain a copy of the first character of a string, use an expression such as:

```
<MvASSIGN NAME="firstchar" EXPR="{substring(mytext, 1,
1)}">
```

See Also `gettoken()`

tan()

Compute tangent

This function returns the tangent of a number.

Syntax `tan(num)`

Arguments *num* Number whose tangent is to be returned.

Example To compute the tangent of an angle expressed in degrees, rather than radians, use a statement such as:

```
<MvASSIGN NAME="y" VALUE="{tan(theta / 57.2958)}">
```

See Also `acos() asin() atan() atan2() cos() cosh() sin() sinh() tanh()`

tanh()

Compute hyperbolic tangent

This function returns the hyperbolic tangent of a number.

Syntax `tanh(num)`

Arguments *num* Number whose hyperbolic tangent is to be returned.

Example

```
<MvASSIGN NAME="y" VALUE="{tanh(theta)}">
```

See Also `acos() asin() atan() atan2() cos() cosh() sin() sinh() tan()`

time_t_dayofmonth() time_t_dayofweek() time_t_dayofyear() time_t_hour() time_t_min() time_t_month() time_t_sec() time_t_year()

Return the portions of a time/date value

These functions extract various values from a number representing a time and date in universal format.

Syntax

`time_t_year(`*`time, zone`*`)`	Returns year (4 digits).
`time_t_month(`*`time, zone`*`)`	Returns the month (from 1 to 12).
`time_t_dayofmonth(`*`time, zone`*`)`	Returns the day of the month (from 1 to 31).
`time_t_dayofweek(`*`time, zone`*`)`	Returns the day of the week (Sunday = 1, Monday = 2, etc.).
`time_t_dayofyear(`*`time, zone`*`)`	Returns the day of the year (from 1 to 366).
`time_t_hour(`*`time, zone`*`)`	Returns the hour (from 0 to 23).
`time_t_min(`*`time, zone`*`)`	Returns the minute (from 0 to 59).
`time_t_sec(`*`time, zone`*`)`	Returns the second (from 0 to 59).

Arguments

`time`	Variable or other expression representing a time/date in universal format.
`zone`	Number specifying the time zone in which to evaluate the time and date.

Discussion

Miva supports storing times and dates in a universal format consisting of a single large number representing the number of seconds since midnight, January 1, 1970, universal time (also called Greenwich Mean Time or GMT). These functions allow you to extract the individual values contained in one of these numbers. Note that you must specify the time zone, so that Miva can adjust from universal time to the local time zone.

Caution: Miva time functions cannot be used with dates earlier than January 1, 1970, or later than January 19, 2038.

Example

This example prints the current date and time:

```
The time is now
<MvEVAL EXPR="{time_t_hour(time_t, z)}"> :
<MvEVAL EXPR="{time_t_min(time_t, z)}"> :
<MvEVAL EXPR="{time_t_sec(time_t, z)}"> on
<MvEVAL EXPR="{time_t_month(time_t, z)}"> /
<MvEVAL EXPR="{time_t_dayofmonth(time_t, z)}"> /
<MvEVAL EXPR="{time_t_year(time_t, z)}"> . <P>
```

This script obtains the current time and date from the Miva system variable `time_t`. It then uses various functions to extract the individual values for hour, minute, etc. (The variable `z` is assumed to contain the correct local time zone.) The resulting display looks something like this:

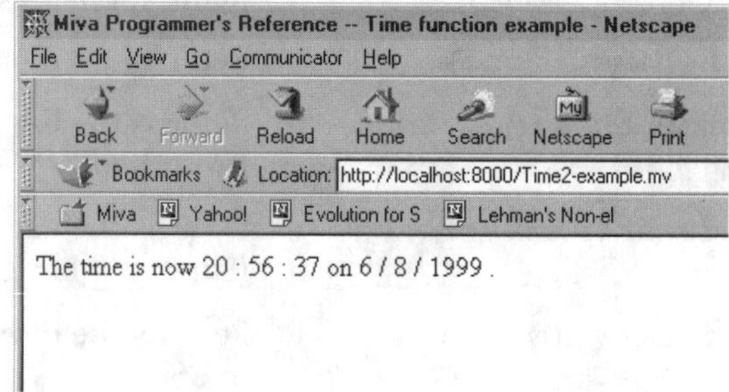

See Also `mktime_t() timezone()`

timezone()

Return the local time zone

This function returns a number specifying the local time zone.

Syntax **`timezone()`**

Arguments None.

Discussion This function returns an integer representing the difference between local time and universal time (also known as Greenwich Mean Time or GMT). For example, on a system in Greenwich, England, `timezone()` returns 0. On the U.S. east coast, 4 hours behind Greenwich, `timezone()` returns –4.

Caution: This function does not discriminate between Standard Time and Daylight Savings Time.

Example To obtain the current time zone, use a script such as:

```
<MvASSIGN NAME="myzone" VALUE="{timezone()}">
```

See Also `mktime_t() time_t_dayofmonth() time_t_dayofweek() time_t_dayofyear() time_t_hour() time_t_min() time_t_month() time_t_sec() time_t_year()`

tolower()

Convert letters to lowercase

This function returns a copy of a string in which all uppercase letters have been changed to their lowercase equivalents.

Syntax **`tolower(`*`str`*`)`**

Arguments *`str`* String to be converted.

Discussion Since users often type an irregular mixture of upper- and lowercase, it is useful to convert user input to a single case, in order to make sorting and searching easier. (To convert letters to uppercase, use `toupper()`.)

Any characters other than uppercase letters are included unchanged in the result.

Example This example converts a person's name to lowercase before storing it in a database:

```
<MvASSIGN NAME="customers.d.name"
VALUE="{tolower(username)}">
```

(The variable `username` is assumed to contain the name that was passed to the script after the user typed it into an HTML form.)

See Also `glosub()` `toupper()`

toupper()

Convert letters to uppercase

This function returns a copy of a string in which all lowercase letters have been changed to their uppercase equivalents.

Syntax **`toupper(`*`str`*`)`**

Arguments *`str`* String to be converted.

Discussion Since users often type an irregular mixture of upper- and lowercase, it is useful to convert user input to a single case, in order to make sorting and searching easier. (To convert letters to lowercase, use `tolower()`.)

Any characters other than lowercase letters are included unchanged in the result.

Example This example converts a person's name to uppercase before storing it in a database:

```
<MvASSIGN NAME="customers.d.name"
VALUE="{toupper(username)}">
```

(The variable `username` is assumed to contain the name that was passed to the script after the user typed it into an HTML form.)

See Also `glosub()` `tolower()`

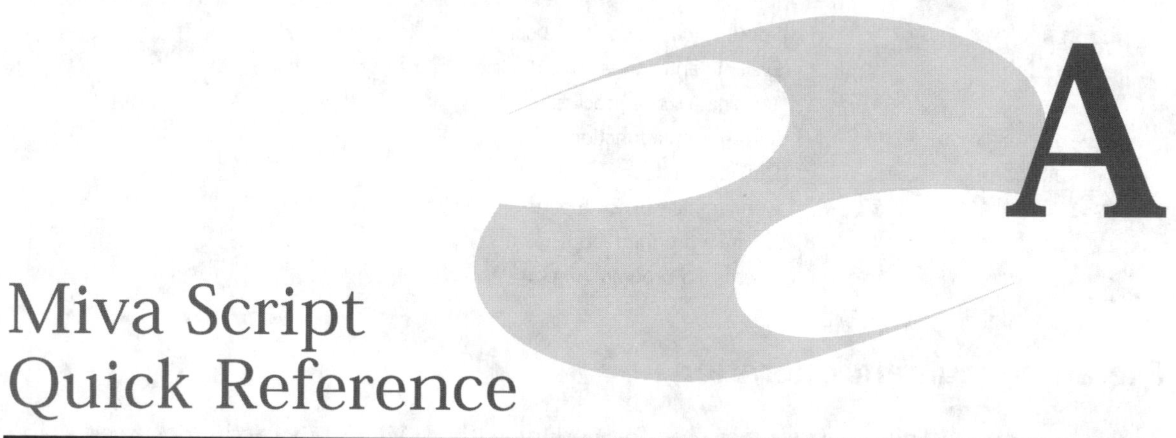

Miva Script Quick Reference

This Appendix provides reference information about Miva Script tags and system functions. For complete information, all tags and functions are described in detail, and listed in alphabetical order, in the Reference section of this manual.

Summary of Miva Tags

The following tables give quick lists of Miva Script tags, divided into categories by their usage.

Basic structure and control

This table lists tags used for basic program functions such as working with variables and creating loops.

Tag	Function
<MIVA>	Configure Miva processing
<MvASSIGN>	Assign a value to a Miva variable
<MvCOMMENT>	Provide descriptive text

Tag	Function
<MvELSE>	Specify alternate part of a conditional block
<MvEVAL>	Evaluate an expression and place it in the output stream
<MvEXIT>	Terminate script processing
<MvFUNCRETURN>	Return from a function
<MvFUNCTION>	Define a function
<MvIF>	Conditionally execute parts of a script
<MvWHILE>	Create a program loop
<MvWHILESTOP>	Interrupt a program loop

File and document operations

This table lists tags used for working with HTML or Miva Script documents, and other files containing text.

Tag	Function
<MvCALL>	Send an HTTP request
<MvCALLSTOP>	Interrupt an HTTP request
<MvDO>	Run a script in an external file
<MvEXPORT>	Write data to an external file
<MvHIDE>	Add hidden data to a form
<MvIMPORT>	Read data from an external file
<MvIMPORTSTOP>	Interrupt reading of an external file
<MvLOCKFILE>	Request exclusive use of a file

Database operations

This table lists tags used for working with database files.

Tag	Function
<MvADD>	Add a record to a database
<MvCLOSE>	Close a database
<MvCLOSEVIEW>	Close a database view
<MvCREATE>	Create a database
<MvDELETE>	Mark a database record for deletion
<MvFILTER>	Apply a filter to a database
<MvFIND>	Find a database record
<MvGO>	Access a specific record in a database

Tag	Function
<MvMAKEINDEX>	Create a database index
<MvOPEN>	Open a database
<MvOPENVIEW>	Create a view of a database and run an SQL query
<MvPACK>	Compress a database
<MvPRIMARY>	Select a primary database
<MvQUERY>	Submit an SQL query
<MvREINDEX>	Rebuild database index files
<MvREVEALSTRUCTURE>	Read database record format
<MvSETINDEX>	Select indexes for database navigation
<MvSKIP>	Move sequentially through a database
<MvUNDELETE>	Restore deleted records to a database
<MvUPDATE>	Modify a database record

E-mail and e-commerce

This table lists tags used for accessing mail servers and performing e-commerce transactions.

Tag	Function
<MvCOMMERCE>	Perform an e-commerce transaction
<MvCOMMERCESTOP>	Interrupt an e-commerce transaction
<MvPOP>	Read e-mail
<MvPOPDELETE>	Delete an e-mail message from a server
<MvPOPSTOP>	Stop reading e-mail
<MvSMTP>	Send e-mail

Summary of System Functions

The following tables give quick lists of Miva Script system functions, divided into categories by their usage.

Time and date operations

This table lists functions for working with times and dates in universal format.

Name	Action
mktime_t()	Create a universal time/date value
time_t_dayofmonth()	Returns the day of the month (from 1 to 31)
time_t_dayofweek()	Returns the day of the week (Sunday = 1, Monday = 2, etc.)
time_t_dayofyear()	Returns the day of the year (from 1 to 366)
time_t_hour()	Returns the hour (from 0 to 23)
time_t_min()	Returns the minute (from 0 to 59)
time_t_month()	Returns the month (from 1 to 12)
time_t_sec()	Returns the second (from 0 to 59)
time_t_year()	Returns year (4 digits)
timezone()	Return the local time zone

String manipulation

This table lists functions for working with text in string variables.

Name	Action
asciichar()	Convert a number to a character
asciivalue()	Convert a character to a number
decodeattribute()	Convert URL to normal text
decodeentities()	Convert entity-encoded characters to normal text
encodeattribute()	Convert normal text to URL format
encodeentities()	Convert normal text to entity-encoded format
gettoken()	Find a token in a string
glosub()	Perform global substitution on a string
isalnum()	Returns 1 if all characters in the string are alphanumeric (letters or digits).
isalpha()	Returns 1 if all characters in the string are letters.
isascii()	Returns 1 if all characters in the string are valid ASCII characters (values 0-127).
iscntrl()	Returns 1 if all characters in the string are control characters (values 0-31 or 127).
isdigit()	Returns 1 if all characters in the string are decimal digits.
isgraph()	Returns 1 if all characters in the string are graphic characters (values 33-127).
islower()	Returns 1 if all characters in the string are lowercase letters.
isprint()	Returns 1 if all characters in the string are printable characters (values 32-127).
ispunct()	Returns 1 if all characters in the string are punctuation symbols (graphic characters that are not letters or digits).
isspace()	Returns 1 if all characters in the string are white space: space (32), tab (9), vertical tab (11), Newline (10), or form feed (12).
isupper()	Returns 1 if all characters in the string are uppercase letters.
isxdigit()	Returns 1 if all characters in the string are hexadecimal digits: decimal digits, or letters A-F (upper or lowercase).

Name	Action
`len()`	Return the length of a string
`ltrim()`	Remove spaces from the left (front) of a string
`padl()`	Pad a string with characters at the left (beginning)
`padr()`	Pad a string with characters at the right (end)
`rtrim()`	Remove spaces from the right side (end) of a string
`substring()`	Return part of a string
`tolower()`	Convert letters to lowercase
`toupper()`	Convert letters to uppercase

Mathematical functions

This table lists functions for performing mathematical and numeric operations.

Name	Action
`abs()`	Compute absolute value
`acos()`	Compute arccosine
`asin()`	Compute arcsine
`atan()`	Compute arctangent
`atan2()`	Compute arctangent of quotient
`ceil()`	Compute "ceiling" (lowest greater integer) of a number
`cos()`	Compute cosine
`cosh()`	Compute hyperbolic cosine
`exp()`	Compute *e* to the power of a number
`floor()`	Compute "floor" (greatest lower integer) of a number
`fmod()`	Compute floating-point remainder
`int()`	Return integer part of a number
`log()`	Compute natural logarithm
`log10()`	Compute base-10 logarithm
`power()`	Raise a number to a power
`random()`	Generate a random number
`rnd()`	Round a number to a specified number of decimal places
`sin()`	Compute sine
`sinh()`	Compute hyperbolic sine
`sqrt()`	Compute square root
`tan()`	Compute tangent
`tanh()`	Compute hyperbolic tangent

File system operations

This table lists functions for working with files on the Miva server's disk drives.

Name	Action
fchmod()	Change permissions of a file in the data directory
fcopy()	Copy a file in the data directory
fdelete()	Delete a file in the data directory
fexists()	Check whether a file exists in the data directory
fmkdir()	Create a subdirectory in the data directory
fmode()	Check permissions on a file in the data directory
frename()	Rename or move a file in the data directory
fscopy()	Copy a file from the data directory to the scripts directory
fsize()	Check size of a file in the data directory
fsrename()	Rename or move a file from the data directory to the scripts directory
fsymlink()	Create a link or alias to a file in the data directory
schmod()	Change permissions of a file in the scripts directory
scopy()	Copy a file in the scripts directory
sdelete()	Delete a file in the scripts directory
sexists()	Check whether a file exists in the scripts directory
sfcopy()	Copy a file from the scripts directory to the data directory
sfrename()	Rename or move a file from the scripts directory to the data directory
smkdir()	Create a subdirectory in the scripts directory
smode()	Check permissions on a file in the scripts directory
srename()	Rename or move a file in the scripts directory
ssize()	Check size of a file in the scripts directory
ssymlink()	Creat a link or alias to a file in the data directory.

Miscellaneous functions

This table lists some other useful Miva Script functions.

Name	Action
makesessionid()	Return a session identifier
miva_getvarlist()	Return a list of script variable names

abs(*num*)

Compute absolute value

num Number whose absolute value is to be returned.

Acos(*num*)

Compute arccosine

num Number whose arccosine is to be returned.

asciichar(*num*)

Convert a number to a character

num ASCII value.

asciivalue(*str*)

Convert a character to a number

str String expression or variable containing a single character.

asin(*num*)

Compute arcsine

num Number whose arcsine is to be returned.

atan(*num*)

Compute arctangent

num Number whose arctangent is to be returned.

atan2(*num1, num2*)

Compute arctangent of quotient

num1, num2 Numbers whose arctangent is to be returned (see Discussion).

ceil(*num*)

Compute "ceiling" (lowest greater integer) of a number

num Number whose ceiling is to be returned.

cos(*num*)

Compute cosine

num Number whose cosine is to be returned.

cosh(*num*)

Compute hyperbolic cosine

num Number whose hyperbolic cosine is to be returned.

decodeattribute (*str*)

Convert URL to normal text

str String to be decoded.

decodeentities (*str*)

Convert entity-encoded characters to normal text

str String to be decoded.

encodeattribute (*str*)

Convert normal text to URL format

str String to be encoded.

encodeentities (*str*)

Convert normal text to entity-encoded format

`str`	String to be encoded.

exp(*num*)

Compute a power of *e*

`num`	Exponent.

fchmod(*path, num*)

Change permissions of a file in the data directory

`path`	Pathname of the file whose permissions are to be changed. The path is specified relative to the Miva data directory.
`num`	Number specifying the new permissions to set.

fcopy(*from, to*)

Copy a file in the data directory

`from`	Pathname of the file to copy. The path is specified relative to the Miva data directory.
`to`	Pathname of the file to create. The path is specified relative to the Miva data directory.

fdelete(*path*)

Delete a file in the data directory

`path`	Pathname of the file to delete. The path is specified relative to the Miva data directory.

fexists(*path*)

Check whether a file exists in the data directory

`path`	Pathname to check, specified relative to the Miva data directory.

floor(*num*)

Compute "floor" (greatest lower integer) of a number

`num`	Number whose floor is to be returned.

fmkdir(*path*)

Create a subdirectory in the data directory

`path`	Pathname of the directory to create. The path is specified relative to the Miva data directory.

fmod(*num1, num2*)

Compute floating-point remainder

`num1`	Dividend.
`num2`	Divisor.

fmode(*path*)

Check permissions of a file in the data directory

`path`	Pathname of the file to check. The path is specified relative to the Miva data directory.

frename(*from, to*)

Rename or move a file in the data directory

`from`	Pathname of the file to rename or move. The path is specified relative to the Miva data directory.
`to`	New name and/or location of the file. The path is specified relative to the Miva data directory.

fscopy(*from, to*)

Copy a file from the data directory to the scripts directory

from	Pathname of the file to copy. The path is specified relative to the Miva data directory.
to	Pathname of the file to create. The path is specified relative to the Miva scripts directory.

fsize(*path*)

Check size of a file in the data directory

path	Pathname of the file to check. The path is specified relative to the Miva data directory.

fsrename(*from, to*)

Rename or move a file from the data directory to the scripts directory

from	Pathname of the file to rename or move. The path is specified relative to the Miva data directory.
to	New name and/or location of the file. The path is specified relative to the Miva scripts directory.

gettoken(*str, separators, n*)

Find a token in a string

str	String to search for the token.
separators	String containing characters to be considered as separators between tokens.
n	Number specifying which token to return.

glosub(*str, old, new*)

Perform global substitution on a string

str	String to search.
old	Substring for which to search.
new	Substring to replace occurrences of *old*.

int(*num*)

Return integer part of a number

num	Number whose integer part is to be returned.

is---(*str*)

Test characters in a string

isalnum(*str*)	Returns 1 if all characters in the string are alphanumeric (letters or digits).
isalpha(*str*)	Returns 1 if all characters in the string are letters.
isascii(*str*)	Returns 1 if all characters in the string are valid ASCII characters (values 0–127).
iscntrl(*str*)	Returns 1 if all characters in the string are control characters (values 0–31 or 127).
isdigit(*str*)	Returns 1 if all characters in the string are decimal digits.
isgraph(*str*)	Returns 1 if all characters in the string are graphic characters (values 33–127).
islower(*str*)	Returns 1 if all characters in the string are lowercase letters.
isprint(*str*)	Returns 1 if all characters in the string are printable characters (values 32–127).
ispunct(*str*)	Returns 1 if all characters in the string are punctuation symbols (graphic characters that are not letters or digits).
isspace(*str*)	Returns 1 if all characters in the string are white space: space (32), tab (9), vertical tab (11), Newline (10), or form feed (12).
isupper(*str*)	Returns 1 if all characters in the string are uppercase letters.
isxdigit(*str*)	Returns 1 if all characters in the string are hexadecimal digits: decimal digits, or letters A–F (upper- or lowercase).
str	String to be tested.

len(*str*)

Return the length of a string

str	String to measure.

log(*num*)

Compute natural logarithm

num Number whose natural logarithm is to be returned.

log10(*num*)

Compute base-10 logarithm

num Number whose base-10 logarithm is to be returned.

ltrim(*str*)

Remove spaces from the left (front) of a string

str String to be "trimmed."

makesessionid()

Return a session identifier

makesessionid()

<MIVA

Configure Miva processing

INTERPRET="*str*"	macros tags
STANDARDOUTPUTLEVEL="*str*"	html text
ERROROUTPUTLEVEL="*str*"	expression runtime syntax
ERRORMESSAGE="*messagetext*"	
*tagname*_ERROR="*str*"	fatal nonfatal display nodisplay

>

miva_getvarlist(*scope*)

Return a list of script variable names

scope String that specifies the scope:

local or *l*	Local variables.
global or *g*	Global variables.
system or *s*	System variables.
database or *d*	Database variables.

mktime_t(*yr, mo, dy, hr, min, sec, zone*)

Create a universal time/date value

yr	Year.
mo	Month.
dy	Day of the month.
hr	Hour.
min	Minute.
sec	Second.
zone	Time zone.

<MvADD

Add a record to a database

NAME="*alias*" If omitted, add to the primary database

>

<MvASSIGN

Assign a value to a Miva variable

NAME="*var*"
VALUE="*expr*"

>

<MvCALL

Send an HTML request

ACTION="*URL*"	
METHOD="*str*"	`GET POST`
FIELDS="*var1,var2,var3...*"	Miva variables to include in the request
FILES="*file1,file2,file3...*"	Files to upload with the request

>

...

</MvCALL>

Variables

`callobjecttype`	`text tag`
`callvalue`	Actual text of the entire object
`callobjectelement`	The tag name, without angle brackets
`callobjectnumattributes`	The number of attributes for the tag
`callobjectattribute(1, 2, ...)`	The name of tag attribute number 1, 2, ...
`callobjectvalue(1, 2, ...)`	The value assigned to tag attribute number 1, 2, ...
`callnumberofheaders`	The number of HTTP headers received
`callreturnheader(1, 2, ...)`	The text of header number 1, 2, ...

<MvCALLSTOP>

Interrupt an HTML request

```
<MvCALL attrs>

  ...

  <MvCALLSTOP>

  ...

</MvCALL>
```

<MvCLOSE

Close a database

NAME="*alias*"	If omitted, close the primary database

>

<MvCLOSEVIEW

Close a database view

NAME="*alias*"	If omitted, close the primary database
VIEW="*viewname*"	

>

<MvCOMMENT>

Provide descriptive text

```
    ... any type of text ...
  </MvCOMMENT>
```

<MvCOMMERCE

Perform an e-commerce transaction

```
    ACTION="URL"
    METAMETHOD="str"                    SCMP CyberCash UPSCost
    FIELDS="var1,var2,..."
>
    ...
  </MvCOMMERCE>
```

Variables (Depends on protocol; see Chapter 8.)

<MvCOMMERCESTOP>

Interrupt an HTML request

```
  <MvCOMMERCE attrs>
    ...
   <MvCOMMERCESTOP>
    ...
  </MvCOMMERCE>
```

Variables (Depends on protocol; see Chapter 8.)

<MvCREATE

Create a database

```
    NAME="alias"
    DATABASE="pathname"
    TYPE="str"                Currently, xbase3 is the only supported value.
    FIELDS="name1 type1,      (See table below)
    name2 type2, ..."
>
```

type Specifier	Meaning
CHAR(*n*)	The field may contain a string of up to *n* characters. The maximum value for *n* is 254.
NUMBER	The field may contain a number up to 19 digits long. The value may not include a decimal point, i.e., integer value only.
NUMBER(*n*)	The field may contain a number up to *n* digits long. The value may not include a decimal point, i.e., integer value only.
NUMBER(*m*.*n*)	The field may contain a number with up to *m* digits before the decimal point, and up to *n* digits after it.

type Specifier	Meaning	
BOOL	The field may contain a logical or Boolean value: 0 representing false, and 1 representing true.	
DATE	The field may contain a date and time in universal format. When you create a DATE field with name *dvar*, Miva also creates the following variables to provide a convenient way to read and change the value:	
	*dvar*_year	Specifies the year as a 4-digit number.
	*dvar*_month	Specifies the month as a 2-digit number.
	*dvar*_day	Specifies the day of the month as a 2-digit number.
	*dvar*_raw	Specifies the entire date as an 8-character string: 'YYYYMMDD' for year, month, and day.
	For more details on storing times and dates in databases, see Chapter 6.	
MEMO	This field may contain a string of any size; unlike CHAR, there is no limit on MEMO fields. This flexibility comes at the cost of some additional overhead, since the fields are stored in a separate file from the rest of the database. This file will have the same name as the main database file, but with an extension of .dbt. For efficiency, you should use CHAR fields when possible.	

<MvDELETE

Mark a database record for deletion

NAME="*alias*"	If omitted, delete from the primary database

>

<MvDO

Run a script in an external file

FILE="*pathname*"	
NAME="*var*"	Name of a variable to receive the result returned by the function
VALUE="{*func*(*args*)}"	

>

<MvELSE>

Specify alternate part of a conditional block

```
<MvIF EXPR="{expr}">

  ... "true" part ...

<MvELSE>

  ... "false" part ...

</MvIF>
```

<MvEVAL

Evaluate an expression and place it in the output stream

EXPR="{*expr*}"

>

<MvEXIT>

Terminate script processing

<MvEXPORT

Write data to an external file

```
FILE="pathname"
FIELDS="var1,var2,..."
DELIMITER="str"
```

>

<MvFILTER

Apply a filter to a database

`NAME="alias"`	If omitted, filter the primary database
`FILTER="{expr}"`	If omitted, Miva remove any filter that may currently be in effect for this database connection

>

<MvFIND

Find a database record

`NAME="alias"`	If omitted, use the primary database
`VALUE="str"`	
`EXACT="EXACT"`	

>

<MvFUNCRETURN>

Return from a function

```
<MvFUNCTION attrs>

 ...

 <MvFUNCRETURN

  VALUE="{expr}"

 >

 ...

</MvFUNCTION>
```

<MvFUNCTION

Define a function

```
NAME="funcname"
PARAMETERS="var1,var2,..."
STANDARDOUTPUTLEVEL="str"
ERROROUTPUTLEVEL="str"
```

>

```
 ...

</MvFUNCTION>
```

<MvGO

Access a specific record in a database

```
NAME="alias"                If omitted, use the primary database
ROW="position"
VIEW="viewname"
>
```

<MvHIDE

Add hidden data to a form

```
FIELDS="var1,var2,..."

>
```

<MvIF>

Conditionally execute parts of a script

```
<MvIF

 EXPR="{expr}">

>

 ... "true" part ...

<MvELSE>

 ... "false" part ...

</MvIF>
```

<MvIMPORT

Read data from an external file

```
FILE="filename"
FIELDS="var1,var2,..."
DELIMITER="str"
FILTER="{expr}"
>

 ...

</MvIMPORT>
```

Variables `recno` Count of records read, starting with 1

<MvIMPORTSTOP>

Interrupt reading of an external file

```
<MvIMPORT attrs>

 ...

 <MvIMPORTSTOP>

 ...
```

```
</MvIMPORT>
```

Variables `recno` Count of records read, starting with 1

<MvLET>

(Replaced by <MvASSIGN>)

Supported for compatibility with older scripts

<MvLOCKFILE

Request exclusive use of a file

```
FILE="filename"
>
...
</MvLOCKFILE>
```

<MvMAKEINDEX

Create a database index

Attribute	Description
`NAME="alias"`	If omitted, use the primary database
`INDEXFILE="pathname"`	
`EXPR="{expr}"`	Miva key expression to use for sorting database records

`FLAGS="str"`	`ascending` (default)
	`descending`
	`unique`
	`nounique` (default)
	`string`

>

<MvOPEN

Open a database

Attribute	Description
`NAME="alias"`	
`DATABASE="pathname"`	
`TYPE="str"`	`xbase3` (default) `odbc`
`INDEXES="file1,file2,..."`	
`USER="str"`	User name (optional; for ODBC only)
`PASSWORD="str"`	Password (optional; for ODBC only)

>

<MvOPENVIEW

Create a view of a database and run an SQL query

Attribute	Description
`NAME="alias"`	If omitted, use the primary database
`VIEW="viewname"`	
`QUERY="str"`	SQL query that is used to request data

>

<MvPACK

Compress a database

`NAME="alias"`	If omitted, use the primary database

>

<MvPOP

Read e-mail

```
MAILHOST="host"
LOGIN="username"
PASSWORD="pwd"
DIRECTORY="path"
```

>

```
...

</MvPOP>
```

Variables		
	`messagebody`	Name of the filename in which the message is stored
	`messagesubject`	Contents of the message's `Subject:` field
	`messagereplyto`	Contents of the message's `Reply-To:` field
	`messagesender`	Contents of the message's `From:` field
	`messagedate`	Contents of the message's `Date:` field

<MvPOPDELETE>

Delete an e-mail message from a server

```
<MvPOP attrs>

 ...

 <MvPOPDELETE>

 ...

</MvPOP>
```

Variables See <MvPOP>

<MvPOPSTOP>

Stop reading e-mail

```
<MvPOP attrs>

 ...

<MvPOPSTOP>

 ...

</MvPOP>
```

Variables See <MvPOP>

<MvPRIMARY

Select a primary database

NAME="*alias*"

>

<MvQUERY

Submit an SQL query

NAME="*alias*"	If omitted, use the primary database
QUERY="*str*"	SQL query string

>

<MvREINDEX

Rebuild database index files

NAME="*alias*"	If omitted, use the primary database

>

<MvREVEALSTRUCTURE

Read database record format

NAME="*alias*"	If omitted, use the primary database
DATABASE="*pathname*"	

>

Variables Each record of the newly created database contains fields that give information about one field of the database being examined:

field_name	Name of the field	
field_type	C	CHAR
	N	NUMBER
	D	DATE
	L	logical (BOOL)
	M	MEMO
field_len	Length of the field	
field_dec	Number of digits after the decimal point (NUMBER fields only)	

<MvSETINDEX

Select indexes for database navigation

NAME="*alias*"	If omitted, use the primary database
INDEXES="*file1,file2,...*"	

>

<MvSKIP

Move sequentially through a database

NAME="*alias*"	If omitted, use the primary database
ROWS="*num*"	
VIEW="*viewname*"	

>

<MvSMTP

Send e-mail

```
    TO="dest1,dest2,..."
    SUBJECT="text"
    CC="dest1,dest2,..."
    MAILHOST="host"
    FROM="addr"
>

     ... headers ...

    (blank line)

     ... message body ...

    </MvSMTP>
```

<MvUNDELETE

Restore deleted records to a database

```
    NAME="alias"                If omitted, use the primary database
>
```

<MvUPDATE

Modify a database record

```
    NAME="alias"                If omitted, use the primary database
>
```

<MvWHILE

Create a program loop

```
    EXPR="{expr}"    If omitted, use the primary database
>

     ...

    </MvWHILE>
```

<MvWHILESTOP>

Interrupt a program loop

```
    <MvWHILE EXPR="{expr}">

     ...

     <MvWHILESTOP>

     ...

    </MvWHILE>
```

padl(*str, len, char)*

Pad a string with characters at the left (beginning)

str	String to be padded.
len	Number specifying the desired length of the string.
char	Character to use for padding.

padr(*str, len, char*)

Pad a string with characters at the right (end)

str	String to be padded.
len	Number specifying the desired length of the string.
char	Character to use for padding.

power(*base, exp*)

Raise a number to a power

base	Number to be raised.
exp	Power value (exponent).

random(*max*)

Generate a random number

max	Maximum value for the returned number.

rnd(*val, precision*)

Round a number to a specified number of decimal places

val	Number to round.
precision	Number specifying how many digits to leave after the decimal point.

rtrim(*str*)

Remove spaces from the right side (end) of a string

str	String to be "trimmed."

schmod(*path, num*)

Change permissions of a file in the scripts directory

path	Pathname of the file whose permissions are to be changed. The path is specified relative to the Miva scripts directory.
num	Number specifying the new permissions to set.

scopy(*from, to*)

Copy a file in the scripts directory

from	Pathname of the file to copy. The path is specified relative to the Miva scripts directory.
to	Pathname of the file to create. The path is specified relative to the Miva scripts directory.

sdelete(*path*)

Delete a file in the scripts directory

path	Pathname of the file to delete. The path is specified relative to the Miva scripts directory.

sexists(*path*)

Check whether a file exists in the scripts directory

path	Pathname to check, specified relative to the Miva scripts directory.

sfcopy(*from, to*)

Copy a file from the scripts directory to the data directory

`from`	Pathname of the file to copy. The path is specified relative to the Miva scripts directory.
`to`	Pathname of the file to create. The path is specified relative to the Miva data directory.

sfrename(*from, to*)

Rename or move a file from the scripts directory to the data directory

`from`	Pathname of the file to rename or move. The path is specified relative to the Miva scripts directory.
`to`	New name and/or location of the file. The path is specified relative to the Miva data directory.

sin(*num*)

Compute sine

`num`	Number whose sine is to be returned.

sinh(*num*)

Compute hyperbolic sine

`num`	Number whose hyperbolic sine is to be returned.

smkdir(*path*)

Create a subdirectory in the scripts directory

`path`	Pathname of the directory to create. The path is specified relative to the Miva scripts directory.

smode(*path*)

Check permissions of a file in the scripts directory

`path`	Pathname of the file to check. The path is specified relative to the Miva scripts directory.

sqrt(*num*)

Compute square root

`num`	Number whose square root is to be returned.

srename(*from, to*)

Rename or move a file in the scripts directory

`from`	Pathname of the file to rename or move. The path is specified relative to the Miva scripts directory.
`to`	New name and/or location of the file. The path is specified relative to the Miva scripts directory.

ssize(*path*)

Check size of a file in the scripts directory

`path`	Pathname of the file to check. The path is specified relative to the Miva scripts directory.

substring(*str, pos, len*)

Return part of a string

`str`	String from which to copy the substring.
`pos`	Number specifying the position of the substring to copy.
`len`	Number of characters to copy.

tan(*num*)

Compute tangent

`num`	Number whose tangent is to be returned.

tanh(*num*)

Compute hyperbolic tangent

num	Number whose hyperbolic tangent is to be returned.

time_t_---- (*time, zone*)

Return the portions of a time/date value

time_t_year(*time, zone*)	Returns year (4 digits).
time_t_month(*time, zone*)	Returns the month (from 1 to 12).
time_t_dayofmonth(*time, zone*)	Returns the day of the month (from 1 to 31).
time_t_dayofweek(*time, zone*)	Returns the day of the week (Sunday = 1, Monday = 2, etc.).
time_t_dayofyear(*time, zone*)	Returns the day of the year (from 1 to 366).
time_t_hour(*time, zone*)	Returns the hour (from 0 to 23).
time_t_min(*time, zone*)	Returns the minute (from 0 to 59).
time_t_sec(*time, zone*)	Returns the second (from 0 to 59).
time	Variable or other expression representing a time/date in universal format.
zone	Number specifying the time zone in which to evaluate the time and date.

timezone()

Return the local time zone

timezone()

tolower(*str*)

Convert letters to lowercase

str	String to be converted.

toupper(*str*)

Convert letters to uppercase

str	String to be converted.

B

The ISO 8859-1 Latin 1 Character Set

The following table shows the entity codes you can use in HTML documents to represent characters in the ISO 8859-1 Latin 1 character set. For instance, in order to create the Yen character (¥) you would enter `¥` into the HTML source code.

Some characters have alternatives. For instance, in order to create the pound-sterling symbol (£) you can use either `£` or `£`. Several of these alternatives were provided in order to allow HTML authors to "escape" various characters that are used in HTML tags (the <, >, &, and " characters).

Note: The entity codes `&130;` to `&159;` won't work in some browsers, as these were not part of HTML 2. Also, `&153;` does not work in Netscape Navigator version 4.

Entity Code	Character	Description	Alternative
`� – `		Unused	
` `		Horizontal tab	
`
`		Line feed	
` – `		Unused	
`
`		Carriage Return	
` `		Unused	
` `		Space	
`!`	!	Exclamation mark	
`"`	"	Quotation mark	`"`
`#`	#	Number sign	
`$`	$	Dollar sign	
`%`	%	Percent sign	
`&`	&	Ampersand	`&`
`'`	'	Apostrophe	
`(`	(	Left parenthesis	
`)`	)	Right parenthesis	
`*`	*	Asterisk	
`+`	+	Plus sign	
`,`	,	Comma	
`-`	-	Hyphen	
`.`	.	Period	
`/`	/	Solidus-slash	
`0`	0	Digit, 0	
`1`	1	Digit, 1	
`2`	2	Digit, 2	
`3`	3	Digit, 3	
`4`	4	Digit, 4	
`5`	5	Digit, 5	
`6`	6	Digit, 6	
`7`	7	Digit, 7	

Entity Code	Character	Description	Alternative
8	8	Digit, 8	
9	9	Digit, 9	
:	:	Colon	
;	;	Semicolon	
<	<	Less than	<
=	=	Equals sign	
>	>	Greater than	>
?	?	Question mark	
@	@	"at" sign	
A	A	Letter A	
B	B	Letter B	
C	C	Letter C	
D	D	Letter D	
E	E	Letter E	
F	F	Letter F	
G	G	Letter G	
H	H	Letter H	
I	I	Letter I	
J	J	Letter J	
K	K	Letter K	
L	L	Letter L	
M	M	Letter M	
N	N	Letter N	
O	O	Letter O	
P	P	Letter P	
Q	Q	Letter Q	
R	R	Letter R	
S	S	Letter S	
T	T	Letter T	
U	U	Letter U	

Entity Code	Character	Description	Alternative
`V`	V	Letter V	
`W`	W	Letter W	
`X`	X	Letter X	
`Y`	Y	Letter Y	
`Z`	Z	Letter Z	
`[`	[	Left square bracket	
`\`	\	Reverse solidus-backslash	
`]`	]	Right square bracket	
`^`	^	Caret	
`_`	_	Horizontal bar-underline	
``	`	Grave accent-back apostrophe	
`a`	a	Letter a	
`b`	b	Letter b	
`c`	c	Letter c	
`d`	d	Letter d	
`e`	e	Letter e	
`f`	f	Letter f	
`g`	g	Letter g	
`h`	h	Letter h	
`i`	i	Letter i	
`j`	j	Letter j	
`k`	k	Letter k	
`l`	l	Letter l	
`m`	m	Letter m	
`n`	n	Letter n	
`o`	o	Letter o	
`p`	p	Letter p	
`q`	q	Letter q	
`r`	r	Letter r	
`s`	s	Letter s	

Entity Code	Character	Description	Alternative
t	t	Letter t	
u	u	Letter u	
v	v	Letter v	
w	w	Letter w	
x	x	Letter x	
y	y	Letter y	
z	z	Letter z	
{	{	Left brace	
		|	Vertical bar	
}	}	Right brace	
~	~	Tilde	
— 		Unused	
‚	‚	Single low-9 quotation mark	‚
ƒ	ƒ	Latin small letter f with hook	ƒ
„	„	Double low-9 quotation mark	„
…	…	Ellipsis	…
†	†	Dagger	†
‡	‡	Double dagger	‡
ˆ	ˆ	Modifier letter-circumflex accent	ˆ
‰	‰	Per mille sign	‰
Š	Š	Latin capital letter S with caron	Š
‹	‹	Single left-pointing angle quotation mark	‹
Œ	Œ	Latin capital ligature OE	Œ
—		Unused	
‘	‘	Left single "curly" quotation mark	‘
’	’	Right single "curly" quotation mark	’
“	“	Left double "curly" quotation mark	“
”	”	Right double "curly" quotation mark	”
•	•	Bullet	•
–	–	En dash	–

Entity Code	Character	Description	Alternative
—	—	Em dash	—
˜	˜	Small tilde	˜
™	™	Trademark sign	™ and ™
		Note: Use ™ as &153; and ™ currently do not work in Netscape Navigator 4.	
š	š	Latin small letter s with caron	š
›	›	Single right-pointing angle quotation mark	›
œ	œ	Latin small ligature OE	œ
		Unused	
ž		Unused	
Ÿ	Ÿ	Latin capital letter Y with diaeresis	Ÿ
		Nonbreaking space	
¡	¡	Inverted exclamation	¡
¢	¢	Cent sign	¢
£	£	Pound sterling	£
¤	¤	General currency sign	¤
¥	¥	Yen sign	¥
¦	¦	Broken vertical bar	¦
§	§	Section sign	§
¨	¨	Umlaut-diaeresis	¨
©	©	Copyright	©
ª	ª	Feminine ordinal	ª
«	«	Left angle quote, guillemet left	«
¬	¬	Not sign	¬
	-	Soft hyphen	
		Note: Use rather than to ensure compatibility with largest number of browsers.	
®	®	Registered trademark	®
¯	¯	Macron accent	¯
°	°	Degree sign	°

Entity Code	Character	Description	Alternative
`±`	±	Plus or minus	`±`
`²`	²	Superscript two	`²`
`³`	³	Superscript three	`³`
`´`	´	Acute accent	`´`
`µ`	µ	Greek "mu," micro- sign	`µ`
`¶`	¶	Paragraph sign	`¶`
`·`	·	Middle dot	`·`
`¸`	¸	Cedilla	`¸`
`¹`	¹	Superscript one	`¹`
`º`	º	Masculine ordinal	`º`
`»`	»	Right angle quote, guillemet right	`»`
`¼`	¼	Fraction, one-fourth	`¼`
`½`	½	Fraction, one-half	`½`
`¾`	¾	Fraction, three-fourths	`¾`
`¿`	¿	Inverted question mark	`¿`
`À`	À	Capital A, grave accent	`À`
`Á`	Á	Capital A, acute accent	`Á`
`Â`	Â	Capital A, circumflex accent	`Â`
`Ã`	Ã	Capital A, tilde	`Ã`
`Ä`	Ä	Capital A, diaeresis or umlaut mark	`Ä`
`Å`	Å	Capital A, ring	`Å`
`Æ`	Æ	Capital AE diphthong, ligature	`Æ`
`Ç`	Ç	Capital C, cedilla	`Ç`
`È`	È	Capital E, grave accent	`È`
`É`	É	Capital E, acute accent	`É`
`Ê`	Ê	Capital E, circumflex accent	`Ê`
`Ë`	Ë	Capital E, diaeresis or umlaut mark	`Ë`
`Ì`	Ì	Capital I, grave accent	`Ì`
`Í`	Í	Capital I, acute accent	`Í`
`Î`	Î	Capital I, circumflex accent	`Î`

Entity Code	Character	Description	Alternative
Ï	Ï	Capital I, diaeresis or umlaut mark	Ï
Ð	Ð	Capital Eth, Icelandic	Ð
Ñ	Ñ	Capital N, tilde	Ñ
Ò	Ò	Capital O, grave accent	Ò
Ó	Ó	Capital O, acute accent	Ó
Ô	Ô	Capital O, circumflex accent	Ô
Õ	Õ	Capital O, tilde	Õ
Ö	Ö	Capital O, diaeresis or umlaut mark	Ö
×	×	Multiply sign	×
Ø	Ø	Capital O, slash	Ø
Ù	Ù	Capital U, grave accent	Ù
Ú	Ú	Capital U, acute accent	Ú
Û	Û	Capital U, circumflex accent	Û
Ü	Ü	Capital U, diaeresis or umlaut mark	Ü
Ý	Ý	Capital Y, acute accent	Ý
Þ	Þ	Capital Thorn, Icelandic	Þ
ß	ß	Small sharp s, German, sz ligature	ß
à	à	Small a, grave accent	à
á	á	Small a, acute accent	á
â	â	Small a, circumflex accent	â
ã	ã	Small a, tilde	ã
ä	ä	Small a, diaeresis or umlaut mark	ä
å	å	Small a, ring	å
æ	æ	Small ae diphthong, ligature	æ
ç	ç	Small c, cedilla	ç
è	è	Small e, grave accent	è
é	é	Small e, acute accent	é
ê	ê	Small e, circumflex accent	ê
ë	ë	Small e, diaeresis or umlaut mark	ë
ì	ì	Small i, grave accent	ì

Entity Code	Character	Description	Alternative
`í`	í	Small i, acute accent	`í`
`î`	î	Small i, circumflex accent	`î`
`ï`	ï	Small i, diaeresis or umlaut mark	`ï`
`ð`	ð	Small eth, Icelandic	`ð`
`ñ`	ñ	Small n, tilde	`ñ`
`ò`	ò	Small o, grave accent	`ò`
`ó`	ó	Small o, acute accent	`ó`
`ô`	ô	Small o, circumflex accent	`ô`
`õ`	õ	Small o, tilde	`õ`
`ö`	ö	Small o, diaeresis or umlaut mark	`ö`
`÷`	÷	Division sign	`÷`
`ø`	ø	Small o, slash	`ø`
`ù`	ù	Small u, grave accent	`ù`
`ú`	ú	Small u, acute accent	`ú`
`û`	û	Small u, circumflex accent	`û`
`ü`	ü	Small u, diaeresis or umlaut mark	`ü`
`ý`	ý	Small y, acute accent	`ý`
`þ`	þ	Small thorn, Icelandic	`þ`
`ÿ`	ÿ	Small y, diaeresis or umlaut mark	`ÿ`

Color Codes

You can specify colors in scripts either by entering the hexadecimal representation of the color or by entering the color names. Colors are used by HTML tags such as `<BODY BGCOLOR="bisque">` and `<FONT COLOR="seagreen">`. The actual color displayed will depend to some extent on the user's computer and software.

The table below lists each color's red, green, and blue hexadecimal values. It's generally easier to use the color name. However, if you want to use a hexadecimal value, enter the six hex digits together, preceded by a pound sign. For instance, to use `aliceblue`, you would enter `#F0F8FF`.

Color name	Red	Green	Blue
aliceblue	F0	F8	FF
antiquewhite	FA	EB	D7
aqua	00	FF	FF
aquamarine	7F	FF	D4
azure	F0	FF	FF
beige	F5	F5	DC
bisque	FF	E4	C4
black	00	00	00
blanchedalmond	FF	EB	CD

Color name	Red	Green	Blue
blue	00	00	FF
blueviolet	8A	2B	E2
brown	A5	2A	2A
burlywood	DE	B8	87
cadetblue	5F	9E	A0
chartreuse	7F	FF	00
chocolate	D2	69	1E
coral	FF	7F	50
cornflowerblue	64	95	ED
cornsilk	FF	F8	DC
crimson	DC	14	3C
cyan	00	FF	FF
darkblue	00	00	8B
darkcyan	00	8B	8B
darkgoldenrod	B8	86	0B
darkgray	A9	A9	A9
darkgreen	00	64	00
darkkhaki	BD	B7	6B
darkmagenta	8B	00	8B
darkolivegreen	55	6B	2F
darkorange	FF	8C	00
darkorchid	99	32	CC
darkred	8B	00	00
darksalmon	E9	96	7A
darkseagreen	8F	BC	8F
darkslateblue	48	3D	8B
darkslategray	2F	4F	4F
darkturquoise	00	CE	D1
darkviolet	94	00	D3
deeppink	FF	14	93

Color name	Red	Green	Blue
deepskyblue	00	BF	FF
dimgray	69	69	69
dodgerblue	1E	90	FF
firebrick	B2	22	22
floralwhite	FF	FA	F0
forestgreen	22	8B	22
fuchsia	FF	00	FF
gainsboro	DC	DC	DC
ghostwhite	F8	F8	FF
gold	FF	D7	00
goldenrod	DA	A5	20
gray	80	80	80
green	00	80	00
greenyellow	AD	FF	2F
honeydew	F0	FF	F0
hotpink	FF	69	B4
indianred	CD	5C	5C
indigo	4B	00	82
ivory	FF	FF	F0
khaki	F0	E6	8C
lavender	E6	E6	FA
lavenderblush	FF	F0	F5
lawngreen	7C	FC	00
lemonchiffon	FF	FA	CD
lightblue	AD	D8	E6
lightcoral	F0	80	80
lightcyan	E0	FF	FF
lightgoldenrodyellow	FA	FA	D2
lightgreen	90	EE	90
lightgrey	D3	D3	D3

Color name	Red	Green	Blue
lightpink	FF	B6	C1
lightsalmon	FF	A0	7A
lightseagreen	20	B2	AA
lightskyblue	87	CE	FA
lightslategray	77	88	99
lightsteelblue	B0	C4	DE
lightyellow	FF	FF	E0
lime	00	FF	00
limegreen	32	CD	32
linen	FA	F0	E6
magenta	FF	00	FF
maroon	80	00	00
mediumaquamarine	66	CD	AA
mediumblue	00	00	CD
mediumorchid	BA	55	D3
mediumpurple	93	70	DB
mediumseagreen	3C	B3	71
mediumslateblue	7B	68	EE
mediumspringgreen	00	FA	9A
mediumturquoise	48	D1	CC
mediumvioletred	C7	15	85
midnightblue	19	19	70
mintcream	F5	FF	FA
mistyrose	FF	E4	E1
moccasin	FF	E4	B5
navajowhite	FF	DE	AD
navy	00	00	80
oldlace	FD	F5	E6
olive	80	80	00
olivedrab	6B	8E	23

Color name	Red	Green	Blue
orange	FF	A5	00
orangered	FF	45	00
orchid	DA	70	D6
palegoldenrod	EE	E8	AA
palegreen	98	FB	98
paleturquoise	AF	EE	EE
palevioletred	DB	70	93
papayawhip	FF	EF	D5
peachpuff	FF	DA	B9
peru	CD	85	3F
pink	FF	C0	CB
plum	DD	A0	DD
powderblue	B0	E0	E6
purple	80	00	80
red	FF	00	00
rosybrown	BC	8F	8F
royalblue	41	69	E1
saddlebrown	8B	45	13
salmon	FA	80	72
sandybrown	F4	A4	60
seagreen	2E	8B	57
seashell	FF	F5	EE
sienna	A0	52	2D
silver	C0	C0	C0
skyblue	87	CE	EB
slateblue	6A	5A	CD
slategray	70	80	90
snow	FF	FA	FA
springgreen	00	FF	7F
steelblue	46	82	B4

Color name	Red	Green	Blue
tan	D2	B4	8C
teal	00	80	80
thistle	D8	BF	D8
tomato	FF	63	47
turquoise	40	E0	D0
violet	EE	82	EE
wheat	F5	DE	B3
white	FF	FF	FF
whitesmoke	F5	F5	F5
yellow	FF	FF	00
yellowgreen	9A	CD	32

For More Information

The scripts shown in the Listings are available online at this manual's companion Web site:

http://TopFloor.com/Miva/

For more information on HTTP protocols, see the Wold Wide Web Consortium's Web site at:

http://w3.org/

For more information about cookies, see the online reference at:

http://www.netscape.com/newsref/std/cookie_spec.html

For complete information on Quick Cost, UPS's documentation is available online at:

http://www.ups.com/tools/tools.html

The UPS OnLine Tools page at

http://www.ec.ups.com/ecommerce/ontools/index.html

has additional information about their e-commerce software and services.

For complete information on CyberSource services, see their Web site at:

http://www.cybersource.com/

Online documentation is available at:

http://www.cybersource.com/manuals/StartHere.html

Additional reference information is available on Miva's Web site at:

http://www.miva.com/commerce/cybersource/docs.html

A list of the ISO standard abbreviations for country names can be downloaded from:

ftp://ftp.ripe.net/iso3166-countrycodes

Index

Symbols and Numbers

A

B

C

D

E

I J K

V

POOR RICHARD'S WEB SITE:
SECOND EDITION

Geek-Free, Commonsense Advice on Building a Low-Cost Web Site

Poor Richard's Web Site is the *only* book that explains the entire process of creating a Web site, from deciding whether you really need a site—and what you can do with it—through picking a place to put the site, creating the site, and bringing people to the site. It is full of commonsense advice that Amazon.com called an "antidote to this swirl of confusion" and "straightforward information." Praised by *BYTE magazine, Publisher's Weekly,* and *USA Today, Poor Richard's Web Site* can save you thousands of dollars and hundreds of hours.

"**Poor Richard's Good Advice.** With all great new things comes a proliferation of hucksters and snake-oil salesmen, and the Internet is no exception. The antidote to this swirl of confusion lies in Peter Kent's *Poor Richard's Web Site.* The analogy to Ben Franklin's volume is appropriate: the book is filled with the kind of straightforward information the Founding Father himself would have appreciated."

—Jennifer Buckendorff
amazon.com

"We highly recommend this book."

—Peter Cook & Scott Manning
Philadelphia Inquirer

"We highly recommend that you get a copy."

—*Marketing Technology*

"Very well written."

—*Library Journa*

"Buy This Book! . . . The lessons of just the first three chapters, alone, saved us thousands of dollars and many hours of work."

—David Garve
The New England Nonprofit Quarterl

"I've found a great book that explains it all—*Poor Richard's Web Site.* This is a practical, no-nonsense guide that lucidly covers topics like how to set up a domain with the InterNIC, how to promote your Web site, and how to actually use all those features that hosting services provide."

—David Methvi

Poor Richard's Web Site
is available in bookstores both online and offline, and at http://PoorRichard.com/

Poor Richard's Web Site:
Geek-Free, Commonsense Advice on Building a Low-Cost Web Site
by Peter Kent ISBN: 0-9661032-8-9

POOR RICHARD'S INTERNET MARKETING AND PROMOTIONS:

How to Promote Yourself, Your Business, Your Ideas Online

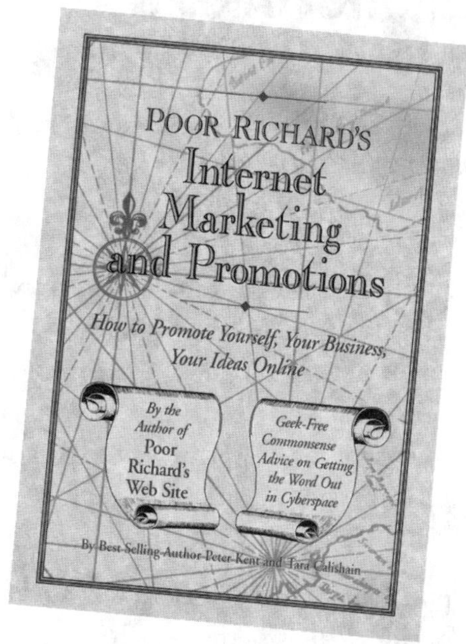

Much of what you've read about marketing on he Internet is wrong: registering a Web site vith the search engines *won't* create a flood of orders; banner advertising *doesn't* work for most companies; online malls *do not* push large amounts of traffic to their client Web sites. . . .

What you really need is some geek-free, commonsense advice on marketing and promoting on the Internet, by somebody's who's actually done it! Most books and articles are written by freelance writers assigned to nvestigate a particular subject. *Poor Richard's nternet Marketing and Promotions* is written by small-business person who's been successfully marketing online for a decade.

Poor Richard's Internet Marketing and Promotions uses the same down-to-earth style o highly praised in *Poor Richard's Web Site.* You'll learn how to plan an Internet marketing campaign, find your target audience, use giveaways to bring people to your site, integrate an email newsletter into your promotions campaign, buy advertising that works, use real-world PR, and more.

You'll also learn to track results, by seeing who is linking to your site, by hearing who is talking about you, and by measuring visits to your site.

If you are planning to promote an idea, product, or service on the Internet . . . you need *Poor Richard's Internet Marketing and Promotions!*

Poor Richard's Internet Marketing and Promotions
is available in bookstores both online and offline, and at
http://TopFloor.com/ AVAILABLE FEBRUARY 1999

Poor Richard's Internet Marketing and Promotions:
How to Promote Yourself, Your Business, Your Ideas Online
by Peter Kent and Tara Calishain
ISBN: 0-9661032-7-0

POOR RICHARD'S E-MAIL PUBLISHING

Creating Newsletters, Bulletins, Discussion Groups and Other Powerful Communication Tools

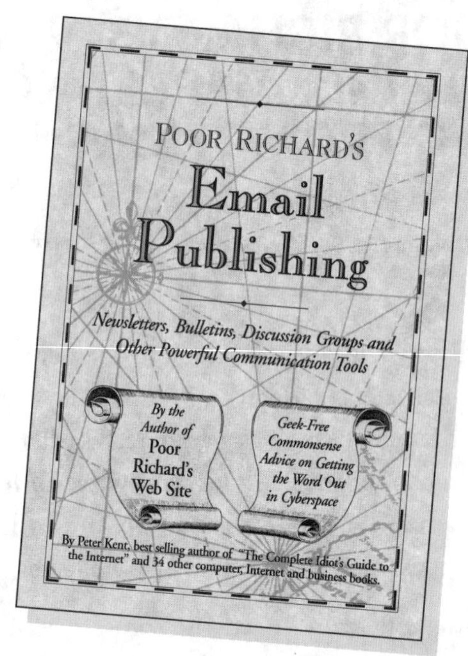

E-mail publishing is booming—it's growing faster than the World Wide Web. Publishing newsletters, bulletins, and announcements, and running mailing-list discussion groups is a powerful way to promote a product or service … it's also a cheap and relatively low-tech tool.

E-mail publishing can also be a simple one-person business. Newsletters such as *This is True* and *Joke of the Day* have subscription lists well over 100,000 people, in over a hundred countries around the world, yet are run by individuals working on their own or even part time. These entrepreneurs are using their e-mail newsletters to generate a comfortable income in advertising sales and ancillary product sales.

You can learn everything you need to know about e-mail publishing the way these people did: the hard way, by trial and error. Or you can read *Poor Richard's Email Publishing* for geek-free common-sense advice on how to publish using e-mail. Written by a successful e-mail newsletter publisher, *Poor Richard's Email Publishing* will explain how to host a simple newsletter or mailing list using a free or low-cost e-mail program; how to find people to sign up for your service; how to write an e-mail message so that it won't get messed up en route to the subscribers; how to find articles and information; how to find an e-mail publishing service when your list grows too large; an plenty more.

You'll even find out how to sell advertising, i both newsletters and discussion groups. You' also learn how to host a mailing list discussio group. Hundreds of thousands of discussio groups are run through the Internet's e-mai system. You'll find out how to moderate a lis how to encourage people to join; how to us the list to promote a product withou alienating members of discussion groups; ho to find advertisers; how to price your ads, th different types of ads; etc.

If you want to get in on the fastest growin area of Internet communications … you nee *Poor Richard's Email Publishing!*

Poor Richard's Email Publishing
is available in bookstores, both online and offline,
and at http://PoorRichard.com/pr/email
by Chris Pirillo
ISBN: 0-9661032-5-4, $29.95